Penny
March 21, 2019 Cornwell

YOU CAN NEVER DIE

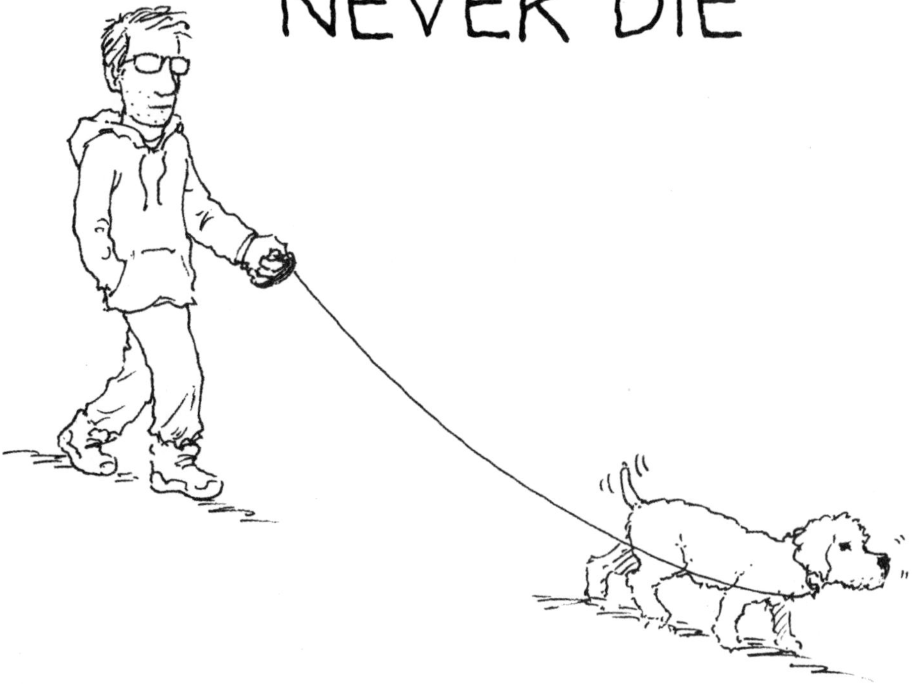

"SITTING HERE WITH YOU IS SO PERFECT . . .
WHICH REMINDS ME: YOU CAN NEVER DIE."

ALSO BY HARRY BLISS

CARTOON COLLECTIONS

Death by Laughter

WITH STEVE MARTIN

A Wealth of Pigeons

Number One Is Walking

BOOKS FOR CHILDREN

Illustrations by Harry Bliss

Diary of a Spider

Diary of a Fly

Diary of a Worm

Louise, The Adventures of a Chicken

Sorry (Really Sorry)

By Harry Bliss

Luke on the Loose

Bailey

Bailey at the Museum

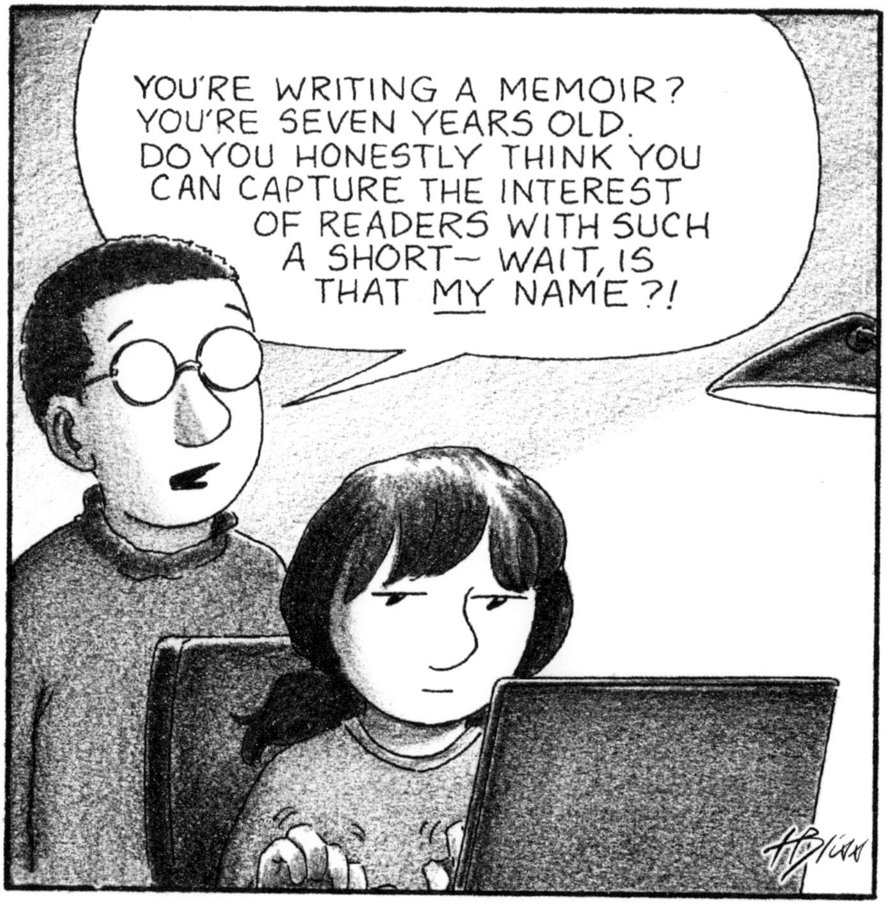
YOU'RE WRITING A MEMOIR? YOU'RE SEVEN YEARS OLD. DO YOU HONESTLY THINK YOU CAN CAPTURE THE INTEREST OF READERS WITH SUCH A SHORT— WAIT, IS THAT MY NAME?!

YOU CAN
NEVER DIE

A GRAPHIC MEMOIR

HARRY BLISS

CELADON
BOOKS

NEW YORK

www.celadonbooks.com

Designed by Michelle McMillian

Grateful acknowledgment is made for permission to reproduce the following art:
Roz Chast on page 192, *The New Yorker* on page 213,
the Maurice Sendak estate on page 243, and the Ed Koren estate on page 319.

Library of Congress Cataloging-in-Publication Data

Names: Bliss, Harry, 1964– author.
Title: You Can Never Die: a graphic memoir / Harry Bliss.
Description: First edition. | New York : Celadon Books, 2025.
Identifiers: LCCN 2024022332 | ISBN 9781250883681 (hardcover)
Subjects: LCSH: Bliss, Harry, 1964– | Cartoonists—United States—Biography. | Dog owners—United
States—Biography. | Dogs—Caricatures and cartoons. | LCGFT: Autobiographies.
Classification: LCC NC1429.B623 A2 2025 | DDC 741.5/6973[B]—dc23/eng/20240523
LC record available at https://lccn.loc.gov/2024022332

Our books may be purchased in bulk for promotional, educational, or business use.
Please contact your local bookseller or the Macmillan Corporate and
Premium Sales Department at 1-800-221-7945, extension 5442, or
by email at MacmillanSpecialMarkets@macmillan.com.

First Edition: 2025

10 9 8 7 6 5 4 3 2 1

For Rozzy and Cheetah

There in that land of mine is buried the first good half
of my life and more. It is as though half of me were buried there,
and now it is a different life in my house.

—Pearl S. Buck, *The Good Earth*

INTENTION

I'm not going to call this an introduction, even though technically that's what it is. I don't like the word *introduction*. It feels cold to me. I put a lot of stock in words. As a cartoonist, I have to. *Introduction* feels like an off chord or a rim shot where a soft kick-bass belongs. So, let's lose *introduction* and instead call this my intention. What are my intentions with you? I would like you to better understand me, connect with me. I'm a believer in taking the time to understand the nuances in our world. If I can make a connection with you here in the pages that follow, we've got intimacy, and intimacy is my intention.

Included here are selected essays from my life. The essays are excerpts from my journals. I write in my journal every day. I've kept a journal for more than a decade now—I have two dozen Moleskines filled with drawings and writing. For example, writing about my dog, Penny. My relationship with her altered the way I understand and carry on in an unanticipated and profound way. There are other reflections . . . giving my baby up for adoption, communing with trees, comic books, life-drawing classes, virginity, drugs, the Mafia, two hours with Andrew Wyeth, making books with Steve Martin, working with a famous porn star (great guy), and other reflections that, honestly, I should have been incarcerated for.

I started keeping a journal because I didn't want to forget things. There came a point in my life when I realized that memory is all we have. Our life consists of our memories. If we cannot make some account of these memories, contextualize them within our own framework, how will we know how and why they happened? As I get older, my memory slips, thus the need for me to record this curious existence I've still yet to make any sense of. There are no facts in this life; it's all a mystery (that's a fact). My journal memories provide clues to the mystery. I can go back to a journal and reflect on a dream I had, a dreadful restaurant experience, a book I loved, a beautiful poop of Penny's, a dead bird I found, a sore neck from watching a barred owl in a tree, a Modigliani nude, my wife's eyes, a snowfall—all clues to life's intention.

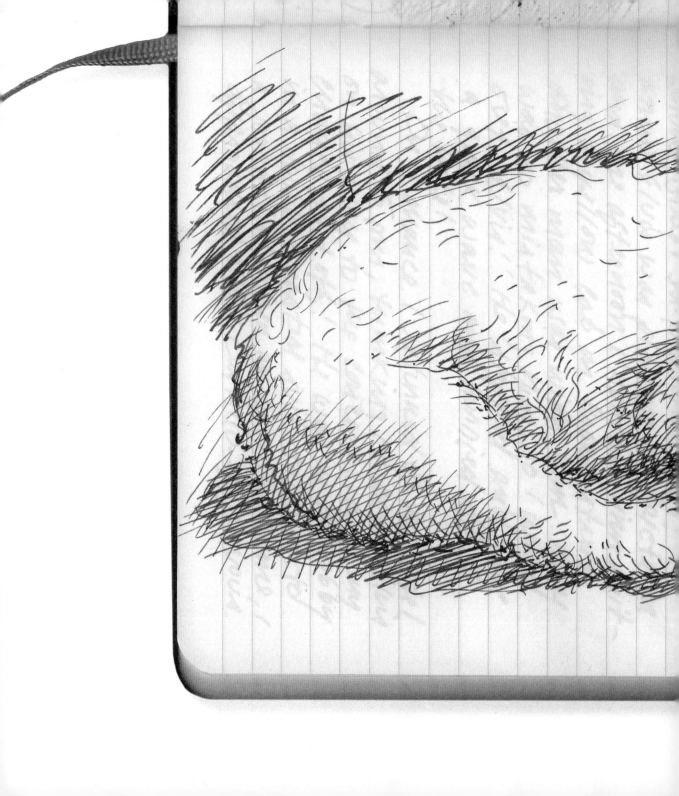

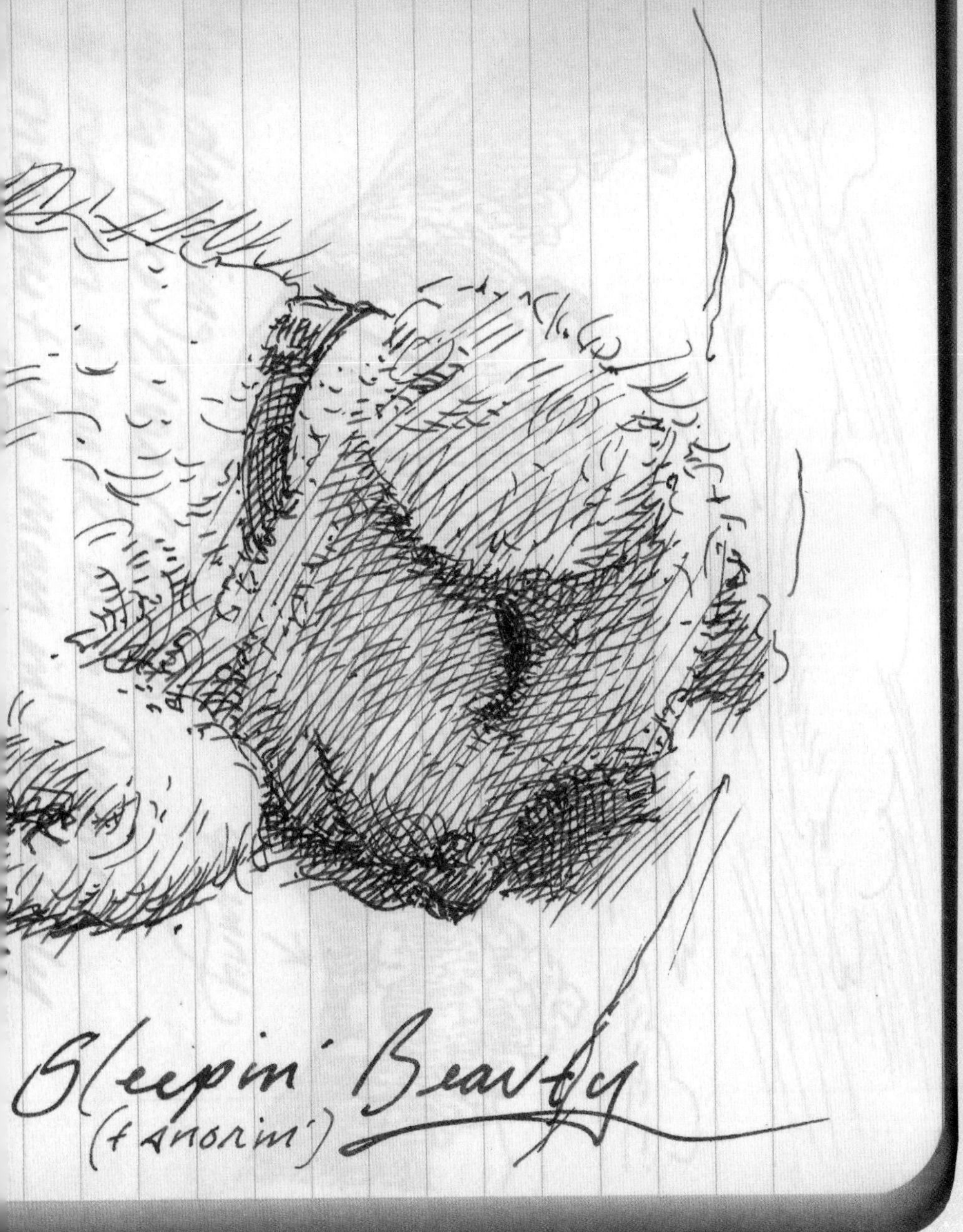
Sleepin' Beauty
(+ snorin')

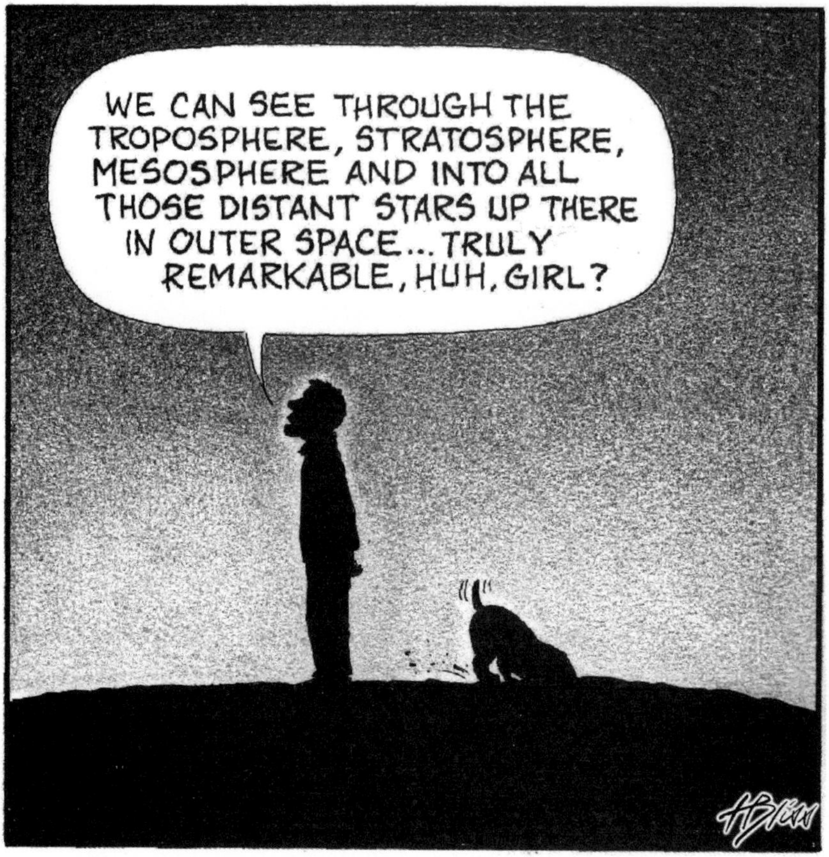
WE CAN SEE THROUGH THE TROPOSPHERE, STRATOSPHERE, MESOSPHERE AND INTO ALL THOSE DISTANT STARS UP THERE IN OUTER SPACE... TRULY REMARKABLE, HUH, GIRL?

PENNY UP AT NIGHT

Like most nights when I'm alone here in New Hampshire with my dog, Penny, she wakes me up at 4:15 a.m. for her breakfast, insulin shot, and to go out beneath the star-filled sky to squat and pee. She's fifteen, an old lady, but with glimmers of spunk still present.

There was a time, last year, when I would wake up angry at her for disrupting my sleep. She always knew I was not pleased, dogs know us better than we know ourselves.

I suppose I'm mellowing as I grow older myself. Now, when I hear her rumbling at the foot of the bed, I slowly wake up, turn on the light, and calmly say, "Okay, I'm up." I'll put last night's clothes back on and finish it all off with a warm terry-cloth bathrobe I purchased last year (get one, you won't regret it). I pick her up off the bed (she can't jump, it's too high—she'd break her goddamn leg). Penny knows the drill; we've been doing this for more than a year now.

This morning, when I picked her up and cradled her in my arms to head downstairs, she was so warm, like a furry little baby—totally resigned and vulnerable. She stared up at me with her cataract eyes, and it was lovely. I stopped at the top of the stairs and took a moment to stare back at her. I felt an absolute presence, like an inexplicable mutual understanding.

I wondered if it was actually happening.

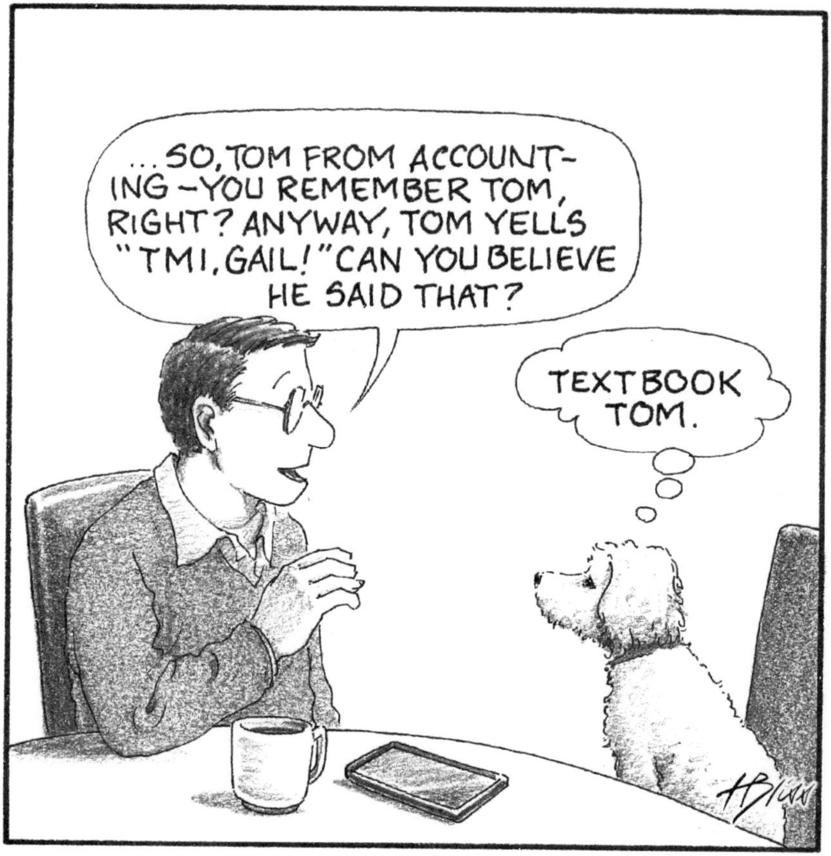
...SO, TOM FROM ACCOUNTING – YOU REMEMBER TOM, RIGHT? ANYWAY, TOM YELLS "TMI, GAIL!" CAN YOU BELIEVE HE SAID THAT?
TEXTBOOK TOM.

TALKING TO DOGS

Raise your hand out there if you talk to your dog . . . so much so that some-times you wonder if you're insane. Most of the time I'm not aware I'm doing it. I like to think that my fifteen-year-old companion enjoys it—like I'm pay-ing attention to her and treating her as an equal. The reality is that I'm talking to myself and the dog knows this, because she looks at me with eyes filled with a curious sadness that say, *You're scaring me.*

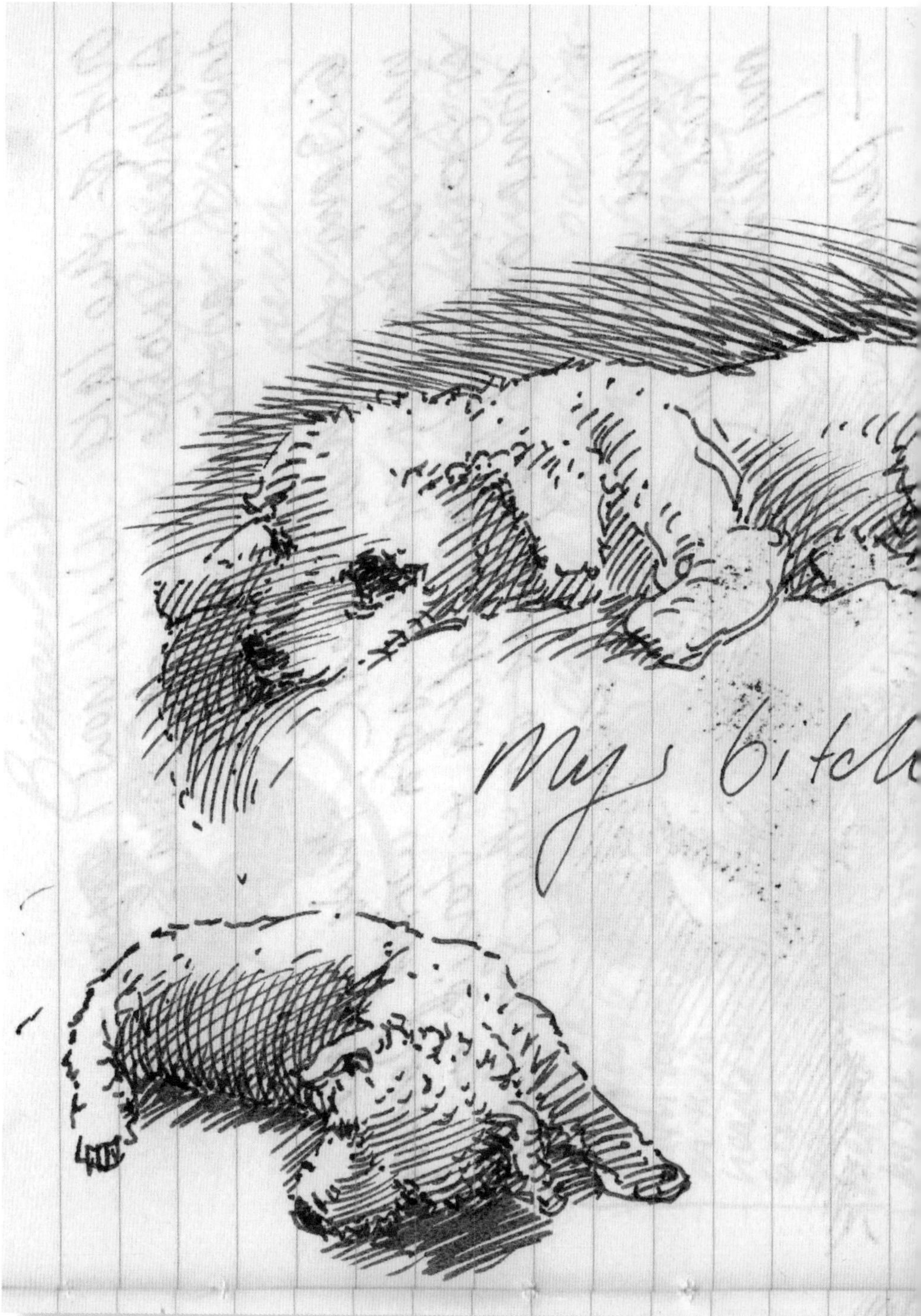
My bitch

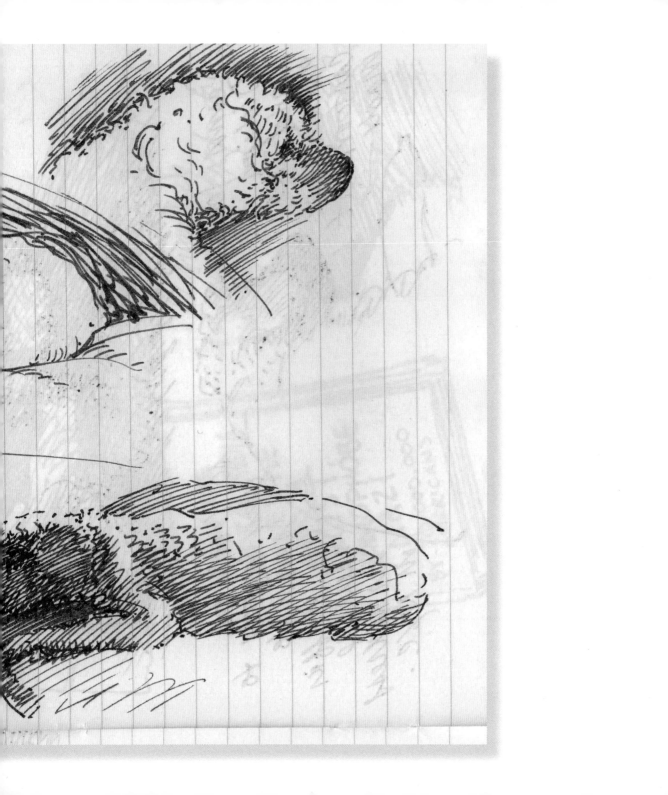

Here's Penny sleeping before
to an outbreak of a new
disease in China, where a c...
of 11 million people are now
quarantined...

not
on some
species deser...

on the sofa as I listen

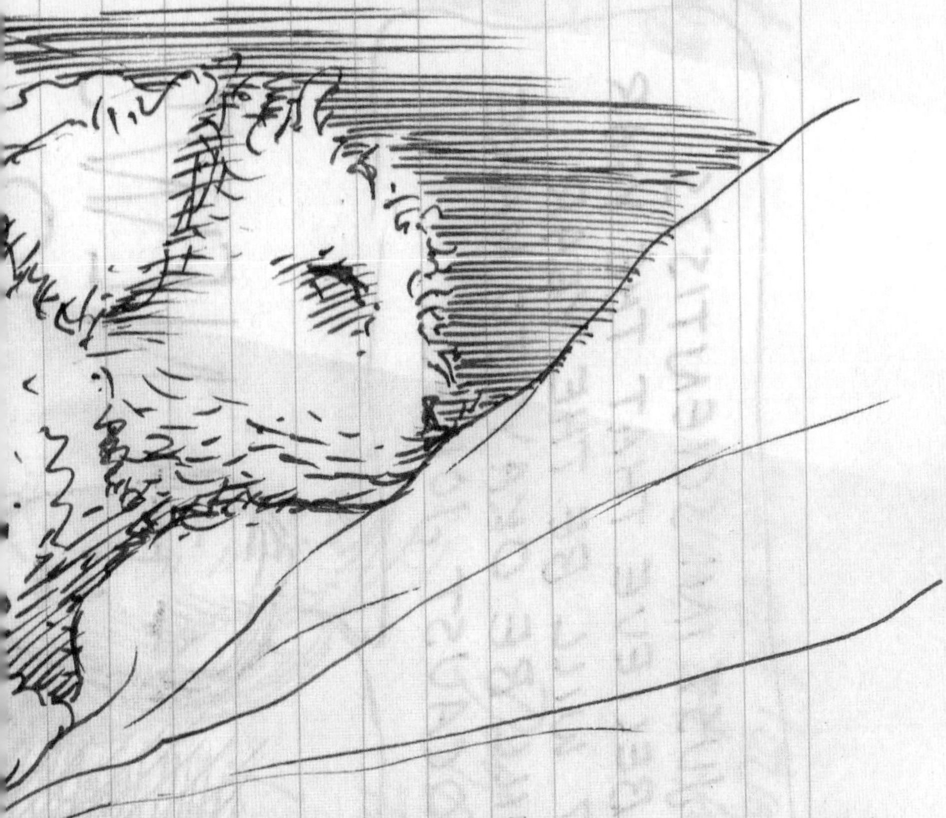

I've had this feeling as of
e that the end of days is
away. Either climate, war
is near. I feel we as a
whatever fate comes.

Regular Penny

Popcorn Penny
(trip to the groomer overdue)

Tony Soprano Penny

The Thing Penny

Mickey Mouse Penny

Rabid Penny

Beautiful Penny

head resting on Eeyore.

The ear resting on the cushion is classic Penny

"Baby Got BACK!"

Penny, post breakfast, sawing logs. She seems to be improving little by little, is able to stand on the hind leg and not instantly fall back down, so, this is a sign of some return to her previous strength — not there yet.

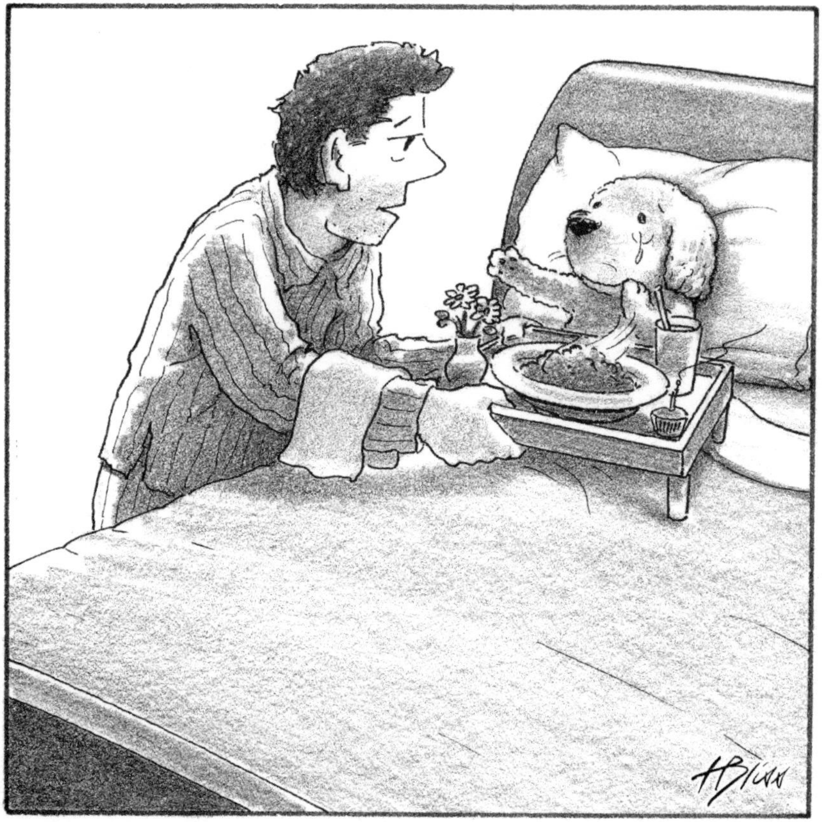
H Bliss

"HAPPY 126TH BIRTHDAY, GIRL!"

PENNY SURGERY

Penny is having surgery today. Nothing serious—I'm not even sure they have to put her under. But she's an old lady. Just driving by the vet's office makes her so anxious. My mind goes to the worst-case scenario, and I see the dramatic Hollywood scene unfold: Penny having a massive heart attack and the nurses pumping her with jolts of electricity. "Clear!" the vet yells.

Why do my thoughts torture my brain? Is this normal?

Inevitably, I start to worry about what my life will be like without Penny, and I get sad. How will I ever get over the grief? Will I ever stop crying? Will I see her furry face everywhere I go—in the trees, the clouds, the ocean? Should I take her to a taxidermist? Is that sick? I don't think my wife, Sofi, would like for me to have Penny stuffed. . . . Maybe I wouldn't have to tell her.

Who am I kidding? She'd find out.

"NEXT WALK, WE'RE GOING TO THE PARK."

THERAPY

When I first returned to therapy in 2017, I told my psychoanalyst about a dream I had had earlier in the week. In the dream I was walking with Penny in a desert. Far off in the distance I could see a sandstorm slowly moving in our direction. I knew Penny wouldn't be able to breathe air dense with so much sand.

So I reached down, scooped her up in my arms, and held her close. As the storm approached, I knelt on the warm sand and covered her body with my body. I closed my eyes, and there we waited for the sandstorm to come.

My analyst suggested the notion that Penny represented me, a boy who had experienced childhood abuse, and that in the dream I was trying to protect myself. Was he right? Am I so sensitive to Penny because I see her as an innocent surrounded by the ever-present prospect of unanticipated cruelty? It's possible. I'd felt this way before, when I would visit elementary schools, looking out at all those children. I often felt a sadness for each and every one of them because I knew they had suffering waiting for them.

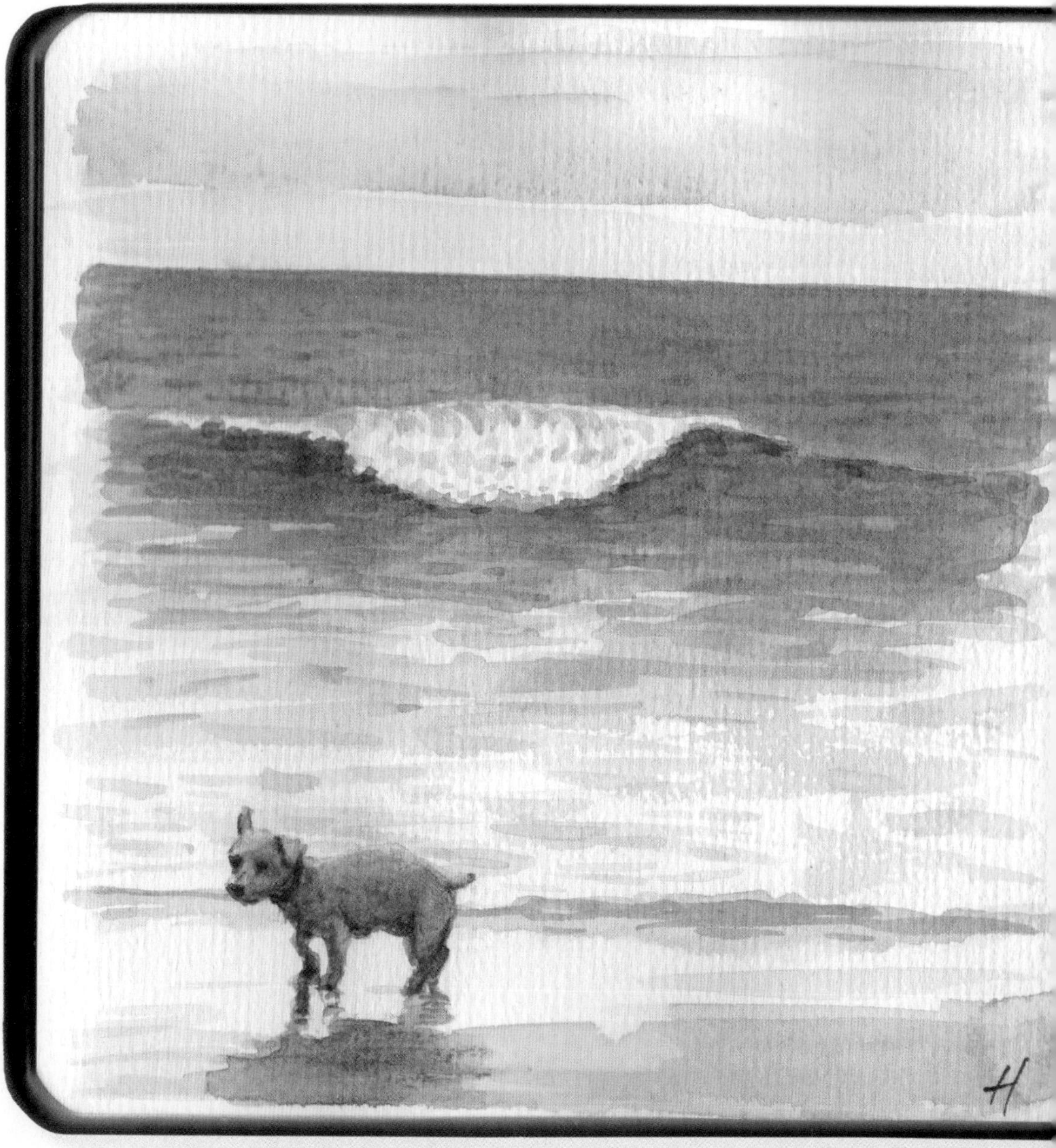
H

These days, every time I see Penny I'm reminded of the inevitable grief I most certainly will feel when she dies. I honestly don't know how I'll manage. I nearly cried painting this damn thing! God bless this miraculous animal.

"SOMETHING VERY BIG BURIED A LOT
OF BONES HERE!"

GOOD OLD DAYS

When I stop and think about my "good old days," I was always alone. In elementary school, on the way home in my snowsuit, I'd stop by the side of the road after a big storm and start digging tunnels in the snow with my mittens, humming songs to myself as I worked. I imagined that after I left, tiny families would come and shelter in the tunnels, protected from the cold.

FIRST FUNNY

One of my earliest memories growing up at 165 Colony Lane in Henrietta, New York, was entertaining my family. I was six or seven, and the youngest of my siblings: John, Charley, and Rachel. Perhaps this memory is so clear because it's one of a handful of memories in which we were all happy as a family. No one was punching or yelling or arguing.

I would lie down on one of the beds, feet where the pillow was, head hanging off the other end of the bed. In a rare, loving and coordinated effort, my father and mother would cover my body with sheets, leaving only my chin exposed. Then, my father would draw eyes on the top of my chin and other features around my mouth.

The effect created a strange character with a misshapen head and a massive mouth. Sometimes my father would add a mustache or glasses, even a tiny hat that sat on my chin (the top of mouth-man's head). My siblings cracked up as my father interviewed me with silly questions. I'd contort my mouth, laugh like a hyena, stick out my tongue . . . the visual was so absurd, it didn't take much to get giggles out of anyone who was watching. It was the first time I experienced being an entertainer of sorts, making people laugh. I thought to myself, *I'm funny!*

My father liked this act so much, he filmed me on more than one occasion. I imagine those Super 8 reels are packed away in my parents' basement or attic. I suppose, in time, my siblings and I will discover them when we have to empty out the house.

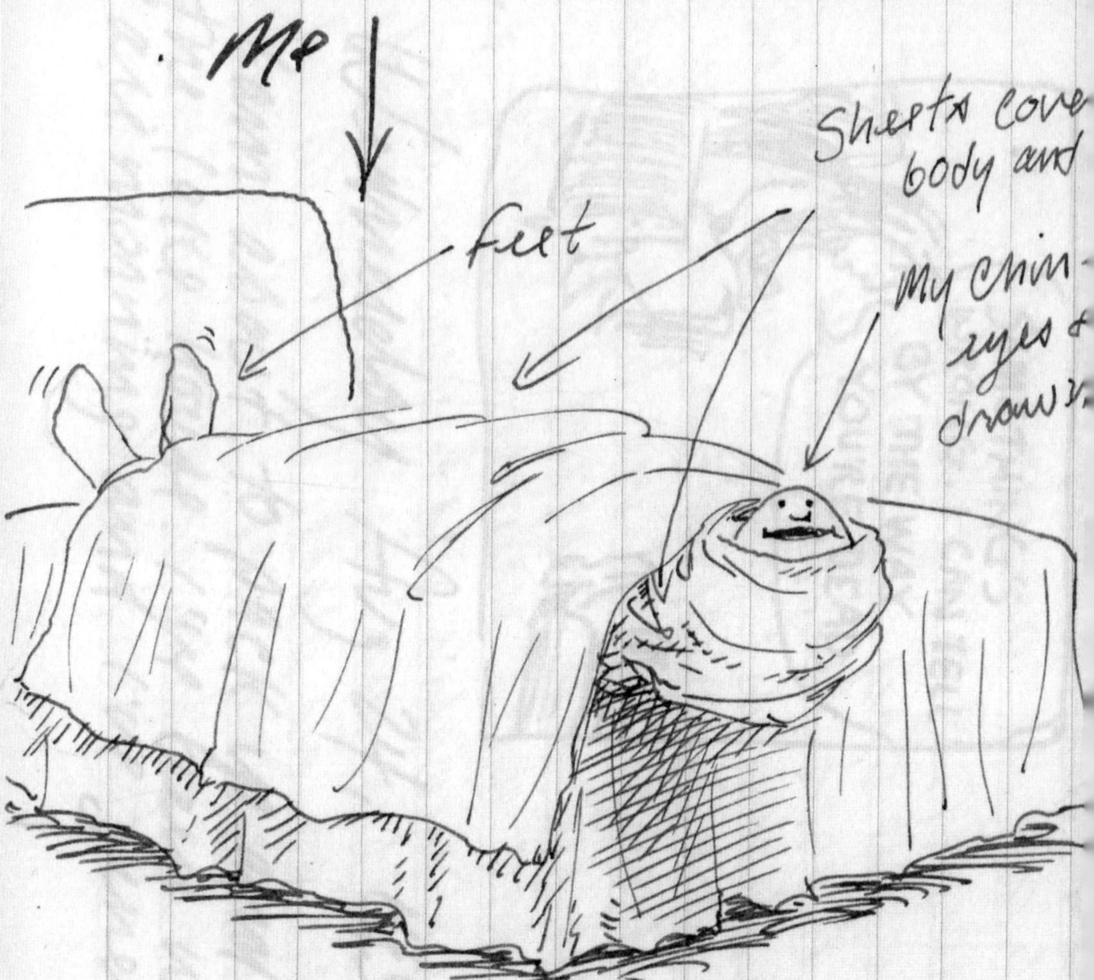

Head rests on edge of bed.

our do
Sonja

mom
SO, BIGMOUTH, WHAT BRINGS YOU TO THIS PART OF THE HOUSE? HAVE YOU SWEPT OUT THE GARAGE LIKE I ASKED?
John
Charley
Rachel

"PROMISE YOU WON'T GET MAD . . ."

SCOTCH TAPE YOUTH

We had a light fixture in our family room growing up, and every time my parents left the house we kids broke the shit out of it. It must've been eight feet off the floor, a sort of wrought iron chandelier with milk glass covers around two light bulbs.

I don't know what sort of games we used to play, something that involved a ball, I'd guess. Precisely how we successfully broke the milk glass each week still boggles my mind. The amazing part is that we repaired the damn thing every time we broke it, before our parents returned home.

Jesus, I can remember the fear and anxiety on my siblings' faces as they struggled to get those things glued back together. I was the baby—too damn young to fix myself a glass of milk, but my older brothers handled it. The old man did some of his graphic design work in the house, so we had glues, tapes, and X-Acto knives readily available to us if we needed to get creative or kill one another.

Many years later, when we were all grown and out of the house, my father had that stupid chandelier replaced with a modern one. When they took down those two milk glass covers, the old man took a closer look.

He couldn't believe how many cracks were in them. He told us he laughed his ass off studying our handiwork. "You idiots even used Scotch tape," he said.

ROAD TRIP

Growing up, if there wasn't fighting going on in the car, it felt as though something was wrong. Our de facto normal was dysfunction. Kids constantly fighting. Mom criticizing Dad's driving. And my father, when he wasn't singing to drown out his children, was angry at my mother for her poor directions.

My father, Jack, was an impressive multitasker. He would steer the car with his left hand, and with his right hand, hit us, randomly, just trying to get a piece of any of his children as he looked straight ahead, lost and stressed-out in some unknown city. . . . I would never attribute the trait of determination to my father, but in those moments he was truly gifted.

As you may have guessed, most of our road trips were fairly traumatic. Yet we still ventured off as a family, for reasons totally unknown to me. Maybe Jack and my mother, Roslyn, felt they needed to fill in some piece of the puzzle that is the American dream. On one of these unholy journeys my father became so angry at my three older siblings, he pulled the car over to the side of the road and made all three of them get out. I was the youngest, probably four years old at the time, so I was still pretty innocent—a voyeur in the car, simply watching with excited fear at all the dysfunction. My three siblings got out of the 1972 Fleetwood Estate wagon and shut the door. Then, my father stepped on the gas, pedal to the metal style, and took off.

I have a clear memory of my father speeding away, my mother yelling at him to slow down. The whole scene is fairly hilarious to me now, but at the time I was terrified. I looked back at my siblings on that street corner and thought, *I'll never see them again.*

As it turned out, my father listened to his wife, slowed down, made a left turn, and another left turn, and eventually I was reunited with my brothers and sister—still on that same street corner, yelling and pushing one another. The wagon pulled up, and my father told them to "Get the hell back in the car." They were quiet as mice until the state line.

"WELL HE DIDN'T DROWN."
"WHO KNEW MICE COULD DO
THE BREASTSTROKE?"

POOL TOSS

Some things you can't forget. This doesn't necessarily make them true. I'm working on my second Negroni and I feel pretty goddamn good, but despite my high, I feel as though my recollections here are fairly accurate.

I don't remember my exact age, maybe five or six—1970 feels right. My parents were having an uncharacteristic backyard party—neighbors, relatives . . . Uncle Ken, Uncle Harry, the aunts, cousins, it must have been fifteen to twenty people.

I have this memory of my mother, intoxicated, throwing me into our above-ground pool. I sank very quickly. I struggled like hell to rise to the surface, dog-paddling, kicking furiously.

My mother was there when my head surfaced, drink in her hand, smiling, I think. I know she had sunglasses on, so I couldn't really decipher what her exact expression was, but I instantly retaliated and splashed her with all my might.

I remember her being surprised and upset that she was suddenly soaked. What the fuck did she expect? I didn't care; I was so filled with anger.

I don't believe I would have died. . . . Shit, do I? It was strange because there were plenty of people around. Didn't anyone think, *Holy shit, what the fuck is Roslyn doing to Harry?!*

And why would she do this? Rookie drinker? Possibly. My mother rarely drank. I wasn't a very good swimmer. Was she trying to teach me in a kind of "sink or swim" way?

If I ask her about this now, she'll gaslight me, claiming I'm making it up and that memory is a strange thing—that it can't be trusted. Is she right? This is a difficult part of getting older.

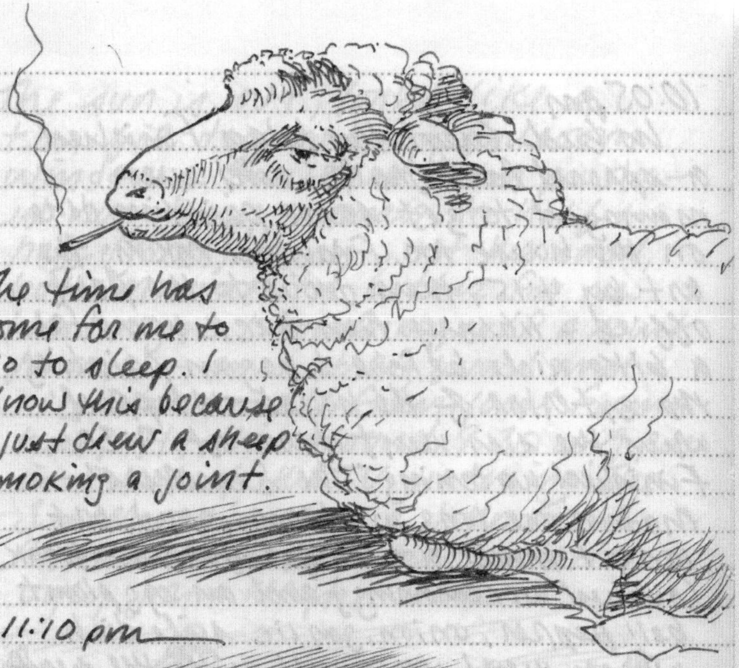

The time has
come for me to
go to sleep. I
know this because
I just drew a sheep
smoking a joint.

11:10 pm

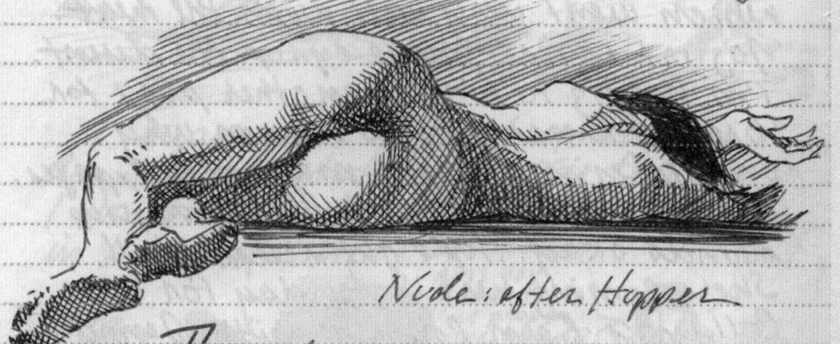

Nude: after Hopper

Thursday 7:30 am

I am officially awake, still in bed, but 'up'. As usual, the morning sun is hitting the sugar maple trees out my window evoking the corpse of Maxfield Parrish. The wind

NAKED

When I was eight, me and my buddies Chris and Jeff, along with our neighbor Patty, would all regularly get naked together. It was summer, our parents were working, and we were left wonderfully unsupervised. Our naked play happened at Patty's house. We three boys loved Patty. She was tough, beautiful, and athletic—the trifecta. Patty's mother, Ms. LaRoka, was a single mom in a rented house raising three kids—she worked all the time. Years later, we'd learned Ms. LaRoka relied on prostitution to make ends meet.

The three of us kids would roam about the LaRokas' two-story home, eventually settling in Patty's mom's bedroom. We'd laugh, get naked, and prance around, showing off our genitals to one another. We jumped on the bed, giggling and silly, all four of us feeling happily and ridiculously misbehaved.

The interesting thing about all our innocent roughhouse exploration is that it wasn't sexual to us at all. We were just exploring our nakedness together. None of us knew how to have sex. None of us had ever had an orgasm, to my knowledge. I certainly hadn't. I only knew that it was fun being naked with my friends.

Not far from Patty's house, in a wooded area, fully clothed, we used to play a game where we would try to grab one another's crotch area for points. Stupid, I know, but we had fun. If Patty was able to grab us and touch our genitals or we were able to jump after Patty and touch near her breasts/genitals, we each got points. We didn't latch on to the genitals, we just had to touch them. It was more like wrestling than anything else. Patty usually won, she was far more athletic. We were all nervously exhilarated about what we were doing, but we didn't know why. There was something beautiful in our collective innocence.

There was another time when I was even younger, maybe six or seven, and I was with my older brothers. We all shared a bedroom in the finished basement of the house. I was naked and so was my older brother Charley, post shower or bath, I'd guess. Charley and I were both showing our father how we could make our penises move. We thought it was hilarious that we could make our penises get slightly hard and move up and down all the while cracking up. I remember my dad looking at us with a really uncomfortable grin—my older brother, John, too. But we didn't know, we thought it was fun. I imagine the activity in the lobes of our young brains in those moments and how electric we once were.

45

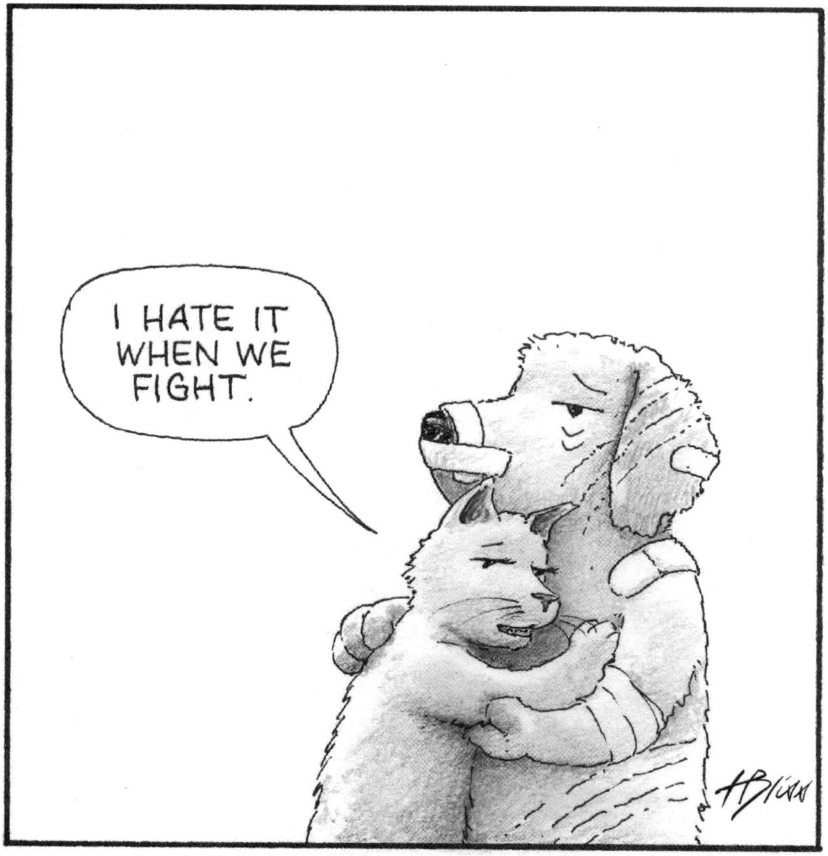
I HATE IT WHEN WE FIGHT.

MOM AND DAD HIT
EACH OTHER

There is a scene in the wonderful film *Defending Your Life* with Albert Brooks and Meryl Streep, a film I've seen half a dozen times, in which the character played by Brooks is recalling his childhood. He watched his parents fight. The parents didn't know he was watching them, and he stood painfully witnessing them yelling at each other and began to cry. His parents turned away from their anger and noticed their son crying.

This scene has always been difficult for me to watch because a similar thing happened to me as a ten-year-old boy.

I was home alone while my parents went out, which was not something they did often. I have many memories of my mother being frustrated with my father for not wanting to leave the house for a party, art opening, or social event of any kind. My Hollywood-raised mother, Roslyn, was more of a social butterfly. This was a stark contrast to my dad's rural, small-town rearing. It made sense that she wanted to spread out a little and have fun. Not Cheetah (my father's childhood nickname). She resented the hell out of him for his unwillingness to let go and try new things.

That night when they came home they were fighting with a quiet hatred-filled calm I'll never forget. At a certain point, I came up from the basement where I shared a bedroom with my brothers (both out getting high/drunk).

I stood in the doorway watching them. My mother called my father "a lousy lover," and slapped his face. My father then slapped my mother across the face. Mom reached up to grab a cast-iron pan hanging on the wall.

Before she was able to hit my father with it they both turned to notice me crying in the hallway. Seeing them seeing me, I instantly ran back down to my bedroom, jumped into my bed and curled up in a fetal position. When I think back now about this incident, I can say with a certain amount of clarity and understanding that I was totally lost. What I'd witnessed was confounding, but there was also a sadness and deep worry.

In time, my father came down and sat on the edge of my bed. The old man said nothing, just sat there quietly. I wished he had said something to me— anything, and for many years I was angry at him for not finding the words to console me or at least communicate to me how difficult things were for him. I feel like it would've helped me in some way.

But now, all these years later, as an older man myself, I'm no longer angry at the guy. I feel bad for the poor bastard. He couldn't figure it out, he didn't know what to do. I see now, we were both lost in that moment. He had never learned how to express himself in a sincere way . . . to anyone. Any contempt or resentment I had for him has since morphed into empathy. Maybe that's the way it should be, after things have settled. We see our parents for the first time.

"WE WERE WATCHING A LATE MOVIE
WHEN JACK HEARD A CRASH IN THE
KITCHEN, LIKE GLASS BREAKING, SO
JACK WENT AND GOT HIS 12 GUAGE
AND SNUCK INTO THE KITCHEN,
CAME NEAR FACE TO FACE WITH A
BURGLER, BUT I YELLED TO JACK
THAT THE GUN WASN'T LOADED
CAUSE I WON'T HAVE A LOADED
GUN IN MY HOUSE... SO, THIS
BURGLER FELLA ESCAPES IN A
HURRY AND JACK BEGINS HOLLER-
ING AT ME FOR TOUCHING HIS GUN,
AND THAT'S WHEN I BLUDGEONED
HIM TO DEATH WITH THE CAST IRON PAN."

"I'M JUST SAYING, IF MY OWNER'S DEAD AND NO ONE'S AROUND TO STOP ME, I'M ROLLING IN HIM."

TUESDAY, NOVEMBER 22, 2022

At the time of this writing, my ninety-two-year-old father, Jack L. Bliss, is killing himself. He stopped eating about a week ago because he's tired of living and hates the current world. "Everyone is nuts, and I'm too fuckin' old," he says. "Why am I still here?! All my friends are dead, goddamnit!"

Dad's not entirely wrong, the world is nuts. But where I push forward with humor, friends, and booze to cope, he finds it all too disheartening. He's been a "glass is half full of horseshit" type of guy for the last thirty-five years. My parents never embraced the retired life. Personally, I cannot wait to try crack on my eightieth birthday!

This whole "I want to die" business started about three weeks ago. My older brothers called and told me that our father really was going to die. So I got in my car and drove six hours home to see him, perhaps for the last time.

He had a urinary infection and said it was the worst pain he'd ever felt. Yet when I arrived at my childhood home, my brothers were there along with our mother (oblivious to the whole situation), and Dad was sitting in a rocking chair and looking like, well . . . not a million bucks but pretty damn good. A VA nurse had arrived before I showed up and removed my father's blocked catheter, which allowed him to pee "like Niagara Falls" (his words).

I sat down in our TV room and listened to my father go on and on about how happy he was that he was no longer in pain and I thought to myself, *I just drove six hours to say goodbye to you and you're healthy and optimistic? What the fuck is happening?!* I had just gotten over the flu a week before, so I wasn't feeling all that great, and the long drive only made things worse. But it was nice to see the old man in good spirits.

My parents hate each other, so I had to visit my dad and then go down into his former painting studio—which my mother has turned into her own little cozy nook of insanity—and separately catch up with her. All in all the visit went pretty well.

That was three weeks ago.

This past week, it seems my dad is again intent on killing himself. He has stopped eating and for six days has had nothing except ice chips soaked in ginger ale. I spoke to him yesterday, and he sounded pretty good. We talked about art and nature, both of which we love. I asked him if he was hungry; he said not really. He lies in bed watching *The Three Stooges*, *The Andy Griffith Show* and Lawrence Welk, which sounds just lovely. I told him I loved him, and we hung up.

Thirty minutes later, I called my mother on her little flip phone. My parents are very competitive about who talks to whom, and if I didn't call my mother after speaking to my father, she would naturally assume that I loved him more than her, and there's a good chance she would've been angry and taken it out on her weak, helpless, soon-to-be-dead husband. I asked my mother if she'll miss Dad when he's gone, and she said no. When I pressed her on this issue, there was a little latitude in her response. As much as she acts like she hates my father—and I do think it's some emotion very close to hatred—when he does die, my mother may encounter a surprising sense of sadness and loss. Or she'll be the happiest eighty-seven-year-old lunatic in upstate New York. Who knows?

I know I'll miss my father when he's gone. Sure, he was the cause of so much of the anxiety and trauma of my youth, but he did all right. I'd like to say he did his best, but I know that's not true. Despite all the abuse—the "spankings" with the belt, having us pick out our own pussy willow branch as a switch, knocking me on my ass a few times in front of my friends . . . you know, that stuff, he was retroactively a pretty lovable guy.

JACK'S BLISS

My fondest memories of my father are of him in our narrow mudroom, half of which he used as his painting studio. The old man would come home from work at six, sit at the head of our dining room table, and try to digest his over-cooked meat while my siblings and I called one another names like pig-whore or idiot-dick . . . we were not nice to one another. Dad would go into his sanctum sanctorum (mudroom studio) after dinner, the first can of Genesee beer pleasantly soaked into his cerebral cortex. Hours later, I'd come in from a friend's house, still baked off my ass, and find him painting a still life while Frank Sinatra played on the turntable. He'd have a pipe going (a terrific, sweet smell I still miss), and be nearing the end of a six-pack by this time, while our wonderful mutt, Igor, would lie sleeping in front of the Franklin stove.

I'd walk into the narrow room, plop down in the chair by Igor and watch my father paint. He was good too. I learned more watching him than any painting class I would later put up with. Sometimes he talked. But mostly he would hum along to the music—happy as a pig in shit. I'd stay with him until my eyelids grew heavy over my bloodshot eyes, then off to bed, leaving him in his zone.

He lived through the Depression, one of five boys raised by a single mother in a rural town outside of Warren, Pennsylvania. The Korean War, the GI Bill, the wrong wife, and four unholy kids followed. Still, despite all the hardships, he was able to find peace in that bastardized studio of his. It was peaceful too;

I felt it. How was he able to find calm when it seemed so many things in his life were out of control? Beer? Maybe. Beer may have saved my father the death of a thousand stress arrows. It's ironic, because his father was an abusive alcoholic—in and out of prison, a real piece of work. Late one night in 1935, walking home drunk from the local tavern, a tractor trailer hit him in the middle of the road; he died instantly.

Cornish   Paganini

Tuesday, 5:00 am
  Woke up too early and now
here I am writing in this
journal with my head-
lamp on... again. It's
fine—I just popped a
valium to quell the
racing mind and
I'm sure in no
time, I'll be back
sleeping. In the
mean time

  I prefer to
not simply lay
prone in the dark
like an idiot, and
instead get a few things
off my chest because
life is too short to <u>not</u>
be watching the ink
flow from this perfect
Mont Blanc Meisterstück
fountain Pen! Ah,
there it is... now I
feel it... the good
old diazapam has
hit the cerebral cortex—— at last!

Picasso's father was a rather accomplished painter of birds... until he witnessed the stunning talent his young son, Pablo displayed in his early teens. Don José Ruiz Blasco was so blown away by his son's talent, the old man stopped painting. Was he depressed? Jealous?

As years passed, each time I returned home, I feared looking at my father's latest work — I knew it wouldn't impress me and I'd have to lie to him, tell him how much I liked it. I wonder if he knew...

My old man was/is an artist, though he's 90 and no longer makes art, hasn't for over a decade. I recall the first time I returned home to look at his paintings, hung throughout my parents home, and finding flaws in his work. His art no longer impressed me and I began to see each one of his efforts mere attempts at something beyond his reach.

DRUGSTORE PRIDE

There came a point in my childhood when I realized the uniqueness of the Bliss family. There were no fewer than ten working artists in my immediate and extended family. It wasn't uncommon for people to refer to the Blisses as "the Wyeths of Rochester."

I remember going to the drugstore with my older brother Charley and my dad. Drugstores in the '70s were like tiny little Walmarts, only less evil. I recall seeing one of my father's graphic illustrations for French's—a little character holding a bottle of mustard—on a cardboard display, hanging above one of the shelves. My father (who always seemed to be searching for pepperoni and cans of Pennzoil) casually pointed to it and said, "I drew that guy."

Seeing my father's artwork up there brought a big smile to my eight-year-old face. I was proud of the old man. I thought, my dad is kind of famous! People see his artwork every time they come into this drugstore.

This gave me a certain pride, not just in my father but in my whole family. My two cousins, Jim and Phil, were successful illustrators. They did terrific advertising art for Genesee beer. I still have two of their posters, both takeoffs on *Star Wars*. Instead of *Star Wars*, the poster reads, "Beer Wars." I know—cheesy, but that's not their fault—blame it on the copywriter.

My uncles' graphic art and advertising work for Kodak, their biggest client, was fairly lucrative, and they did well. Not bad for three boys raised in the Depression by a single mother. Their combined portfolios have hundreds of art illustrations and graphic designs for Xerox, Kodak, French's mustard, Bausch + Lomb, and many other companies in and around Rochester.

Aside from their advertising work, my uncles and cousins were successful painters and watercolorists. Their artworks were regularly shown in the annual juried show at the Rochester Memorial Art Gallery. (I would later get into this show as an eighteen-year-old—the youngest artist to get work accepted into the show.)

Not long after that Key Drugs visit, if I had a friend over to goof off or break stuff, I would bug my father to draw us something—some hot rod character, or the Incredible Hulk—whatever, and he would do it. It was magic. We were transfixed watching him draw for us. No mistakes and fast. He was good.

TEARS

My sweet Penny has passed on. My heart is so heavy. Tears. No more words from me. I leave them to E. B. White . . .

"Charlotte," said Wilbur after a while, "why are you so quiet?"

"I like to sit still," she said. "I've always been rather quiet."

"Yes, but you seem specially so today. Do you feel all right?"

"A little tired, perhaps. But I feel peaceful. Your success in the ring this morning was, to a small degree, my success. Your future is assured. You will live, secure and safe, Wilbur. Nothing can harm you now. These autumn days will shorten and grow cold. The leaves will shake loose from the trees and fall. Christmas will come, and the snows of winter. You will live to enjoy the beauty of the frozen world, for you mean a great deal to Zuckerman and he will not harm you, ever. Winter will pass, the days will lengthen, the ice will melt in the pasture pond. The song sparrow will return and sing, the frogs will awake, the warm wind will blow again. All these sights and sounds and smells will be yours to enjoy, Wilbur—this lovely world, these precious days . . ."

Sleeping after
another snack &
goodbye visit
from Delia

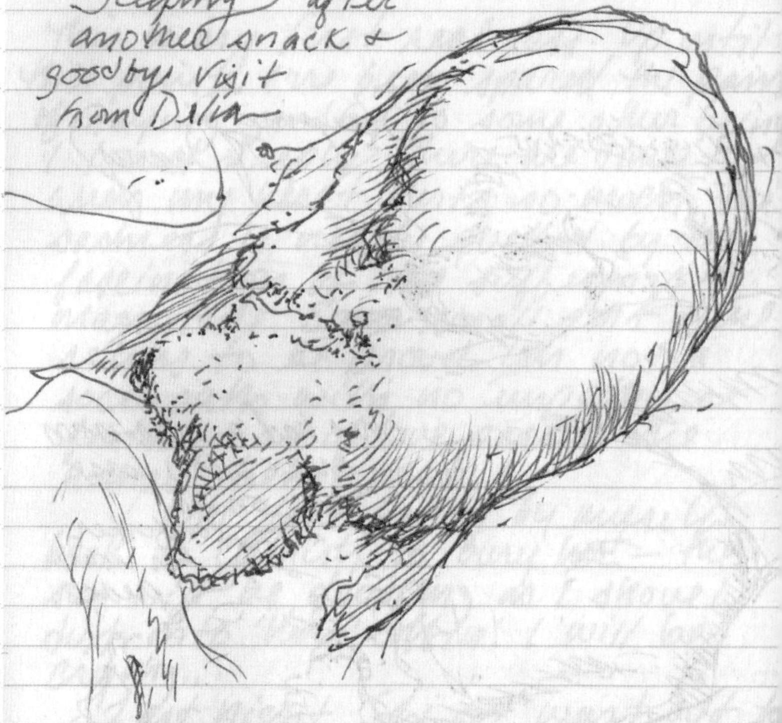

11:30 pm

My sweet Penny is gone. I miss
her beyond words. I'm broken. Christ,
what have I done? I want her back,
I'll put up with all of it. Christ, I'm
devastated. I loved Penny so much,
so much. I honestly don't know
how I can go on. I'm a fucking
mess. I'm alone here in Corinth.
After the doctor came and euthanized
Penny at 6:00pm, I had to drive

...re above w/ Penny — dead, in
...e back of the car. It was dark
...en we arrived. I put a still
...arm Penny on the dining room
table and weeped into her body —
...er smell was still sweet. God, it
...as so hard to bury ~~her~~ her. Her
eyes were gone — lost forever and
...t crushed me so. Her loss is too
...uch — too much. I can't stop cry-
...ng. I loved her so much. I don't
know what to do — I'm practically
suicidal.

Wednesday 9:40 am

Still raw. Managed to sleep.

The last time I
saw my
beautiful Penny.
She was wrapped
in a soft shawl of
Sofia's in a sturdy
wooden chest w/ a
lock on it. In the
earth she went. I
shovelled the earth
over the box and placed a
...ge stone, a flat stone, over her. She was
...ead, her body — she now lives in me and
...eres the rub, a beautiful + heart-wrenching
RUB.

"I KNOW. I MISS HER TOO."

DIGGING HER GRAVE

I never thought I would dig a grave. Who does? I dug Penny's grave two days before she passed. I selected one of my smaller blanket chests. I had no intention of laying Penny directly on the soil, although I don't know why. I suppose I wanted her body to be comfortable. I'm assuming that's why we bury our dead in coffins the way we do. I was just following a ridiculous protocol that made things easier for me. I suppose that's all right.

It's not easy digging a grave, even a dog's grave, which I intentionally made twice the size necessary. All the while I was digging, I was miserable as hell. It's not like digging a hole to plant a tree or any other type of digging for that matter. Digging a grave is a very specific feeling. I was angry and deeply sad in fits and bursts. With each shovelful of dirt I threw aside, I could feel my heavy heart in the back of my throat. I forget how many intervals of tears I shed, and I'm grateful I live in a rural place where I wasn't bothered by anyone. Digging a grave is something you want to do alone or at least in a quiet place.

For the next couple of days, every time I looked out my bedroom window and saw the grave, I cried. It was an inescapable emotion, and I didn't fight it. When she died, the option of having her body taken away was on the table, but I never considered it. For some reason I knew I had to bury our dog in the backyard. Is this because my father buried our dogs in our backyard? Is it because the former owner of my home buried her two pets in the backyard? I honestly can't say. I only knew that I needed to keep Penny's remains close to me.

Tuesday October 12, 2021 9:15 am

Today, we will lose penny to another world. At 4:00 pm a woman will come to our house and while both Sofi & myself hold our dog of 17 years, the woman will inject the 'michael Jackson drug' into Penny — she'll die within 2 minutes. The drug, we were told, will feel very good and it seems our girl will leave us high as fuck.

I woke with Penny this morning, took her out back to pee, fed her... insulin shot, etc. She's sleeping now a few feel away from me — soft piano jazz playing as usual — she seems content. It was strange that she didn't flinch this morning when I gave her the insulin shot, she usually does. maybe she knows it's the last one she'll get and she wanted to make it easy for me. I hate sticking her with the goddamn needles, I hate to hurt her. Showing me some strength and empathy on this, her final day of life.

Last night was not easy. She had both Sofi + me up a few times and the lack of sleep is so difficult for me — torture. Christ, this day is going to be so hard.

I have a nice coffin-ish wooden chest in the back of my wagon, ready to place penny in.

photo Sofi took at golf course in winter
wooden box
Penny's canniuh bed + a few pennies
I'll cover her with my old cashmere sweater.
her favorite piece of rawhide

4 days ago in Cornish I picked a spot out to bury penny. It's a nice place where I can put a stone...

— GRAVE —

Before   After

I plan on making the site a bit of a flowery shrine to her — I'll plant next year...

I had no real understanding of just how much losing Penny would hurt.

66

Penny sleeping
(and snoring) 2/16

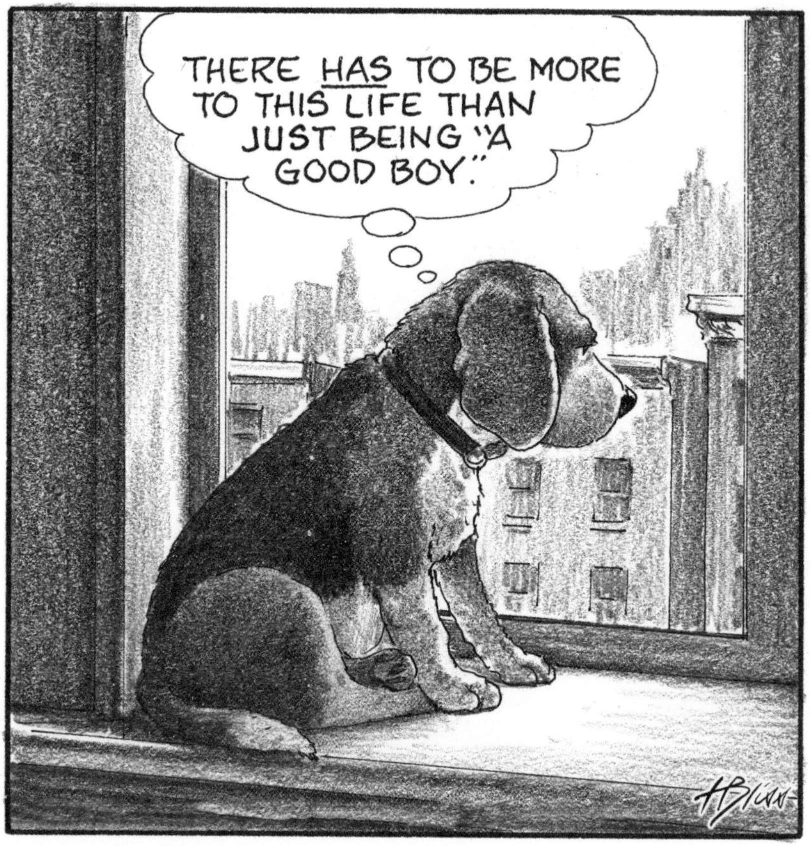
THERE HAS TO BE MORE TO THIS LIFE THAN JUST BEING "A GOOD BOY."

THE PENNY LOOP

Sofi ran into a couple out front of our home in Burlington, Vermont. They asked about Penny. Sofi told them that Penny had passed. The couple was saddened to hear this. They told Sofi they regularly walked different routes in our neighborhood for years and that they always enjoyed seeing Penny on her perch in the window. They called the walk by our home "the Penny Loop."

Sofi and I then imagined all the other people over the years walking by our window, finding Penny laying on her tummy, peering out at them. A scruffy sentinel bringing a smile to countless strangers.

Did Penny change their mood? Make them feel better? When I see a dog, I feel myself becoming tender—I soften. This same shifting-toward-tenderness happens when I see children. The accumulation of this shifting in energy can be significant. Does it make us kinder to each other? Nourish our sense of humanity? Did Penny's furry face in that window make the world kinder? We can never know how many lives our pets touch, but the numbers over those seventeen years of Penny's life cannot be underestimated.

I have therapy with Jacobson at 4 — haven't seen him in a couple of weeks. Then, at 5, I'm off to Cornish.

Penny sleeping on the mulch out front.

And here's Penny at the window on the 'perch' where she keeps an eye out for anything or anyone.

9:45 pm
        In bed here in Cornish listening to 'Slowburn' podcast about Watergate. I'm tired...

fitch on Monday, possible lunch at Marks on Wednesday, two visits from 2 solar panel companies on Thursday & Fridays respectively... A busy week.

Sofi holding Penny. Penny became the defacto baby we regretted not having earlier in our time together. We were too old to conceive when we really wanted our child. Sometimes, I wondered if somehow Penny knew this, though I honestly doubt it. She only knew we loved her & treated her like our baby girl. Humans are odd animals.

"WHEN I GO, I'D LIKE MY ASHES DUMPED ON
TOP OF A SQUIRREL'S HEAD."

MISTAKES MADE

If I could go back to the day Penny died, there are a few things I would've done differently.

For starters, I wouldn't have passed out. You see, when the woman who administered the lethal drug to Penny first injected her, she missed the vein—the needle came out, leaving the lethal dose of what the woman called the "Michael Jackson drug" not in Penny's vein but on her fur. Penny wasn't conscious, she was already sedated.

The woman, a bit distraught, quickly injected another dose and this one "worked." In seconds, I watched Penny's head slowly fall back in a way that I will never forget. It looked like she was injected with heroin, and I like to think that at that moment she was feeling extremely good/high.

But in those last few seconds I became overwhelmed. It was all too much. I began to sweat and feel dizzy—I was going to pass out. Sofi took Penny's body from my arms and placed her on the ground by my feet, then ran to the kitchen to get me a glass of juice. I couldn't be in the moment, I was pale and on the verge of losing consciousness. I just sat there and waited to recover so I could be present again.

I was angry at my mind and body for failing me in that moment. It took a couple of minutes for me to come back—I was soaked with sweat. This has happened before. When my son was born, the nurse couldn't find the vein on my son's mother, Nicole, and she kept having to stick the needle in over and over again . . . I passed out.

When I drove Penny's body from Burlington back here to Cornish, where I would bury her, I should have put her on my lap and not in the back of the car. It kills me now that I didn't do that. She was dead, but she wasn't dead long enough. . . . Instead, she was in a compostable body bag the vet provided. When I got back to Cornish, I took her out of the bag and carefully placed her on my dining room table, where I cried, sobbing with my face against hers.

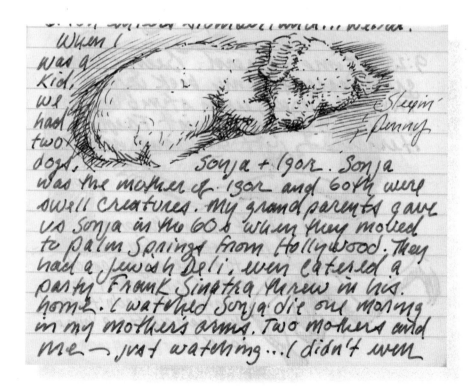

When I was a kid, we had two dogs — Sonja + Igor. Sonja was the mother of Igor and both were swell creatures. My grandparents gave us Sonja in the 60s when they moved to Palm Springs from Hollywood. They had a Jewish deli, even catered a party Frank Sinatra threw in his home. I watched Sonja die one morning in my mother's arms. Two mothers and me — just watching . . . I didn't even

There were traces of blood near her nose. It is extremely difficult for me to revisit all this . . . but, some part of me doesn't want to forget. Maybe we do this with lives we've loved and lost. I don't know.

I carried Penny's body out back to the hole I had dug a few days earlier. It was raining, cold, and dark—miserable. At one point she slipped from my hands and landed on the pile of dirt next to the hole. She didn't fall from a great height, but when I reached down to pick her up, her body was totally limp, as though her bones had melted. Trying to pick her up in that state and then holding her close in the rain was brutal. I held her in my arms and said out loud how sorry I was for letting her slip from my hands. Jesus, that was hard. I then placed her in the blanket chest and covered her just as though she were alive. . . . I stroked her head, nestled her favorite stuffy next to her. . . . I was tucking her in like a child.

"YES, THAT'S A DEAD MOUSE. . . . DON'T EVEN
THINK ABOUT IT."

DEAD MUSKRAT

I just had this memory as I was cartooning here at my desk, and I needed to put it down on paper.

I remember I was ten or eleven years old, hanging out with my friend Jeff and another buddy. The three of us were out walking around in a quasi-rural suburban plot of land, not far from the local strip mall and the Star supermarket (later replaced by the first Wegmans). We were smoking cigarettes and doing whatever stupid shit we did back then. Being destructive was our go-to elixir for boredom (getting high replaced destruction two years later).

I remember us coming upon a shallow well. Inside was dirty water, an empty bottle of beer, and a dead muskrat. Jeff and I stared down at it, wondering if it was alive or not, but I knew it was dead. It must've drowned and couldn't get out. Jeff immediately found rocks and started throwing them at the dead muskrat's backside. Now, I was by no means a "good" or kind kid, but the sort of knee-jerk reaction Jeff had to desecrate a dead animal made me question his mind.

I remember watching Jeff really put a lot of effort into hitting the thing, puncture it or God knows what. The animal was enlarged, and I imagined one of the stones penetrating the bloated carcass, sort of popping it like a balloon and bursting guts all over. It didn't feel right. I didn't feel right. I felt sick. You

The Monroe County Fair 1976
Me in the grandstands at a demolition derby with my older brother, Charley and his friends...
HERE, YA FAGGOT— HIT THIS!
THAT DRIVER IS ON FIRE.
TED NUGENT
GENNY
HOUSE OF GUITARS
GENNY

couldn't see the muskrat's face, only the backside, so it looked like a brown sand-filled balloon covered with patches of fur.

I remember thinking somehow it was wrong to throw the rocks, but I was quiet. I don't remember why it was wrong, and I still don't know why it was wrong. Maybe it wasn't wrong.

I'm not so sure how I feel about putting this "down on paper."

DEMOLITION YOUTH

Last week, I was with my wife, Sofi, driving back from a week in Maine when I started talking about the Monroe County Fair, the fair of my youth. The Cornish Fair that ended this past weekend here in New Hampshire must've resurfaced some memories. Sofi wasn't a county fair kid (she grew up in Rye, New York, less than a mile from Playland!) But we both remembered demolition derbies.

Driving past the impressive White Mountains, we both considered the fucked-up-ness of demolition derbies. People, many of whom lived paycheck to paycheck, handed over their hard-earned money to watch cars crash into other cars . . . with people in the cars. It's like bumper cars for angry drunks. I recall full-blown crashes (the actual point of the thing), fires, brutal injuries, and all those engines smoking like goddamn metallic Detroit dragons. Truly a sight to behold. The smell of gasoline everywhere.

And get this: they served beer. This was some *Mad Max* shit in 1975. My brother Charley was friends with some of these drivers and would airbrush numbers or art on the sides of their cars. I'd sit in the grandstand and watch in awe. I was only ten or eleven, but even then I couldn't believe what I was witnessing was legal. I recall having the thought: *How is this happening?* Don't get me wrong, I loved it. I couldn't look away. It was glorious.

Driving home in our safe, recently inspected Volvo XC70 wagon, Sofi and I surmised that in many ways a demolition derby might be the most American thing we've experienced—like Fourth of July fireworks marinated in anger.

"IF YOU CRASH THROUGH THE DETOUR SIGN, HIT THE ROAD WORKERS, AND SMASH INTO THE CEMENT TRUCK, YOU'VE GONE TOO FAR."

"GO . . . GET . . . YOUR . . . MOTHER."

CRUEL KIDS

When I was in middle school, over the course of a week just before summer began, a group of eighth graders thought it would be fun to find a scrawny seventh-grade boy and crush his testicles. I know this sounds absurd, but I swear to you it's true.

I remember a mob of both boys and girls grabbing a younger student by the legs, hauling the poor child out to our middle school flagpole, and then ramming his genitals against the pole. I know for sure this happened to a couple of boys. I witnessed one incident from a safe distance inside a classroom. I never found out if either kid later fathered children or ended up as a soprano in the local church choir. Perhaps both?

I have a vivid memory of being so frightened that I would fall victim to this middle school sociopathy. I don't think I have ever been more frightened in my life. I felt like I was in *Lord of the Flies*, *A Clockwork Orange*, and Shirley Jackson's "The Lottery" all at the same time. My heart was pounding. I was racing through the halls to get the fuck out of there. I scurried home soaked in sweat, wondering how it was possible that this "activity" was even happening. I could not (then or now) wrap my brain around this violent and disturbing ritual these sick fuckers had concocted (pun intended). Children can be not just cruel but also downright psychotic!

My year at McQuaid Jesuit...
gym class. Hairless Harry?!!

Harry and Brian – two
freshman... same age!

Edward Gorey...

artist. His drawings are so patient in their execution, a lotta love in each one of them. I think that's what I like about them, they're so morbid, yet lovingly rendered.

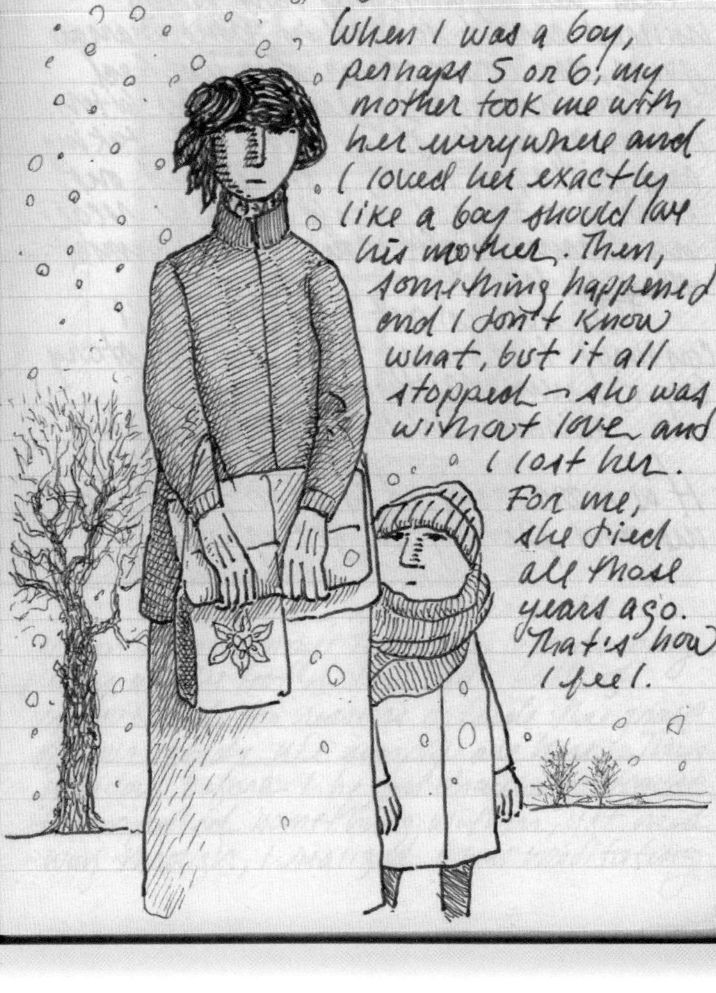

When I was a boy, perhaps 5 or 6, my mother took me with her everywhere and I loved her exactly like a boy should love his mother. Then, something happened and I don't know what, but it all stopped — she was without love and I lost her. For me, she died all those years ago. That's how I feel.

MONOPOLY

Looking back, I'm surprised I had the intelligence to play a board game like Monopoly when I was eleven or twelve. I never thought of myself as smart. Not even close to smart. I saw myself as dumb. Most board games were too complicated for me. Risk, Life, Concentration, Sorry! . . . these names terrified me! Still do. I probably had undiagnosed ADD or a general learning disorder, which was fine because I excelled at daydreaming and drawing. I don't know what it was about Monopoly that made it easy for me to understand, but I understood it well. Maybe it was greed. I don't say that to be funny; I actually think I was a greedy little boy and that inspired my determination for this particular game.

My friend Jeff, my older sister, Rachel, and I would have marathon sessions, playing for seven or eight hours at a time. We wouldn't eat. We feared going to the bathroom in the event one of us would cheat. If one of us had to get up and go to the bathroom or get a glass of milk, each of us would take our pile of money with us. We would threaten one another before we left the room, say things like, "I swear to God if either one of you cheat, I'm gonna fucking kill you." We actually said things like that to one another.

There were some funny moments, but these were scattered across hours of anxiety, paranoia, and name-calling . . . it was kinda fucked-up. At least once during these long sessions, one of us, usually me, would throw the entire board up into the air in frustration when it was clear bankruptcy was inevitable.

I can still recall those plastic and metal game pieces flying in slow motion as a glorious, cathartic, prepubescent hate-filled vindication washed over me. I may have lost the game, but at least I wasn't dumb. Maybe Gordon Gekko was right, greed is good.

"THIS NEXT SONG IS ABOUT UNBRIDLED CORPORATE GREED AND ITS PROPENSITY TO DECIMATE THE PLANET. . . . I HOPE YOU LIKE IT."

"I DON'T CARE ABOUT THE DRUGS OR THE ALCOHOL. JUST TELL ME WHO GAVE YOU THESE AYN RAND BOOKS!"

NARDONES' BASEMENT

Like most little brothers, I wanted to hang around my older brother and his friends. Like most older brothers, Charley didn't want me hanging around. But my persistence paid off over the years, and by the time I was in seventh grade, I was allowed to hang at Johnny Nardone's basement.

Johnny Nardone was Charley's friend, and I was friends with Johnny's little brother, Stevie, and Stevie's best friend, Steve Faggiano, who lived right next door. Steve Faggiano's older brother Mike Faggiano was good friends with Charley . . . it's not that complicated, just imagine two houses next to each other and in each house there were a bunch of kids and all those kids were friends. Plus, two of Johnny's sisters, Terri and Chrissey Nardone, dated two of Charley's friends. There must've been fifteen to twenty friends of Charley's who got together regularly in the Nardones' basement.

At one point, there were seven children living in the Nardone home. By the time I was hanging out there, three of them had grown up and moved out. That left Johnny, Terri, Chrissey, and Stevie and, of course, Mrs. Nardone. When I first started hanging out at the Nardones' house, I had no idea what Mrs. Nardone looked like—she worked all day, came home after dark, and went right upstairs.

Down in the basement we all drank beers, got high, smoked cigarettes, and played pool. Southern rock on the turntable, never too loud. All of us had a deep respect for Mrs. Nardone, and we knew not to piss her off. The basement was like a bar; in fact, there was a bar in the basement. We would go there on the weekends (or weekdays for that matter) around seven or eight and stay till near midnight. Most of the time I walked the mile or two home from their house stoned and ready for bed.

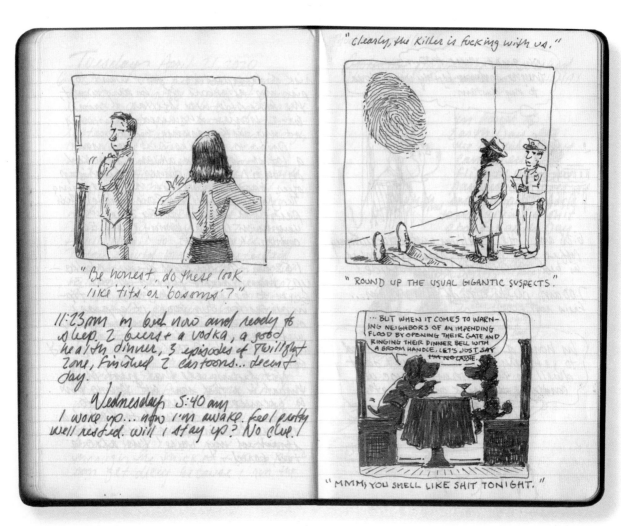

Mrs. Nardone always thought that it was better if we smoked and drank in her home as opposed to getting behind the wheel of an automobile and going from bar to bar. Now, in theory (and reality) this kinda worked, but every now and again reality beat the shit out of the theory and I experienced a few late nights in which one of my brother's friends got behind the wheel of a rusted Gran Torino and went somewhere . . . drunk.

But this was unusual because most of my brothers' friends didn't have any money. They went to school, worked at night, and had to pay for their own cars—fixing them themselves and taking care of them. They didn't want to fuck their cars up in a drunk-driving collision. My brothers' friends worked for everything they had, and a few of them stole for what they couldn't afford.

I had a huge crush on Chrissey Nardone, but she didn't think much of me. In fact, no one thought much of me. My nickname was Gayby. The truth is, the only reason I didn't get the shit beat out of me more often than I did was because my two older brothers were actually cool. Because of them, I was nearly untouchable. I say *nearly untouchable* because I was certainly touchable to my brothers' friends. Those bastards would punch me in the arm every time they saw me. I was in constant fear of being punched by my brothers' friends, and it lasted for years.

Do you have any idea what that kind of fear does to a kid? Forget the fact that both of my parents physically disciplined us, then I had to get it from my brothers' friends. I guess this was par for the course back then. At least it was in our little screwy world.

The Rings of my Regret

* 1970: USED A KITCHEN KNIFE TO OPEN A CAN OF PEACHES.

* 1973: SET OFF A BOTTLE ROCKET IN MY DAD'S BUICK — HE WAS DRIVING.

* 1980: HOSPITALIZED AFTER TELLING TICKET-HOLDERS WAITING TO SEE 'THE EMPIRE STRIKES BACK' THAT DARTH VADER WAS LUKE'S FATHER.

* 2016: TUNED INTO ELECTION RESULTS.

* 2009 INGESTED PSILOCYBIN AT THE OPERA.

* 2003: GAVE MY MOTHER MY CELLPHONE NUMBER.

* 1990: WATCHED 'HENRY: PORTRAIT OF A SERIAL KILLER' FOR THE 5TH TIME.

MARKY

A common refrain from my father that has been repeated countless times for the past twenty years is, "I have no regrets. I've lived a good life. I served my country, had a decent career, a family—no regrets, goddamnit, I've had a good life." Whenever I hear my father say this, I always think, *Is he trying to convince me or himself?* I never take him seriously.

Of course he has regrets. We all have regrets. I'm pretty sure he regrets hitting his children, and I know he regrets not giving his brother Leon—the best of the Bliss brothers—a cigarette on the day he died. When my uncle Leon requested one last smoke, the hospital wouldn't allow it. My father told me he regretted not giving Leon that last cigarette. So there's one regret right there. I have a few, none of them too severe, except one.

For a brief time in my preteens I was a little fucker—I bullied. Hard to imagine me being a bully back then, I had the face of a six-year-old, and I wasn't particularly big; nevertheless, I was successful. Bullies come in all shapes and sizes.

In our neighborhood, there was this kid named Marky. He lived two houses down from us. Marky was always picking his nose and I found it disgusting. I, of course, picked my nose, as did every other person I had ever met in my life, so why I singled out Marky makes no sense to me to this day. I only know that my childhood was so out of control: parents fighting, abuse, constant dysfunction and fear in our home. I think I needed something or someone to have control over. This was before I discovered that art could provide a form of stability for me.

I bullied Marky on and off for over a year. We were alone one summer afternoon outside of our middle school when I held a switchblade to the kid's neck just to see if I could make him afraid of me. It worked. This isn't easy to write about, and honestly I think I've tried to block most of this stuff out because of the shame I have around it. A shame I'll never lose. I had the knife against Marky's neck, and he was looking at me with a sort of sad, pleading expression. Then he said, "Can we still be friends?" I didn't know how to react—it really confused me. Empathy wasn't in my emotional wheelhouse, so I couldn't feel that. I went blank. I didn't say anything to Marky. I folded the knife up, put it in my pocket, and walked home.

A few weeks later, during one of our neighborhood soccer games on the front lawns, Marky was playing with us. At one point he tripped and fell on the ground. I piled on top of him, gave him a few punches in his ribs, and when we both got up, I kicked him back to the ground. I was surprised to find his father watching the whole thing. Marky's father came over and helped his son off the ground, and as he did this, he leaned over to me and said softly, "Harry, don't you ever lay a hand on my son again." When he said this, I was silent; I didn't respond. I believe I was in shock. He put his arm around his son, and together they walked back to their home. I simply turned around and walked back to my house.

The whole thing felt so strange. I didn't know what to make of any of it. I went into my bedroom, shut the door, and sat on the edge of my bed. I have a vivid memory of crying, bawling my eyes out. It wasn't the kind of crying I was used to—angry crying. This was another kind, maybe it was shame crying. I bawled in that room for about ten minutes. I remember this because I put on "Riders on the Storm" by the Doors to drown out my sobs so that no one in the house could hear me. I know that song is about eight minutes long.

Something had happened to me. I realized that Marky, this poor kid who I bullied, had people who loved him and cared for him. He had a father and a mother and a little brother, a family. If they found out what a bastard I had been to him, it would've broken their hearts. I suppose sitting there on the edge of my bed I understood this, and I couldn't stop crying. I hated myself. I still hate myself for what I put that kid through. Marky's family moved away that year, and I never had the chance to tell him how sorry I was for hurting him. I wish I could go back in time and be Marky's friend, but I can't.

"SORRY, BOY. THE BASEMENT ATE
YOUR TENNIS BALL. . . ."

TENNIS

We were a tennis family thanks to my father, and to this day I love tennis. My oldest brother, John, was a strong tennis player in high school. I recall my mother and father driving John to the various tennis clubs for his tournaments—he did well. Many other parents, most of whom made a hell of a lot more money than my old man did, came up to him after matches and told him how impressed they were with John's playing. I think I was proud too. Though, I always felt a little embarrassed by my dad. (Who isn't embarrassed by their parents?) He wore a beat-up brown leather jacket, jeans, and his shabby Airborne hat with the flaps hanging down over his ears—he looked pretty disheveled compared with the other parents at these elite clubs. I tagged along and watched, but I just wanted to be home with my comic books, watching TV with a massive bowl of Cocoa Puffs.

I played too. I'd hit a tennis ball against the brick wall at my elementary school in the summers. I'd ride my bike up there and practice for over an hour. Looking back, I think part of this activity was a good way for me to get my frustrations out. I couldn't serve for shit, but I could volley. I was young, so I could get around the court fast and chase balls without tearing an ACL. Most of my memories of playing tennis are with my friends Dean and Jeff, or with my father. I played a little in high school in my senior year, and as a freshman in Jesuit school, but I was high most of the time, so . . .

At thirteen I would play with my father and get really angry whenever I

Harry, age 12. Playing tennis with his Father...

my old man's 'Davis Classic'

GUNNA RETURN THIS INTO THE OLD MAN'S TINY BALLS!

Molly Hatchet T-shirt.

Levi jeans

Chuck T Converse

I would often become so enraged with my poor attempts at a back-hand. I'd curse out loud or throw my racket. Others on the courts heard my outbursts and my poor sportmanship embarrassed the old man. I was incapable of learning from my errors. I was filled with rage.

messed up. I was so hard on myself. I'm not sure why I got so angry, maybe it was just a father-son dynamic. Maybe I wanted to impress my father. I don't know, but I said the word *fuck* out loud a lot and threw my racket at the chain-link fence, much to my father's disgust. (It's possible I simply watched too much of John McEnroe's playing.) I recall times when my father had had enough of my antics and simply left, didn't say a word, just walked off the court and got into our flatbed Ford. I followed, feeling disappointed in myself. I got into the passenger seat, and he'd hit me, a firm punch in my arm—it hurt. I know it wasn't the best style of parenting, but I kind of deserved it. I mean, I was a real bastard.

My dad eventually stopped playing with me, but I played with friends. We watched the US Open every year—John McEnroe, Jimmy Connors, Björn Borg, Chris Evert, Billie Jean King—all of them, straight up until Roger Federer and Rafael Nadal. If tennis was on television, I was watching it.

These days I can't play anymore because my shoulders hurt, knees hurt and, well, that physical door has closed for me. Still the game continues to give me joy. It's a strange thing, when I recall all of those times playing dysfunctional tennis with my old man, him hitting me, me crying, hating him all through the silent drive home . . . But the truth is, if it weren't for him, I wouldn't have my love of tennis.

"KIDS, COULD YOU DO MOMMY A HUGE FAVOR AND
GO REALLY FAR AWAY FROM ME? THANKS."

WHOSE KID IS THIS?

I wish I had more nice things to write about my parents. In the early years my mom tucked me in at night, and I know we were close despite the fact that she kept losing me in department stores. Boy, did I cry and get to know plenty of security guards on a first-name basis. Really enjoyed Thomas. A big man with kind eyes and fingers like sausages. Thomas told me stories about growing up in Chicago, his father losing him at a ball game once. Made me feel better, great guy.

When Mom eventually came for me, I know I was happy and relieved. I ran to her. I must've loved her.

Two years ago my mom told me that for most of my life, up until I was in my thirties, my father thought I wasn't his son. I know, crazy! My mom became pregnant with me shortly after a trip to California to visit her parents. So, naturally, Dad always suspected she cheated on him while she was out west . . . traveling with her three kids!

If what Mom told me is true, it explains a lot, mainly why my father treated me like I was the child of another man who fucked his wife.

CHARLIE

When freshman year of high school came around, I was all set to go to public school, but my parents felt a stricter education would benefit me due to the fact that I was turning into a juvenile delinquent. This wasn't solely the opinion of my parents—it was a fact. Even I knew I was a little shit. I was turning out to be a very bad young man. So, as much as I railed against this decision, Jack and Roz won out, and one August morning my parents drove me to meet the admissions man at McQuaid Jesuit High School. I was to be one of three Jewish kids in the entire place—lovely. No more jeans, T-shirts, cigarettes, or Chuck Taylors . . . I had to wear a jacket and tie.

With the benefit of hindsight, and a great deal of self-reflection, I realize now my time at McQuaid was unique, and in many ways surprisingly beneficial to the person I am today. I got respectable grades, participated in athletics, studied, read actual books, made friends, even prayed in the priests' chapel (which no longer exists).

None of these things would've been possible at public school. Public school was all about survival. Public school was about getting through the day without being punched, mocked, or made to feel bad about yourself. At least that was my experience. Our public high school in 1978 wasn't far off from a prison. Hazing, cheating, drugs, and a fight every day after school. Most of the teachers couldn't wait to get the hell out of there. McQuaid had some of these traits as well, but fewer and further between.

If you did mess up at McQuaid, you weren't simply reprimanded or made to stay after school (which, instead of detention was called JUG—judgment under God), you were also hit . . . by an angry priest . . . and it hurt. I would hear a kid crying once a week and occasionally see some poor bastard still whimpering from a visit to the principal's office. I hate violence. I have a hard time watching football because of my fear of witnessing an injury and I'm not a fan of corporal punishment, but I have to tell you, it worked. I quickly learned to stay out of trouble.

Before that year at McQuaid I don't think I'd ever really experienced empathy. I knew laughter and anger . . . nothing in between. At McQuaid we all had to take theology no matter what your religion or belief, like math or English or social studies—a core class. In our first theology class that freshman year, all the students were told to introduce themselves. You had to tell the class your name, where you lived, and what your father did for a living. No mention of our mothers—nothin'. I dreaded having to do this. I hated public speaking. When we had to read out loud in elementary school or middle school it was worse than torture for me. Just having to introduce myself I became nervous and was consumed with fear and self-doubt. But I got through it. In fact, when I mentioned to the class that my father was an artist, some of them were impressed.

After me it was Charlie's turn. Charlie was a very quiet kid in the class, and the reason he was quiet was because he had a stammer—the worst stammer I've ever heard in my life. My father is a stutterer and has been his whole life, so I was familiar with it. But Charlie's stammering was painful to endure. I knew that Charlie was going to be worse off than me, and I suppose this had taken away some of the fear.

When it came time for Charlie to speak, the entire class felt his pain. This sort of thing wouldn't have happened in public school. In public school everyone would've ridiculed Charlie. There would've been students in the class laughing at him, making his pain all the more unbearable. This didn't happen that first day of theology class. In fact, as I sat there listening to Charlie trip over each and every letter of his introduction, another student sitting behind Charlie leaned forward and laid a compassionate hand on Charlie's back, and said, "Take your time, Charlie, you got this."

Up to that point in my life, I had never seen anything like this. I was thirteen years old, and I had just witnessed empathy for the first time. I felt myself become emotional. I kept my emotions in check and, instead, started sweating like a bastard. I didn't dare cry because I had learned over the years that crying was a sign of weakness, or that you were a faggot. The truth is, all of those boys in that class wanted to cry or at least hug Charlie—to be supportive.

Later in the year, the class walked over to the priests' residences to pray in their chapel. This was kind of a big deal. I'm not sure why, but to have an opportunity to pray in a sacred place where your professors prayed wasn't insignificant. I was nervous. I had never been to a church before or prayed. I didn't know how to pray. The only praying I had ever done up to that point was the sort of praying you do when you don't want to get in trouble for doing something really stupid: *Please, God, don't let me get caught burning down the neighborhood. Please, God, don't let me get caught with this cigarette. Please, God, don't let me get caught stealing quarters from my father's top dresser drawer. Please, God, make my erection go away.* That kind of praying.

We all walked through the darkened halls of the residences and entered a small, beautiful wood chapel with soft light coming through long stained glass windows. I have a clear memory of how taken I was with those wonderful depictions of biblical scenes. Our teacher asked us all to find a place to sit and be with our thoughts for a moment. I was nervous, as usual. But after a few minutes of quiet, I felt myself entering a sort of meditation—long before I'd ever heard the word *meditation*. I surprised myself and managed to focus my attention on various people in my life. I thought, *Who should I pray for?* I considered my grandparents, but I really didn't know them very well, and I held resentment for the corduroy pants they sent me every year for my birthday. I thought about my own parents and my siblings, but that felt too easy. I wanted to find something or someone unique to pray for. It didn't take me too long to find the right person—he was sitting in front of me. My thoughts found Charlie.

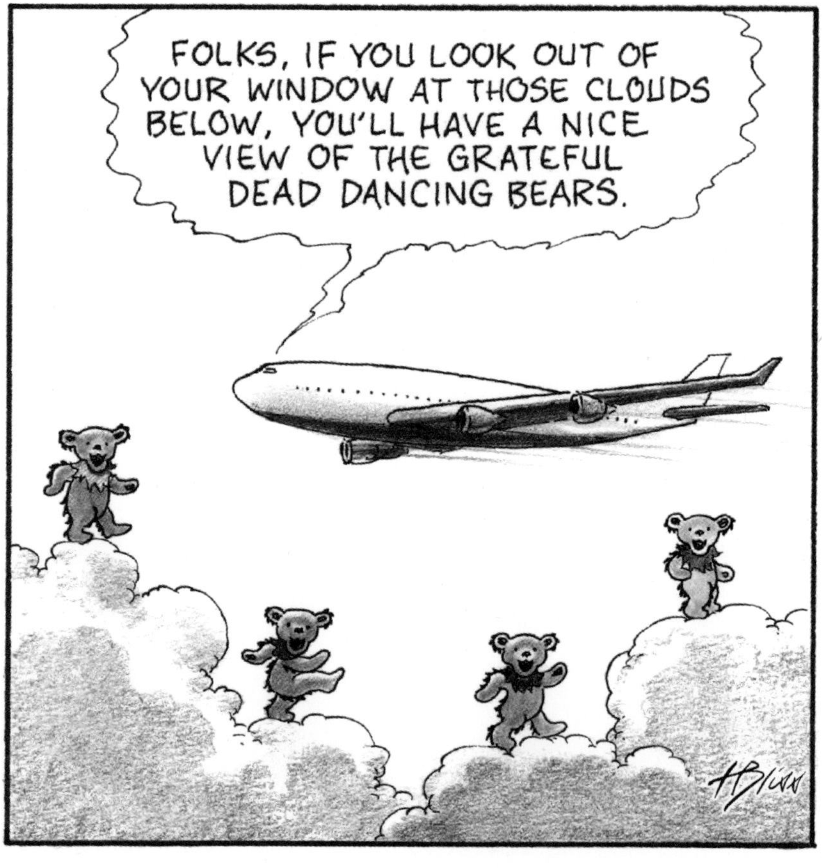
FOLKS, IF YOU LOOK OUT OF YOUR WINDOW AT THOSE CLOUDS BELOW, YOU'LL HAVE A NICE VIEW OF THE GRATEFUL DEAD DANCING BEARS.

SELF-REFLECT BUS

On the ride to McQuaid the bus made about ten stops. The whole trip took forty minutes. At various points the bus would downshift and come to idle in front of houses. I'd study the boys as they sleepily climbed up the bus steps and found a seat. I would watch covertly, but intently, paying attention to each kid, how they walked from their homes, with various gestures of insecurity. I liked studying things and making a mental picture of them.

At first, I resented everything about leaving the familiarity of public school, but in time I found I enjoyed sitting on the bus and looking out the window. Maybe it was the quiet of the morning, before the unruliness would take over.

Looking out the window, I noticed all sorts of things: farms, cows, different houses and neighborhoods, mothers with their little kids waiting for their school bus, joggers, terrific trees and skies—all of it. My mind would start turning things over and I'd consider what I saw. I wasn't aware I was doing it, I just did. The most innocuous things on that bus ride could be fascinating to me.

At one house, with an adjacent barn and wooden fence on a more rural road along the way to McQuaid, we picked up one boy whose father accompanied him from their house to the curb where the bus waited. The boy's father looked like a farmer—Tom Joad with a buzz cut—strong, thin arms, worked with his hands, I figured. Guy could've walked out of a Norman Rockwell illustration. He had an odd, loving, concerned look on his face. To my mind, the reason for this look became instantly clear.

His son was very meek. He had a crew cut, wore thick glasses, and was very short. Everyone on the bus eyeballed the kid as he made his way toward the back. I turned and watched the poor son-of-a-bitch plop down like a sack of potatoes. His paper bag lunch fell off the seat, and an orange rolled away from him toward the front of the bus.

I turned back around and pretended not to notice anything. I didn't wanna make the kid feel any worse. There were quiet, cruel laughs. I got sad sitting there, staring out the window. The father still had that concerned look, waving at the bus as it pulled away. Sometimes, if you pay too close attention to things, they can depress the hell out of you.

I've been thinking about those looking-out-the-window bus rides lately. And the walk home from the parking lot where the bus dropped me off. Prior

I MISS OLIVER SACKS... 12:00 NOON

"Creativity is the intellectual capital of any country or group, but it must be funded."

"I think that all children are little scientists and little artists."

"Apprenticeship in art, I think, is a crucial sort of stage in creativity." (7 years, at least)

Oliver Sacks — my hero

"One needs to be impressionable, to be open to influences, to be fertilised by influences, to synthesise them and then to get beyond them."

"Moby Dick is a work of genius."

"Growing up in England in the Jurassic (HA) I was quite fond of P.G. Wodehouse."

"Bach had twenty children—." 'Have intercourse' with the World.'

to those bus rides to McQuaid I don't believe I'd ever self-reflected. Hell, I didn't even know what *self-reflection* meant. I noticed that when I was alone outdoors looking at things, I wasn't anxious. That first week at McQuaid, I sat all by myself on the bus, and when I climbed down off the bus, and

walked home alone . . . I was calm. I'm thinking there's something to this. When I was around people and noise, I'd get nervous and chew my nails. But when I was all alone, I was myself. I'd sing and talk to myself, think up jokes, even laugh out loud. I was creative when I was all by myself.

"SO, IN RARE INSTANCES, THE ATTACKER
MAY OVERPOWER YOU."

STEVE ANDREWS

That's the kid I fought in high school. I started the fight in the cafeteria—I walked up to him and his stoner underclassmen friends and said something simplistically confrontational (I was an idiot). He stood up, we stared red-eyed at each other, and went at it.

Now, I was a senior and had four inches on Steve Andrews, so in my stoned mind I was thinking, *This'll be over in no time.* Well, I was wrong. Little Steven threw a right hook that landed hard on the side on my face, knocking my glasses who-the-fuck-knows-where and leaving me legally blind and panicking. Another punch clipped my jaw. Kids gathered around, and I needed to get in close to this feisty little bastard and hope for an uppercut. So I pulled him in, but all I got was a pathetic flurry of abdominal blows, cutting my drawing hand on the goddamn zipper of his leather jacket.

A teacher broke it up, and we both got sent to the office. I should've been humiliated, letting this sophomore get the better of me, but mostly I was glad it was over. Not ten minutes later we were both in the principal's outer office and this little prick said, "I'm gonna finish you off after school."

I had shit to do after school!

I didn't have time to fuck around. We fought, it didn't go the way I planned, and, as far as I cared, we were done.

Later that day in detention he was still threatening me! Finally, I yelled at the kid, loud, so everyone in detention could hear me, "You won! Okay? I give up—let it go!" Un-fucking-believable. Later in the school year, when Steve Andrews finally did "let it go," we sometimes waved to each other in the hall. There was an unspoken respect between us. I respected him for being a tough little bastard, and he respected me for admitting he was a tough little bastard.

LOST QUOTES of the GREAT ARTISTS...

'Just have _one_ drink with me!
Don't run away... I gave you
my fucking ear!!'
—— Van Gogh

'Man, syphilis sucks'
—— Manet

'Manet's right...'
—— Gauguin

'Now, pretend you're talking
to God, only bend over
and lift up your gown.'
—— Michaelangelo

'I can't reach the
fucking absinthe!'
—— Lautrec

'Just piggy backing on what
Manet and Gauguin said.'
—— Lautrec

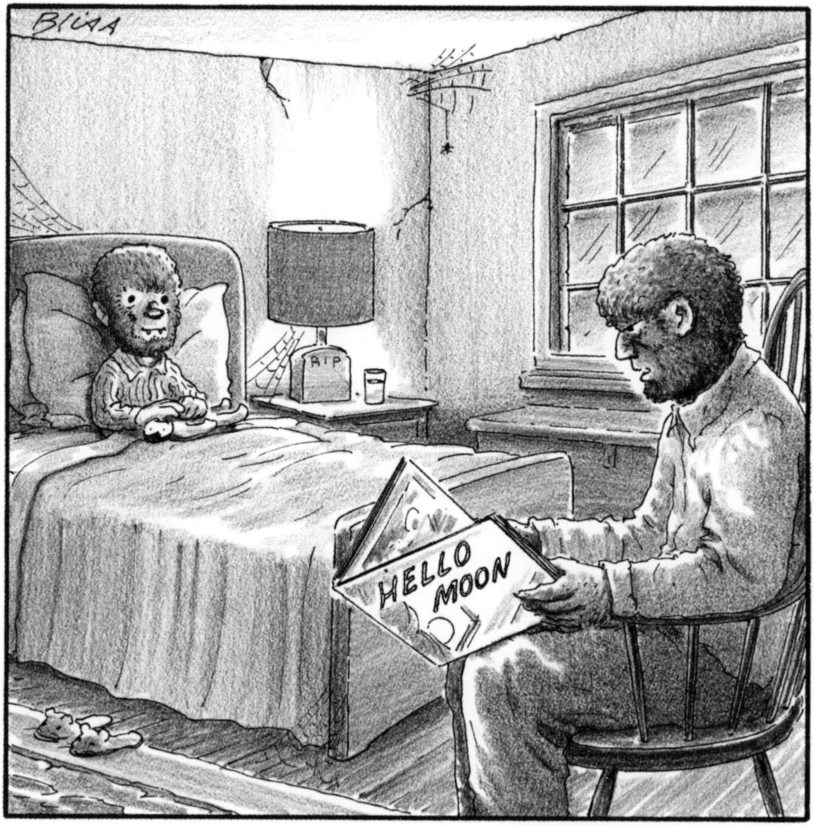
RIP
HELLO MOON

SPERRY LIBRARY

I don't think it's an exaggeration to say that libraries and museums not only kept me from being incarcered but were also sacred places for me. At a very early age, whether I was conscious of it or not, I felt peaceful within their walls.

My mother took me to the library two or three times a week when I was very young. She was, and still is, a voracious reader. In most of my memories of her she is on the couch with a stack of books next to her on the floor.

Once inside the library, she would go off to find her books (fat novels) and I would head to the seven hundreds—the arts section. This is where I found dozens of cartoon books and other illustrated works by Richard Scarry, Maurice Sendak, N. C. Wyeth, and Edward Gorey (which I found both frightening and eerily charming). I would look at any art-related books: how-to books on stained glass, woodworking, ceramics. I marveled at how much there was to choose from.

When I started public high school at fifteen—as difficult as that time was for me—I found the library at James E. Sperry High School to be a beautiful space. I looked forward to the day's end, not because I could go home and watch TV, smoke pot, or destroy things with my friends (again, we were extremely destructive), but because I could go to the library. I knew the Dewey decimal system and had no trouble navigating my way through those stacks. I made that library my bitch. In time, I discovered other sections beyond the

MAUS art spiegelman

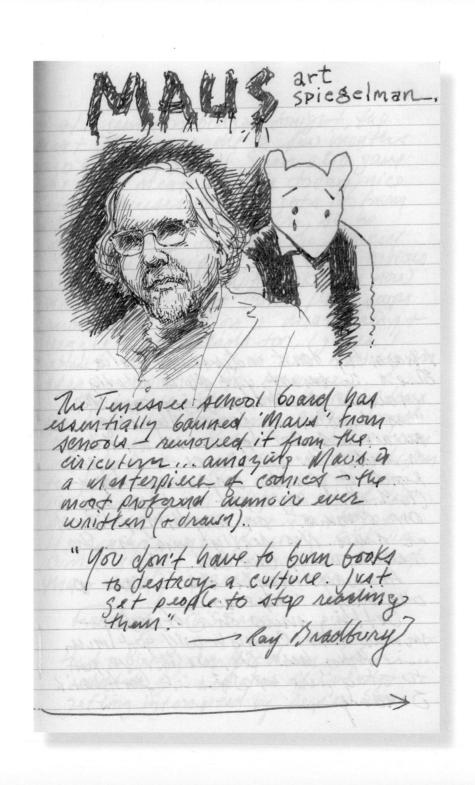

The Tennessee school board has essentially banned 'Maus' from schools - removed it from the curriculum... amazing. Maus is a masterpiece of comics - the most profound memoir ever written (or drawn).

"You don't have to burn books to destroy a culture. Just get people to stop reading them".
— Ray Bradbury

seven hundreds—books on film, animation, photography, architecture, and more.

On most school days I was the last student to leave the library at 5:00 p.m. In all kinds of weather, I would head home carrying at least five and sometimes up to ten oversize, coffee-table art books, struggling with an inordinate determination to reach our kitchen door without dropping that beautiful folio of Toulouse-Lautrec paintings.

Once home, I would dump these books onto my bed and continue to pore over them. I would pull out my sketchbook and copy paintings by Picasso, Toulouse-Lautrec, Daumier, Delacroix, Duchamp, and a slew of other artists I was obsessed with at the time. Homework fell away into the *Fuck it* abyss and was happily replaced by the inspired drawings I would develop. I can still close my eyes and see myself propped up in my bed drawing, the twelve-inch Panasonic TV playing old black-and-white movies into the night.

"I LOVE <u>EVERY SINGLE ONE</u> OF THESE."

HIGHBROW JACK

My father was abusive to me. He could be a real prick when I was a kid, and I doubt he'd disagree with my assessment.

Sure, he was a good provider and there were instances when he was sincerely kind to me, but I can count them all up on two hands. I don't hold on to any of the abuse. I forgive the guy, and these days we get along pretty well . . . when he's not complaining about how shitty the world is or wanting to die.

As I got older, sixteen or so, he and I would find common ground in art. The Blisses couldn't communicate for shit about most things, but when it came to discussions around art and artists, we became passionate, opinionated, and almost coherent. The oldest Bliss brother, my uncle Harry, would hold court after a Thanksgiving meal. No football game for these guys—my father and his brothers would sit around Harry's Fairport, New York, living room discussing art: the Wyeths, popular illustrators, Picasso, Modigliani, Klee, Soutine, Jasper Johns, Rothko, and more. I learned so much just sitting there, watching and listening. I loved all of it.

One of the few things my father bestowed upon me for which I am deeply grateful came one afternoon when he took me and my brother Charley to the Memorial Art Gallery in Rochester, New York (a fantastic museum if you're ever unfortunate enough to find yourself in Rochester). Hanging on the walls of this wonderful museum was a show of comic art. My dad always had respect and enthusiasm for cartoonists like Walt Kelly, Bill Everett, Charles

Schulz, Burne Hogarth, George McManus—great comic strip artists whom I would later learn to love as much or more than my old man did. This experience was profound for me. Here, in this highbrow museum where Monet, Rembrandt, Rothko, and Degas lived, were the ink slingers whose work I knew and relished.

That afternoon, Jack Bliss conveyed to his two sons that comic book artists were just as important, just as gifted and skilled, as some of the "master" painters housed in that museum. Through my father, I understood there was no highbrow or lowbrow art, there was only sublime art and sub-sublime art.

Tuesday 8:30 am May 23, 2017

Christopher Lee
When I was kid growing up in Rochester NY in the 70s, I loved the Hammer Films. No matter how late is was or how high I was on skunk weed, if this guy was on TV, I was watching him. One of the great joys of an otherwise dysfunctional youth.

Every now and again I imagine a figure in my mind and set about putting the vision down on paper. Van Gogh depressed was on my mind this morning — been reading letters...

Am I gifted or am I CURSED?!

SO, here we have one sorry-ass genius whose work remains beyond comprehension. There are 2 or 3 painters I feel have been gifted with divine ability — Vincent is #1 on this list.

EPIPHANY

I would spend all my allowance from cutting lawns on art books and art supplies. I was an art nerd if that was ever a thing. I didn't hang out with other kids who were into art. There wasn't an art club I belonged to, and I didn't talk about it with anyone. It was just something I did all by myself. But, to my surprise, I got attention because I drew well. Even at Jesuit school, all the drawings of priests in various compromising positions won me all sorts of discreet accolades from my classmates. "Drawing good" made me almost cool.

After my sophomore year of high school I went to the Philadelphia College of Art (PCA) for a precollege program. Unlike Jesuit school, I really wanted to go. I knew I wanted to be an artist since I had an epiphany at fourteen:

I'd stayed up all night drawing my feet. There were assorted art books borrowed from my school library scattered around me. I'd draw for about forty-five minutes, then stop and peruse the books for inspiration. Then I'd get back to drawing. I kept this up for hours. The art books were a kind of visual cocaine that kept me going all night. I still have these drawings in a spiral-bound sketchbook.

When dawn came, I was the only one awake. I quietly tiptoed out of the house in my bare feet, up Colony Lane to the elementary school grounds. The morning dew soaked the bottoms of my pajamas, but the sun was warm on my face. I saw no one that morning. When I made it to the schoolyard, I stood in that grassy field, looked up, and said to the world and myself, "I'm going to be an artist and I'm going to leave this place." I felt completely free for the first time in my life.

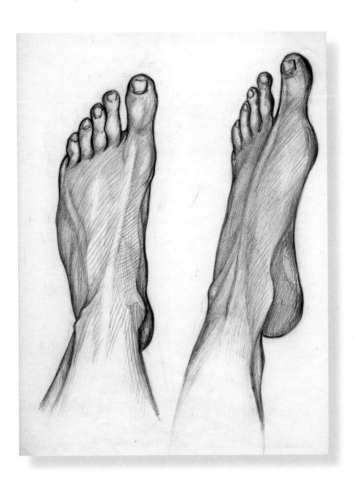

"'COLLEGE FUND'? HAHAHAHAHA!"

PRECOLLEGE

In July 1981, after finishing off my junior year in high school, I was back for my second summer of precollege at PCA. I was fairly obsessed with Bruce Springsteen at the time. Both *Born to Run* and *Darkness on the Edge of Town* were always on my turntable. *The River* had just come out, and I played the shit out of that album.

My older brother John, a Bob Dylan fan, worshipped Bruce Springsteen. He'd seen him perform in 1978 at the Rochester War Memorial. I recall John coming home after the concert and declaring "Bruce Springsteen is a prophet." I guess his cheesy praise inspired me because in no time I felt the same way about Springsteen.

At precollege, in Philly, I would sit up on the roof of our apartment building on Spruce Street with my roommates, Bruce singing through the open windows into the summer night. We sat and took in the city. We smoked cigarettes, talked about art, drank warm beer, and laughed. We were young and thrilled to be on our own.

The apartment I shared was above an oddly quiet leather bar, probably the gayest bar in Philly at the time. This was 1981, and I'll never forget looking out our second-floor window to see a robust, Divine-looking prostitute jerking a guy off in a white Buick . . . at noon! Down the hall from us were three girls, and I became infatuated with a twenty-one-year-old fabrics major. First love!

"SO, OWEN TELLS ME YOU GUYS MET
IN ART SCHOOL."

ART SCHOOL

When high school finished (didn't attend graduation, no senior photo of me),
I was set to get outta Dodge. The car ride from upstate New York to Philadelphia wasn't too bad. In retrospect this is miraculous because my parents
always bickered like psychotic raccoons in the car. Did I have a Walkman?
Did they exist in 1982? Most of the time I just looked out the window. Seven
hours is a long time to look out the window.

Once I saw the skyline of the city, I got really excited. I couldn't wait to
get out of the car and start my new artist life away from my excruciating
suburban pain.

On the first day, I moved into the dorms, which were designed by the
architect Frank Furness. (Furness was also the architect of the Pennsylvania
Academy of the Fine Arts, the oldest art academy in the country and the
school where I would later study.)

I had three roommates. Peter Woodward was a hilarious guy from the UK
who I'm lucky to still be in touch with. Scott Zukin was a Jewish Deadhead
from a quasi-affluent neighborhood outside Philadelphia. Scott was a wood
major and spent his entire freshman year listening to the Grateful Dead,
smoking pot with his girlfriend, and working on a fucking walking cane—
which I have to admit was one of the nicest-looking canes I've ever seen.
Linh Dinh was Vietnamese and wouldn't shut up about what a goddamn
genius Thelonious Monk was. Linh drew beautifully and knew more about

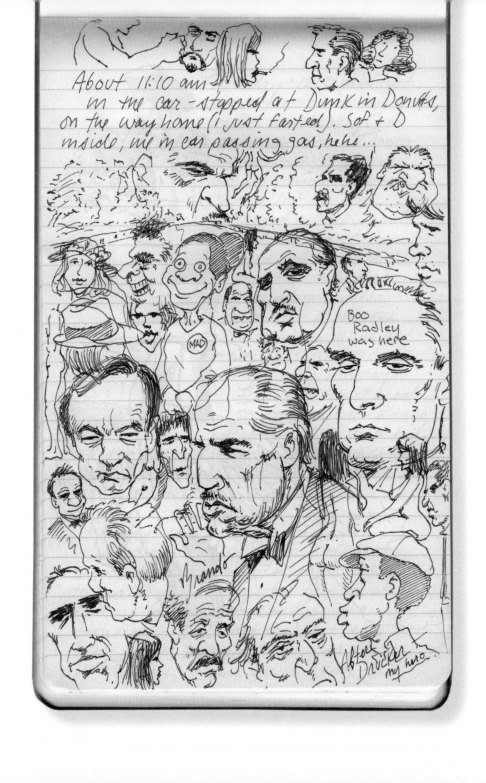

About 11:10 am
in the car - stopped at Dunkin Donuts,
on the way home (I just farted). Sof & D
inside, me in car passing gas, hehe...

BOO
Radley
was here

MAD

Brando

After
Drucker
my hero.

this country's history than I did. But what really impressed me was how Linh would prepare ramen—very methodical and so spicy he'd perspire right back into the bowl. And then there was me, little pasty-face Wonder-Bread Harry. The four of us were like the United Nations. We shared two large rooms, one with a skylight and a small galley kitchen and the other with two bunk beds. That first year was glorious.

My advice for anyone who wants to become an artist is this: move away from your home as soon as you can and have as many experiences as you can—live a life. And then you'll be able to draw from that life to make your art. Here's the rub: you have to live this full life before you're thirty.

Good luck.

"HANDS, RACHEL. CLAP YOUR HANDS. WHY ON EARTH WOULD I SAY, 'IF YOU'RE HAPPY AND YOU KNOW IT, SLAP SAM'?"

TRAUMA GRATITUDE

So much of my childhood was fear-based. There was so much hitting and yelling in our house—so much! It was frightening for little Harry to know that at any turn, one of my parents or siblings (or I!) would turn combustible. I was constantly afraid. It wasn't all horrible—we had laughter, TV, and art. Yet, this constant fear (my psychoanalyst labeled it PTSD) stayed with me.

I was just thinking about this as I was looking out the window at two chipmunks chasing each other around my patio. Should I be grateful for my dysfunctional, loud childhood? The reason I moved to this rural mountaintop was because I was no longer able to tolerate the sounds of cars, leaf blowers, sirens—most of the noises that exist in more populated areas.

And now that I'm here, living off a dirt road, watching the chipmunks, staring out at the sugar maples and birches, the distant mountains on the other side of the Connecticut River, I feel happy. Ironically, it's the trauma that got me here. I feel a strange gratitude for the childhood trauma—it brought me here, and I love being here.

Here is peace.

Maple Tree bark

Ash Tree bark

6:50 pm

I cannot leave
this spot. I
find my surround-
ings remarkable.

A chipmunk is under my chair. I am
surrounded by birds, trees and sunlight with long shadows. This is so
damn entertaining — just sitting here.

Penny
sleeping
Sunday Morn.

Penny
Again...
Monday
10:30
am

10/21/21

I worked in the basement last
night for about 2 hours. Run
Sofi had veggie sushi delivered
and we watch Ted Lasso. I
was pretty sad here after we
arrived at 5 pm. My first time
back since Penny's death. So
many things remind me of her
here. I only know this house with
Penny in it... tough. I took a
bath around 6 pm. Penny would
always come into the bathroom
and lay on the floor to keep me
company. Penny wasn't penciled
in between Sofi & I in bed this
morning like she always was...

slept between
us like a nestled
pencil. Penny also
doubled as a chastity
belt of sorts...

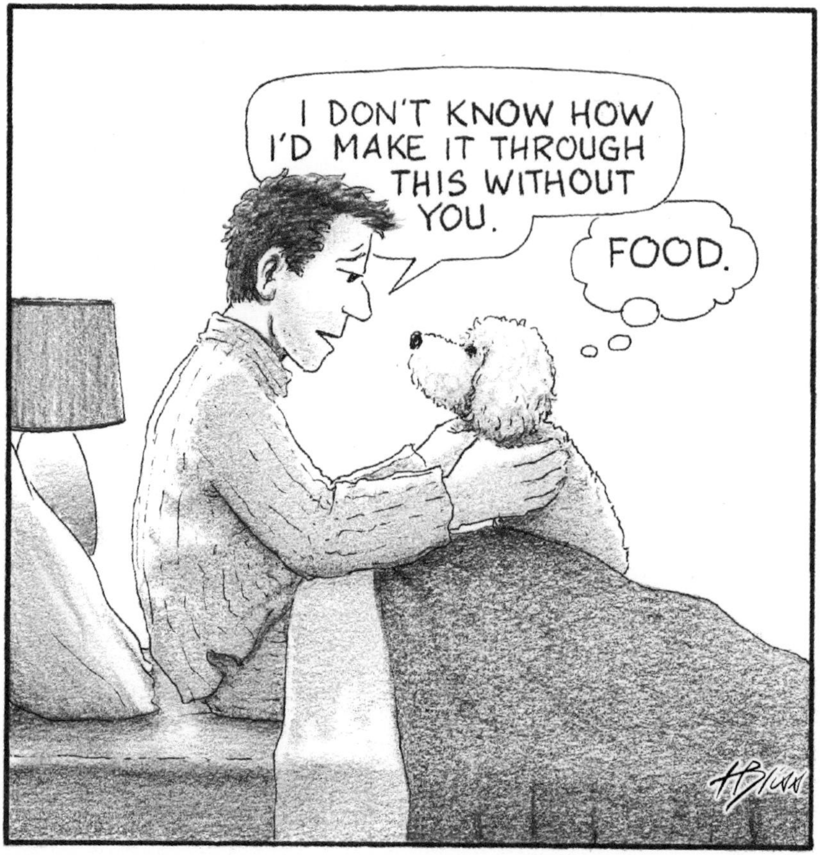
I DON'T KNOW HOW I'D MAKE IT THROUGH THIS WITHOUT YOU.
FOOD.

PENNY GRIEF

Every time I think I should be writing about Penny for this book, I get sad and lose any desire or inspiration. I miss her so much. Seventeen years of my life were spent in close proximity to that furry creature. Just sitting here thinking about chasing each other around the dining room table at our home at Overlake Park fills me with longing to have her back.

Why does this happen? Why can't I remember her without the visceral heartache? Rather than it "getting easier with time," I feel as though the moments of grief are becoming more profound as time passes. Maybe the time spent thinking about Penny decreases, but the intensity of the loss only seems to increase in these moments.

A few minutes ago I stopped writing and had to breathe slowly with goddamn tears in my eyes. My chest is still heavy and weak. These moments have become what I can describe only as a helpless immersion into sorrow. I no longer fight it, I simply allow it, for better or worse, to occupy my body. It's a possession by sadness for which there is no exorcism. Well, vodka helps. Maybe Max von Sydow will show up with a bottle of hooch. Laughter helps. . . .

I'm angry too. I want my dog back. I'm like a child who cannot listen to reason or is unwilling to accept the reality of loss. I want my fucking dog back . . . Right . . . Fucking . . . Now!

There's no question in my mind that if I could have Penny back right now,

I would trade in my parents' lives to make that happen. No question about it. My parents gone, Penny back. No-brainer. Why do I feel so strongly? Because my parents are wasting the precious gift of life. They've been wasting it for the last thirty years.

All my father does these days is complain about how shitty things are, and he wonders why he's still alive. My mother does little else but complain about my father, how he abuses her both physically and verbally. The police have been called—abuse reports filed on both sides. Mom once tried to strangle my father with an extension cord, God bless her.

They never call, write, reciprocate, or contribute in any way to their children, grandchildren, old friends, neighbors, or the world. They never leave their house. They coexist hating each other and spreading vitriol to my two older brothers or anyone else who will listen. They have created a sort of anti-life. Yet, both in their late eighties, early nineties, they remain relatively healthy—no major issues. They can still go to the bathroom, wipe their ass, read a book, watch TV.

Meanwhile, my mother-in-law, Elaine, who recently suffered a stroke, is in a rehabilitation home working hard with whatever ninety-two-year-old fight she has left to get back what she's lost. Unlike my parents, Elaine knows how beautiful it is to be alive. She's waiting for that day when she can once again hold a fork and eat a piece of salmon.

Penny loved life. She really did. In her seventeenth year that tail of hers was still active. Please, God, if you're out there, take my parents and bring back my dog.

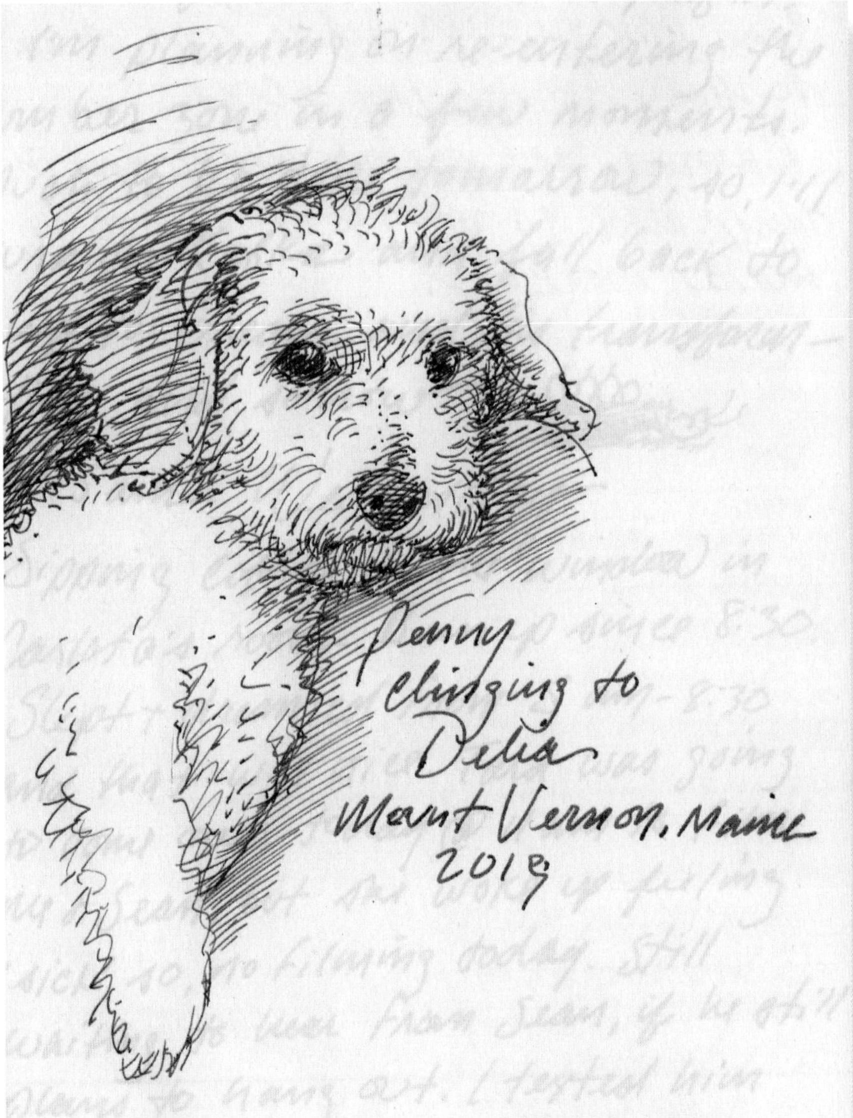
Penny
clinging to
Delia
Mount Vernon, Maine
2019

WIDMER WINES

My very first "big" freelance illustration job came by way of my father. It was a sweet gig. A full-color promotional poster art for Widmer Wines, an upstate New York winemaker. The finished art would hang in the offices of the winery, and my art would get terrific exposure.

My father got the job through the ad agency he was working for at the time. The graphic design company he co-owned and ran with my two uncles for more than twenty-five years, Studio 5 Graphics, had closed, and he was offered a job as a layout designer at one of the larger agencies in Rochester. He could've had a seasoned illustrator do the poster art, or done it himself, but he offered it to me, which was damn nice. It paid $500, and in 1983 that might as well have been $1,550. In fact, I think that's about right—I just googled it.

At the time I was studying painting at the Pennsylvania Academy of the Fine Arts (PAFA) in Philadelphia with my friends Peter and Keith. The three of us left the Philadelphia College of Art (PCA), where we were studying, to take a fine art path. We weren't challenged by PCA and sought the rigor of an academic setting. I was deeply embedded in the European academic painting methods, specifically those of Northern European masters Albrecht Dürer and a handful of Flemish masters. I wanted my illustration for the Widmer Wines poster to be in the old Flemish style, à la Pieter Bruegel, the Elder.

Looking back, I now realize how ridiculous this goal was; there was no way to imitate Bruegel. Not then, not now, not ever. In fact, of all the artists in the history of Western art to choose to replicate, Bruegel is probably the most difficult. One could argue that Hieronymus Bosch is more difficult, but you know . . . six of one, half dozen of the other. I didn't know this back then, being the clueless idiot I was, so I pushed ahead. And to my credit, it was a sincere push. I did my homework.

I went to my instructor, Arthur DeCosta, a legend at PAFA. He's dead now, but this masterful old-relic bastard knew his shit. He was steeped in all the methods of the masters, and he generously gave me specific technical directions on how to prepare the painting surface (a piece of Masonite) prior to the underdrawing and subsequent transparent underpainting. I took notes as DeCosta carefully educated me on the methods and techniques of the old masters. I bought the most expensive gesso available, sanded the surface smooth, and readied it for the layers of transparent oil paint.

I finished a Bruegel-like burnt sienna underdrawing on the gessoed Masonite with a fine quill pen. This drawing took me a week, too long, but the composition was scaffolded out—I was ready to begin the underpainting. Then one day I woke up anxious in my shitty apartment on Fifteenth Street and thought, *Oh fuck, I have no idea what I'm doing—I'll never make my deadline.* But I stuck with it and nervously began adding thin layers of transparent oil paint, each of which took days to dry. Finally, it became clear I was failing. I was in over my head. The deadline was ten days away . . . I didn't know what to do. I called my father and confessed the hole I was in. And in a most uncharacteristically kind gesture, he offered to drive from Rochester to Philadelphia to help me out. Now, to be clear, I think my parents were already planning a trip to visit my older sister, Rachel, who also lived in Philadelphia

A Lake Niagara Tradition

·THE GRAPE HARVEST·

**Widmer's Wine Cellars
Proudly Presents
The Grape Harvest,
a Limited Edition Print**

at the time, but I can't be sure. I'd like to stick to the memory of my dad just doing this to help me out; it feels nice.

The old man came down and sat in my tiny apartment bedroom on a metal life-drawing stool I'd stolen from PCA and worked on the painting all day. Then he left and came back the next day to finish it up. I'd fetch him lunch or just watch him work. My roommate Marianne, also a painter, watched too. He was affable and charming with us, not the Jack Bliss I was familiar with. He really pulled through for me, and I was grateful.

The finished art looked good, not the Dutch masterpiece I'd envisioned, but it was nice. And he let me keep all the money! Some of my sienna under-drawing was still visible in the finished printed poster, so in a way, we worked on it together—a father-and-son collaboration. Here's the finished poster.

Pieter Bruegel the Elder . . . what the hell was I thinking?

Tom
I am having one hell of a time not
mixing myself another Manhattan.

'Sheepshearing Beneath A Tree'
after Millet

Rolandson

Thomas

Rowlandson
inspired doodles.

I am having one hell of a time keeping this fire going in the bedroom fireplace — keep going out!

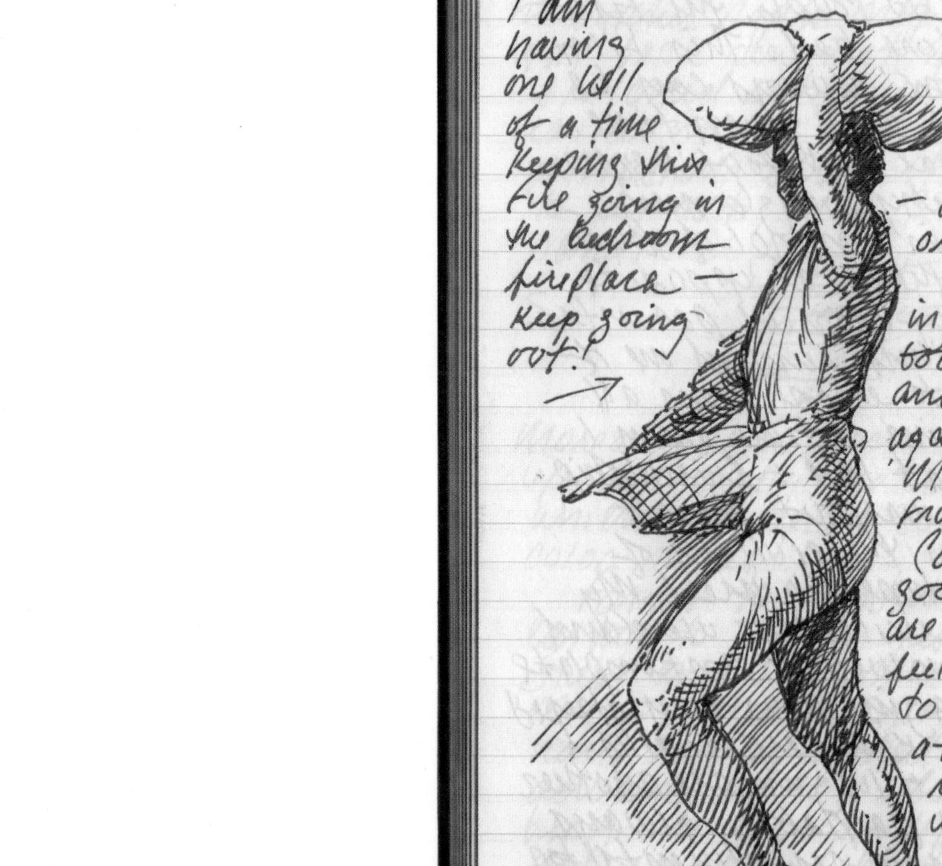

There must be some sort of atmospheric alchemy at work — draft in the fire or something...

I love rediscovering terrific art books I buy, forget and then pick up again. This one — 'Master Drawings from the Thaw Collection' is so good. The images are so delicate, I feel compelled to do my best to attempt my weak reproduction. Oh well, good practice

After Andrea del Sarto 1511-24

I may have to break out the recently repaired Mont Blanc fountain pen due to the fact that this Visconti pen doesn't quite allow me the fine line I'm lookin

..., at least for some of the drawings.
... is a brilliant writing pen, for
...re, but on occasion, it fails to
...mply with my drawing demands,
...ainly fine lines for cross hatching
...man forms. Fuck.. The fire went
...t again
...Okay, it's going again and think
...s time for good.

...mething I enjoy
...ing is
...ying these
...at master
...wings,
...n add
...any
...icl
...nt

...ch
...on,
...for
...s.

Here's a fucking
live bird for baby
Jesus to devour!

FUCK YOU
'WISE'
MAN!!

After François
Boucher
1761
'The Nativity'

...3 am and I'm still in bed...glorious!

After Winslow Homer, Americas
greatest artist!

Sitting outside in the sun with Penny.
The sun is very hot now. She is
laying on the   grass.
must be cool   on her
ever heated   fur.

Washington
Square...
What a beautiful
Day...
"All the mongaloids
are out today!"

GRAND
OPENING

Here is a copy of 'Standing Woman'
by Picasso — ink on paper 1912.
It's been over 35 years since I've
attempted a Picasso cubist copy
— first one or two I'd done around
the age of 14 or 15 when I was
obsessed with his work... totally
over-the-moon with the Spanish
wife beater. In this attempt, rather
than a copy of a figure, I found
it damn challenging. There are so
many connections to make with
the eye & hand, measurments I'm
not familiar with the way I am
with the human form. The spacial
relationships must all line up or
the whole thing begins to lose it's
original structure (scaffolding.
    This particular drawing took me
nearly an hour to complete — non-
stop drawing... my neck hurts!
There are a few mis-steps I made, yet
overall it's fairly accurate. There was
a period in my youth when I did a
fair amount of copying the work
of various cubists: Picasso, Gris,
Metzinger, Braque, Duchamp, etc
Both in Black + White and color —
excellent practice. Not easy, but
a necessary discipline.

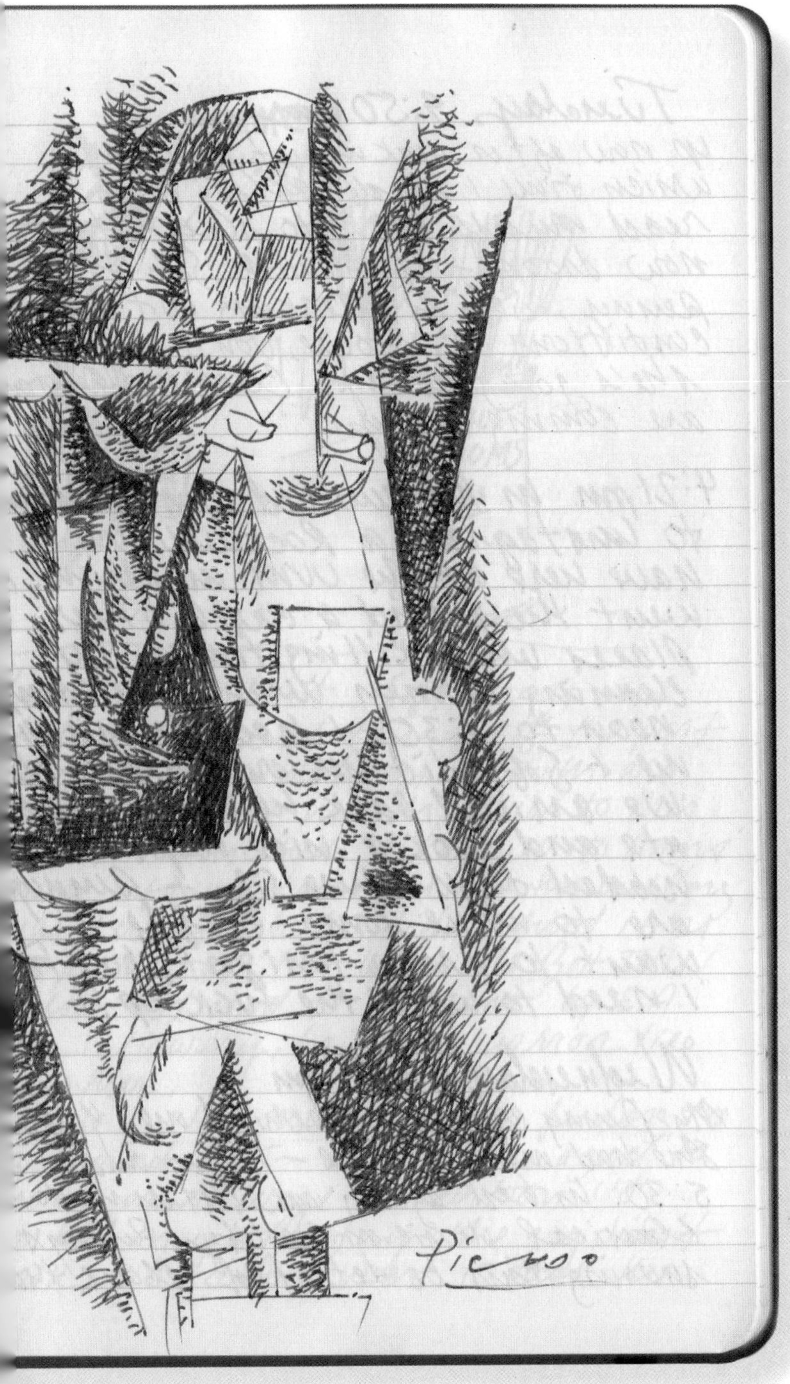
Picasso

"I'D LIKE TO PIGGYBACK ON WHAT PAULY SAID ABOUT DUMPING THE BODY IN JERSEY."

THE WARWICK

In 1986, after leaving the Pennsylvania Academy of the Fine Arts (the second art school I'd abandoned), I worked at the historic Warwick Hotel (now a Radisson). I was a waiter and room service server for the Brasserie, a restaurant in the Warwick. The upper floors were apartments, the lower floors were hotel rooms. Back then, the Warwick Hotel was busy. The Grateful Dead stayed there exclusively. On any given weekend you'd see Joe Frazier, the O'Jays, Phil Lesh, and other local celebrities, like Teddy Pendergrass (pre-wheelchair) all walking across the lobby from Club Elan to our restaurant.

Cocaine and the Mafia were part of the atmosphere. I waited on Nicky Scarfo and his crew often: wiseguys in and out of federal prison like a revolving door. There was always a celebration when one of them was released. Pains in the ass to wait on, but always an excellent tip. On the main table, an eight-seat roundtop where everyone wanted to be seated, the FBI had a hot mic set up.

After my waiter shift was over at the Brasserie around midnight, I would walk across the lobby to Club Elan and earn fifty bucks applying face paint to the scantily clad young men and women who made up the club's cocktail staff. On the weekends, the waitstaff put on a dance performance. It was newly choreographed each week and was kind of a big deal. These smoking-hot men and women would come in for fifteen minutes and suck on their Newports while I applied different colors to their faces with an airbrush. I have no idea if the paint was toxic or not. I'm still alive . . . Jesus, I hope they are.

I was virtually sober back then. I drank a little beer but no drugs. My pot-smoking days were pretty much behind me. It's not much of an exaggeration to say that everybody who worked at that club was wired. I'd be sitting across from a beautiful waitress applying paint to her face after she'd been serving some Mafia prick who kept pinching her ass.

"I hate this fucking pig," she'd complain, "but he's a big tip."

Penny as puppy

This whole room smells like warm corn chips... come on!!

you know that
expression or saying,
'Cleanliness is next to Godliness'?
I think that's a crock of shit.
Drawing your dog to McCoy Tyner
is about as close to 'Godliness' as
you're gonna get.

CLIFF AND JOSE WANT ME GAY

While I was a waiter at the Brasserie I worked the breakfast shift with two other waiters, Cliff and Jose, both gay men. I was twenty-two and they were pushing thirty. I loved them. They were hilarious, smart, constantly bickering in their flamboyant way. Cliff was more feminine—fit, short, blond hair. Jose had a loud nasally voice and a Puerto Rican accent.

These guys were stellar servers, very professional and hilariously obnoxious. They made my work shift a blast. But they both sexually harassed me for at least a year.

Did it make me uncomfortable? A little bit, yes.

On most mornings when I walked into the kitchen at six after walking sixteen blocks from the apartment I shared with my girlfriend, I'd find Cliff spread-eagle on the stainless steel worktable with Jose thrusting into his ass (fully clothed) . . . just for me to witness. Both of them would be groaning, asking me if I wanted to join in. This happened almost every time we worked those morning shifts together, all pre-coffee.

Reflecting on this now, it's all hilarious to me, and I wish I could go back and not be uncomfortable. This is true for most of my life—I want to go back and be relaxed! Jose would always ask me if I wanted a blow job—always. He'd say, "Come on, Harry, you know you want me to suck your dick. Don't you know men know better what they want than women?"

I mean, it made sense then and still does . . . Whatever!

I don't wanna harbor too much on the sexual-harassment thing, I really liked Cliff and Jose. They were my friends, and I miss them. I hope they're still out there, and if they read this, get in touch, because I'd really like that blow job.

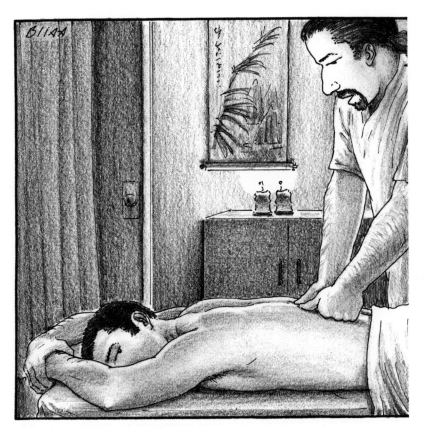

"YOU'RE HOLDING A LOT OF HOMOPHOBIA
IN YOUR LOWER BACK."

DRUM LESSONS

In 1985, when I was 21, I had decided that I would no longer be a visual artist. I was going to play the drums. This didn't come from out of nowhere, I had been banging on stuff my entire life, even had a drum kit when I was a boy.

I began taking drum lessons with a terrific player whose name I cannot recall. He lived by the Philadelphia Museum of Art, and I would ride my bike twice a week to meet with him for an hour. He was a classically trained jazz drummer—a short, kind, Italian guy whose playing made him a giant in my mind. He had done some session work in the late seventies and early eighties, but mostly disco stuff that didn't give him the opportunity to show off his versatility and skill. He was a very good teacher, and I loved the lessons.

One day I was riding my bike to a lesson and I noticed far in the distance a large cloud of smoke coming from West Philadelphia. When I arrived he was watching TV and asked me if I had "seen this." At the time I didn't have a TV, so I didn't know what "this" was. We both sat down and watched the news. Mayor Wilson Goode and the police had dropped a bomb on the MOVE house—the base for the MOVE political organization. An entire city block had gone up in flames, and the subsequent fire burned out of control. Five children and six adults were killed. Sixty-one homes were burned to the ground over two city blocks. After my lesson, the cloud of smoke was still visible over West Philly. When I got home I stayed in my crappy little apartment bedroom for hours, working on my paradiddles and double-stroke rolls.

I wish I could recall my drum teacher's name—he was a cool guy. I haven't forgotten Ramona Africa's name.

The nice thing about drawing cats is that they don't move. This fucking cat stayed in this exact position 3 hours after I finished this study. I think it's dead.

Unknown Pussy 12/15/19

12:30 pm Still enjoying being in this bed with this fire... drawing. This is a lovely way to spend a Sunday morning.

After Millet 1866

Here is a drawing I tried to copy by Tiepolo! The original was in ink + wash, but I did my best to render it all in ink. The original is such a compelling image — just leapt off the page. I adore Tiepolo's wash & ink drawings!

I MISS RANDY SPEARS

In the early nineties I was working at an Italian restaurant called Ralph's when they hired a famous porn star as a new waiter. I'm gonna go ahead and use his real name and his film name here, because it's not a secret at this point. In the films he was known as Randy Spears, but I knew him as Greg.

At the end of his first shift we had a meeting upstairs with all the busboys and waiters. My boss, Jimmy, introduced Greg to everybody, and disclosed that Greg had spent years in the adult-film business along with his wife, Danielle. Every guy at the meeting already knew this information. I was probably the only person in the room who didn't know Greg was a former adult-film god.

Greg and Danielle had two young kids and were trying to start a new life together—a clean and sober life far away from the porn industry. I had never seen any of Greg's films, and I kind of didn't want to. I have no issues with pornography, but I wasn't comfortable or cavalier enough with my own sexuality to venture far into pornography. A few magazines is all I needed . . . and my imagination.

Anyway, Greg was an absolute blast to work with. After a few weeks of waitering, he was one of us, only an ex–porn star. He soon opened up a martial arts gym in South Philadelphia, just a few blocks from the restaurant, and seemed to have found his new beginning.

Greg would sometimes regale us with stories from his adult-film life. In the restaurant business there's always an hour or two before the crowd shows up—servers sit around and shoot the shit. Once he told us that after a day's shoot he would be offered as pay $500 in cash or cocaine.

A few of the other waiters who were way too familiar with Greg's work asked about specific female costars. He never disclosed too much; he was fairly respectful of those he knew and worked with, but he did tell us about how AIDS changed the business. I remember him finishing a funny story, shaking his head, and saying out loud, "Ah, the good old days," and then quickly correcting himself: "I mean, the bad old days, the bad old days!" Greg was very funny, a natural raconteur and one of the smartest guys I knew.

Inevitably, on a busy night there was always some twentysomething guy with his girlfriend at the bar who would notice Greg from his film work. I watched this happen. The guy would sneak four or five glances, followed by a kind of pathetic look of eureka. They would always point and say, "I know you!" Greg would look back at the idiot with a wry smile and say, "No, not me, but I wish I had his money." Some of the guys knew Greg was bullshitting them, but it rarely continued past one or two lines exchanged. If it went any further, these guys would have to cop to sitting around watching porn. That's not a great first-date conversation.

Years later, I learned just how big of a star Greg was. He had won the equivalent of the adult-film Oscars for three or four years in a row; he was a superstar. Since those days at Ralph's, I have watched one or two of his films, and he was really good!

At some point during his time in South Philadelphia, Greg borrowed money from a loan shark (I know this loan shark) and struggled to pay it back. You know in the movies when they say if you don't pay back the loan, they'll break your legs? Well, that actually happens. The last thing I knew, Greg had left town with his wife and his two kids—gone.

Jump ahead to 1999. I'm living in Nyack, New York, and I'm just starting to work for *The New Yorker*. I was also doing cartoons for *Playboy* and *Penthouse*. Bob Guccione was still the editor in chief at *Penthouse*, and he liked my work. Each time you'd contribute cartoons for either of those magazines, they sent you a complimentary issue and a nice thank-you note (I still have all of mine). In one of the issues of *Penthouse*, there was a photo-essay spread called "Eyes Wide Open," a spoof on the Stanley Kubrick film *Eyes Wide Shut*. The photo essay featured Greg and another woman in masks at a posh mansion. I remember thinking at the time, *Look at that, Greg and I are in the same issue!*

I tried to get in touch with him but never heard back. We had a lot of fun together, and he was a terrific waiter. Greg, if you're out there, get in touch, because I have a screenplay I'd like you to read.

BOOKWORM

In the seven years I worked at Ralph's on and off, we had a regular customer we called the bookworm. Soft-spoken, kind, pudgy, with a manicured beard and always wearing a scarf. He came in once a week all alone with a book. Always a five-dollar tip and the same meal every time. An appetizer of roasted peppers, followed by lasagna, half a carafe of Cribari (cheap) Chianti. No coffee or dessert. I later learned his name was Brian.

He would read mostly plays. I remember one of the last times I saw him he was reading George Bernard Shaw. I felt a solidarity with the bookworm. I liked his quiet demeanor, his need for privacy, and his authentic gratitude for the food and our service. He was a rare, intelligent guest in our restaurant—very different from the obnoxious goombah pricks or crooked attorneys (our main clientele). We never had in-depth conversations, only what I interpreted to be an unspoken appreciation for each other.

At a certain point, the bookworm disappeared. For four or five months I wondered what happened. Maybe he moved away. Then, on what could've been the hottest day I had ever experienced in the city, I noticed what appeared to be a walking Giacometti sculpture heading toward the restaurant. I was midway through a slow lunch shift. I stood in the foyer in my bow tie and waiter vest, thankful to be in the air-conditioning.

The man struggled to open the front door and eventually made his way inside, where I greeted him. It was the bookworm. We exchanged some pleasantries, and I guided him to a seat in the dining room where, drenched in sweat and clearly grateful to be out of the heat, he requested half a carafe of Chianti and his usual lasagna.

When I walked away from the table after taking his order, I stood for a moment back at the service bar, alone. I was overwhelmed with sadness and dread. What I knew then and know now about his disease doesn't make my recollection of that afternoon any easier to recall. AIDS had reduced what was once a healthy young man into an emaciated near skeleton. I had never seen anyone so close to death in my life, and it frightened me.

I went into the kitchen and told Jamie, a nineteen-year-old waiter from the neighborhood, that the bookworm was out there and that I thought he was dying of AIDS. Jamie instantly freaked out—disgusted, and said to me, "I'm not clearing his plate." One of the chefs in the kitchen, a big guy, George, was near us eavesdropping and had the same

11:10 pm In bed listening to a piece on ravens from The Atlantic. I finished 4 cartoons today + cleaned the gutters. I'll finish 3 more tomorrow before I head to Burlington for the week.

Tower of London Raven

disgusted look on his face. Then, I started to become freaked out. I thought, *Could I catch AIDS by touching his plate? Are there particulates in the air I could breathe in and become infected and in time, transform into a walking Giacometti?* I'm ashamed looking back now, but this is what happened.

In the alley behind the restaurant, I smoked a cigarette to kill time. Twenty minutes later, I went back out to his table to clear his plate and found him sort of hunched over his meal. He'd hardly touched his food. I thought he died right there. He had fallen asleep. I carefully woke him by asking if I could get him anything else. His eyelids opened slowly, and a smile formed. He shook his head, and I brought the check. I took his money along with the usual five-dollar tip and went back to cash it in with the bartender. I walked back to the dining room, and he was gone.

Greg, Dominic, John, Cheech, two Pauls, John's boyfriend, and Cheech's boyfriend whose name is also John. I can't remember all the other men I knew who are now gone.

Fred Gwynne ... "Herman"

Fred was a radioman on a submarine chaser in WWII. Attended Harvard on the GI Bill and drew cartoons for The Harvard Lampoon!

Fred also illustrated children's books wrote a few as well, in fact many of his ideas for these books were way ahead of their time. I recall seeing one years back, thinking "shit, this is fucking great!"

When I was a kid, I always wanted to live with The Munsters in that glorious house.

I have a friend who would run into Gwynne in the Parson's school art supply store, told me he was a terrific guy. He died in 1993 at 67.

"IF YOU DON'T MIND, JUST FOR TODAY'S SESSION, CAN YOU PRETEND TO BE TERRY GROSS?"

FRESH AIR WITH TERRY GROSS: UNAIRED EXCERPT

Terry Gross: My guest Harry Bliss is an internationally syndicated cartoonist and cover artist for *The New Yorker* magazine. He's illustrated more than twenty-one covers and has also published twenty-six books for children. In 2019 Amazon Studios turned one of Bliss's illustrated books into an animated series for children called *Bug Diaries*. He's currently collaborating with actor/comedian Steve Martin on a series of books that have become *New York Times* bestsellers. In 2016 Bliss moved to Cornish, New Hampshire, where he lives in the former home of J. D. Salinger and set up a cartoonist residency program called the Cornish CCS Residency Fellowship. He has a new cartoon memoir out called *You Can Never Die*, about the passing of his beloved dog Penny. Harry Bliss, welcome to *Fresh Air*!

Harry Bliss: Thank you, Terry. I know a lot of your guests say this, but: it's an honor to be here. I'm a longtime listener and have always admired your professionalism. Plus, it's great to be back in Philadelphia, where I made some of my best mistakes.

TG: Haha, yes, your new memoir describes some of those years in Philly, particularly when you were working at restaurants in South Philadelphia. . . . Can you talk a little bit about what that time was like for you?

HB: I could, Terry, but then I'd have to kill you.

TG: [laughs]

HB: I worked at a few Italian restaurants when I was living in South Philadelphia. But before that I lived in Center City and worked at the Warwick Hotel. Now, I don't know if you remember the mid-to-late 1980s, but the Warwick Hotel had a club called Elan—

TG: Oh, yes, of course I remember Elan. It was Philadelphia's answer to Studio 54, is that right?

HB: Yes, and remember Elan was at one end of the lobby, and at the other end of the lobby was a restaurant called the Brasserie. When all the mob guys were done partying at Elan, they would stroll across the lobby to the Brasserie, where I was a waiter. The Brasserie was like a high-end International House of Pancakes; it was the place you went to after you got really drunk, only they served eggs Benedict and steaks up until two a.m.

TG: How old were you then?

HB: I was twenty-two, twenty-three, I think. Emotionally I was sixteen.

TG: Did you serve mob guys?

HB: Of course. The mob guys tipped really well, consistently. . . . But they were tricky to wait on.

TG: How so?

HB: Well, they were obnoxious. It's really not that different from *Goodfellas* or *The Sopranos*. These guys just didn't give a shit about me or anybody else, but they had a wad of cash in their pocket, and I needed to pay rent, buy paint, and pay off student-loan debts, so I put up with it. I once had to chase Johnny DiSalvo, a made guy, out onto Seventeenth Street because he left without paying. The bill was over four hundred dollars and that was a lot of money back then—maybe it still is—but when I caught up with him he looked at me and said, "Whaddaya want from me—I'll pay it tomorrow." And then walked away. I went back to my manager, who knew Johnny and his just-released-from-prison brother, Tony DiSalvo, and he said to me, "Don't worry about it."

TG: I'm surprised he didn't get mad at you when you approached him with the bill, kind of like that scene in *Goodfellas*.

HB: Well, that happened too, but not to the extreme the movie portrayed. You develop a sensibility to these guys, and you know when to approach them and when not to. You have to be tuned into the room. It's interesting, Terry, I hadn't thought about this for many years, but being in the restaurant business back then taught me a lot.

TG: Let's take a short break and we'll be back to talk some more in just a minute. I'm Terry Gross, and you're listening to *Fresh Air*.

TG: Let me reintroduce you before we go on. My guest today is Harry Bliss, an internationally syndicated cartoonist and cover artist for *The New Yorker* magazine. His new cartoon memoir, *You Can Never Die*, has just been published. I love this new memoir about your life and grieving over the loss of your dog Penny. It's filled with journal entries and drawings, photographs, prose, cartoons, an interview with me, and it's really beautiful to look through.

HB: Oh, that's very kind, thank you, Terry. Your praise means a lot to me. You saying that probably just made me twenty thousand dollars in royalty payments. Maybe say that again later on toward the end of our interview, but hey—no pressure.

TG: One of the things that really struck me about the book is some of the watercolor portraits and landscapes that you have painted over the years. I would've never thought that a cartoonist could paint that way. It seems as though you could've been a very successful painter or watercolorist and had a gallery, but instead you chose cartooning, why is that? I mean you were academically trained at a painting academy, so why not continue with that?

HB: I've had many people ask this question—I'm paraphrasing here: *You could be a fine artist, why settle for being a cartoonist?* The short answer is: cartooning is much more difficult. The amount of drawing any seasoned cartoonist generates in a day far exceeds that of the fine artist, at least that's been my experience. Of course there are outliers on either side of this, but cartoonists draw a lot. Buried within most of my cartoons or covers or even the children's books is all that academic training. Somehow, Harry the needy class clown had to find a way to make people laugh *and* satisfy his desire to draw lush things.

Plus with cartooning, you're constantly thinking of ideas and digesting the world. A good cartoonist's brain is hardwired to seek out mirth twenty-four/seven; it doesn't stop. . . . I'm like the Terminator looking for Sarah Connor, only I don't want to kill her, I want to study her until she does or says something that I can turn into a cartoon.

TG: That's interesting. So your life is the work.

HB: Yes. It's a disease. Vodka helps.

TG: [laughs] I would think that it would be tricky finding things in your journal to publish and not to publish, some things might be too personal to put out there, but you seem to have curated this really beautifully. How did you decide?

HB: Well, like I said in the opening "intention" of the book, it was very important for me to make a connection to the reader. Intimacy is very important to me, and I can't pull punches if I want that connection. And there are some things I left out. My drug use, I mention it, but I could have said much more. Frankly I'm tired of memoirs going on and on about their dark drug past. I find it all very boring. Just do the drugs and shut up about it.

TG: But in your memoir you write, and I'm quoting from one of your journal entries here, which has a really funny drawing of you snorting a line of cocaine off Betty Boop's rear end: "I don't use drugs anymore, but if someone I trust came up to me with a bump of pharmaceutical cocaine, I'd snort it."

HB: Terry? Are you holding?

TG: [laughs] No, but you seem to speak highly of drugs, specifically cocaine and your relationship with it.

HB: It's a great drug. But I'm too old, and it's risky. These days, risk-taking involves me cleaning the gutters or going down a flight of stairs and not holding on to the railing.

TG: I sneezed last week and injured my back.

HB: [laughs] That's a cartoon! Can I use that?

TG: [laughs] It's yours. I'm curious about a subject you did choose to include—I don't think you've ever written about this or spoken about it in interviews before, but you gave a baby up for adoption in 1986. I want to know if you can talk a little bit about that? What were the circumstances surrounding the adoption? I can only imagine it must've been very difficult for you and the baby's mother.

HB: Yes, this may be the first time I've spoken about it. With the exception of a few isolated therapy sessions, I've not revisited that time in my life. I should note that my biological daughter, Valerie, and I reconnected fourteen years ago. We recently had dinner in the city with my son. But in

'86, I was involved with my first girlfriend, who was six years older than I was—I believe I was twenty-one. I was a virgin, then I wasn't, and she was pregnant. I guess I had really good aim.

TG: [laughs] Wait, so the first time you had sex you got someone pregnant?

HB: I'm sure I'm not the first, and I doubt I'll be the last, but yes. I was batting a thousand at that point in my life. But I was far too immature to be a parent, and I don't think she was ready either. So we decided to go through with the pregnancy and give the baby up for adoption. Abortion wasn't an option—my girlfriend was Catholic.

TG: When she started showing, did you tell people you were going to give your baby up?

HB: Terry, I think a lot of those memories are lost. I was on autopilot, just trying to survive. We were on welfare, living in a two-bedroom apartment in South Philadelphia—right by the Italian market, upstairs from Willie's pork sandwiches. I had a relative who was a successful attorney. I sought his advice and, in time, arranged the adoption. All we asked was for the medical bills to be covered by the adoptive parents, but it was very difficult. I will say that the staff at Pennsylvania Hospital were very good to us. But, no, we told no one what our plans were. I'm not sure that was the right thing to do, because people would ask us about names, due dates . . . all the things that you would say or ask when you see a pregnant woman. All the while we knew we weren't keeping the baby.

TG: It must've been emotionally exhausting for you, no?

HB: Terry, however difficult it was for me, it must've been at least two or three times as difficult for my girlfriend. Those scars don't heal. The day after we had given our baby away, we told people that we'd lost the baby.

TG: What do you mean?

HB: We figured no one would ask questions about it after hearing this. We wouldn't have to explain anything beyond that, and that was pretty much the case.

TG: I see. You told people the baby died in childbirth.

HB: That's right.

TG: Why didn't you tell the truth?

HB: We were ashamed we gave our baby up for adoption. That's the truth. We didn't want people to judge us.

TG: Did your parents or siblings know about the adoption?

HB: Yes. I believe after five or six months, when we made the decision to go ahead with the adoption, I communicated this to my family. I have to be honest though, like most of my memories surrounding that time, it's all blurry. I will tell you that my girlfriend did not like my mother or my sister—there was visceral hostility there. I was caught in the middle of it. Christ, just talking about this makes my stomach hurt.

TG: Oh no. I'm sorry.

HB: It's fine. I'll line up a few shots of Pepto Bismol when I get back to the hotel.

TG: It doesn't sound as though your immediate family was supportive of the decision, is that right?

HB: I seem to recall my family was fairly quiet when they thought we were going to keep the baby, but after they knew we were going to give our baby up, my parents voiced their disapproval. My mother, especially, was angry. I feel my siblings were mainly quiet, which is not uncommon in our family. We're not close in that way. At least we weren't back then. I seem to recall my older sister, Rachel, being fairly supportive through the adoption process. She held Valerie when she was a baby, just a day after she was born.

This is what
(I recall and it's fairly
accurate, I feel. From far off in
the distance as I sat here with →
just below Okemo mountain, what
birds, but they were so far off in
could they appear so large so far
Then, I began to see them with
birds. There were planes. Planes all
Just as I understood what, exactly,
pulled in the drive. The planes moved
of the engines were audible. I then
too saw these military planes
to be artillery...aka, bombs. Why
directly over my fucking house?
were to the sugar maples and pine
estimation...but what the fuck do
watched them in amazement. Still,

Penny snoring on my lap, I noticed
seemed to be 3 or 4 very large
the distance 20-40 miles? How
away? I waited and watched...
more clarity. — These were not
in formation and heading my way.
was in the air. Sofi, John & Rachel!
closer and closer and the sound
called to Sofi to rush over. She
overhead... carrying what I believe
were they here in Cornish? Who
I was floored at how close they
trees — dangerously close, in my
I know? I counted 4 or 5. We all
some part of me was frightened. Still is.

TG: Did you get a chance to hold the baby, Valerie?

HB: Terry, I wasn't that strong. No, I didn't hold her. I waited outside the nursery while my sister was with her, and we both left the hospital together. I'm just now remembering that we named her Rebecca.

TG: Do your parents know you reconnected with Valerie?

HB: Yes. I've kept them up to speed on Valerie and her whole family. They're happy we are in each other's lives. But you have to understand that my parents don't call me. In the past twenty years they've called me maybe ten times.

TG: Have they met her?

HB: No, and I doubt they ever will.

TG: Why not?

HB: Terry, I don't believe my parents are capable of it. They're so deeply entrenched in their own minds . . . they lack the communication skills to connect in a meaningful way. Valerie would have to just show up one day on their doorstep holding their great-grandson.

TG: What would they do?

HB: Well, my mother would say, "You should've called first."

TG: [laughs]

HB: But here's the thing: Valerie is cool. She's funny, pragmatic, and would walk away from that excruciating experience with some wisdom—somehow gleaned from her biological grandparents' solipsistic neuroses.

TG: Valerie sounds great.

HB: She is. I'm glad she found me.

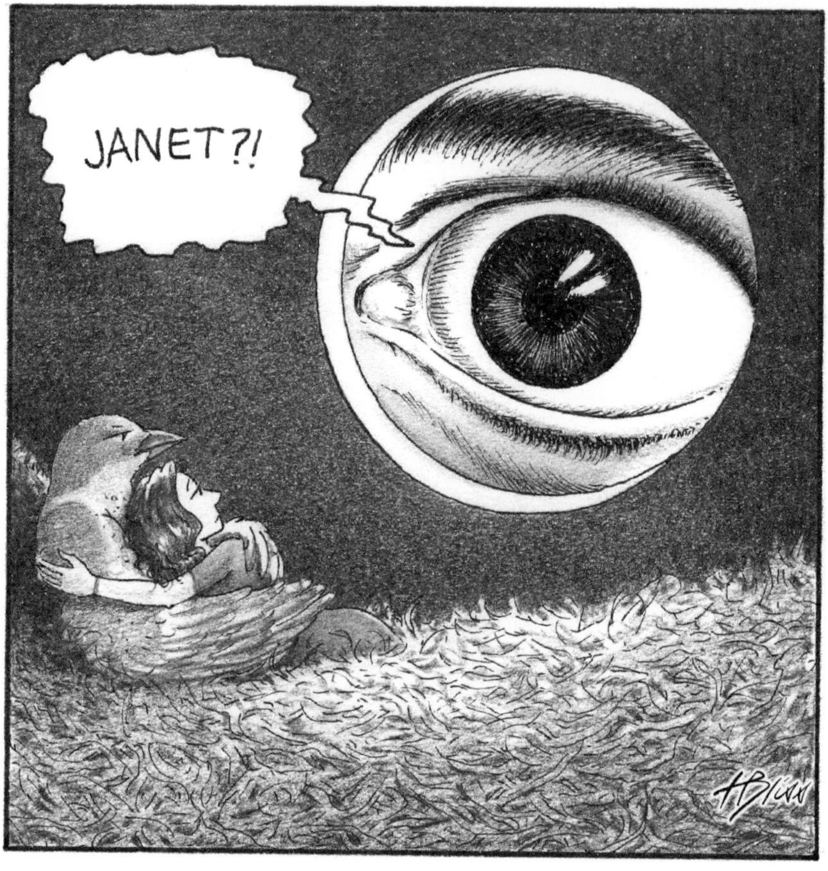
JANET?!

FRIDAY, MARCH 4, 2022

Yesterday, I was driving to the supermarket to pick up some essentials when I noticed a dead bird in the middle of the road. It was a chickadee recently killed. Initially, I passed the bird, but then I slowed down, put the car in reverse, backed up, and retrieved it. I carefully placed the lifeless bird on a T-shirt I had lying on the passenger seat.

This isn't the first time I've found a dead bird. There have been a few over the years, and every time I find one, it's nearly impossible not to hold on to the bird, imbuing this miraculous species with the false hope that someday it will come back to life, thank me, and fly off.

It's ridiculous, I know, but I cannot help myself. There aren't many things in this life that I find more heart-wrenchingly beautiful than a dead bird. When I returned home from the supermarket, I placed the bird in a clear glass jar and set it on the countertop in my kitchen. For the rest of the evening, when I was in the kitchen, I would take a moment to look closely at the bird—its tiny eyes, beak, and feathers. Each time I looked, I found myself unable to keep my emotions in check.

This morning, when I went down to make coffee, I looked again at the bird. Something wasn't right. I knew this delicate lifeless creature had to be outside. I'd had my time with it—it felt necessary to return it to its natural habitat.

I removed the bird from the glass jar and held it in the palm of my hand. I walked outside to the edge of my property, where a flat slab of white marble sits atop an old stone wall overlooking a sloping ravine. An autumn wind was blowing yellow and orange leaves in all directions—a beautiful morning. I carefully placed the bird on the marble and walked away.

Dead Bird. Sendak's Farm.

My friends
think I'm nuts
for keeping dead
birds in my freezer.
Make no mistake, I am nuts, but
not because I find it 'insane' to
not pick up one of the most
incredible/beautiful beings on the
planet. I'm nuts for a host of
other reasons and I'm fine with it.
   This bird I found on a walk near
Maurice Sendak's farm when I was
in residency there for the summer.
I was walking with Nora Krug when
we spotted the fallen bird. Nora
doesn't know this, but later I went
back and put the bird in a zip-lock
bag, kept it all month in the
freezer. When the residency ended,
I put the bird in my freezer — it's
still there. I cannot 'dispose' of
a dead bird, feels all wrong.

Many times, on a
return home we were
greeted with Penny
latching on
like this.
I can only
guess she
was express-
ing her
Joy.

Sofi's
leg.

Sometimes,
these draw-
ings are difficult
for me — so
many emotions
rise up... but,
they make
Penny more
permanent
in my
mind

MISSING PENNY

Today has been a very difficult day for me. For reasons I cannot understand, I have missed Penny throughout the day. There has been a constant presence of grief hovering. The beautiful day here in Cornish couldn't cure this feeling. Tonight, from my bedroom window, I try to relish the moonlight falling onto the yard—it's like a Maxfield Parrish painting . . . but I think of Penny's grave out there, and I want to cry.

Earlier in the day, I cut the lawn. Every time I cut the lawn and I come upon Penny's grave, something in me morphs. I become distant inside myself. The emotion is new and unfamiliar. I feel lost. I don't know what brings about these waves of sadness—why they come when they do. I only know that I am sad now for her. I wish my dog were here with me in this bed. Will the missing her be a forever ache?

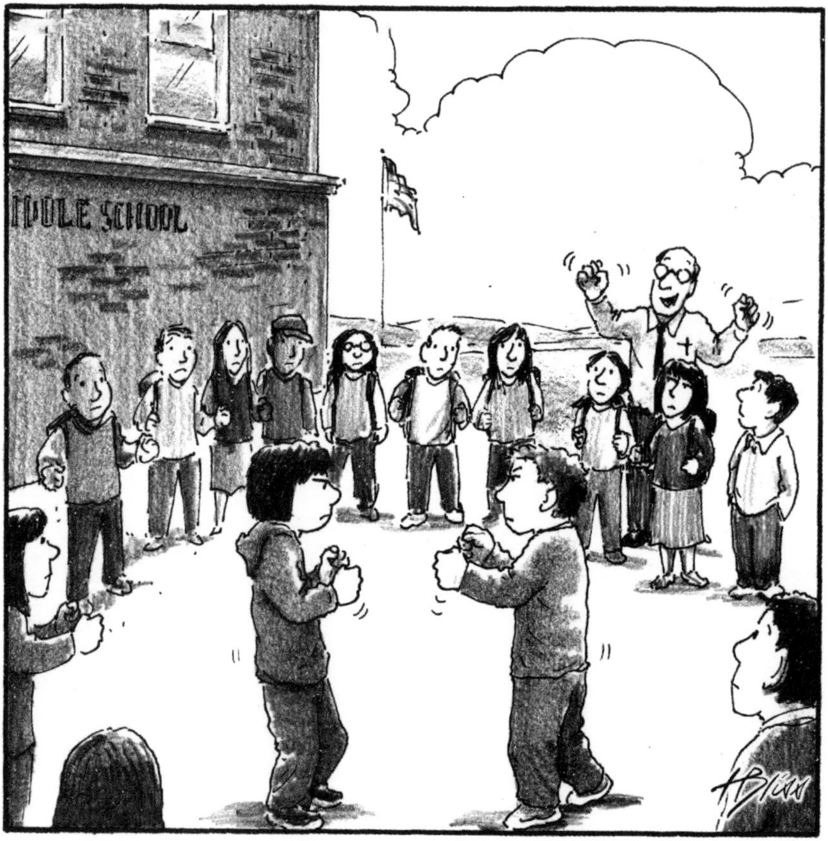
IDDLE SCHOOL

BAD TEACHER

In 1993, after having received my BA from the University of the Arts, and MA from Syracuse University, I was asked to teach at the University of the Arts. I began in the continuing-education department, teaching at night as an adjunct professor. I taught a watercolor class to a handful of students for two nights a week for three semesters.

I was a new father with a one-year-old son, Alexander, and some nights he'd join me in his snuggly while I taught.

I had recently separated from his mother, and every two weeks our son would spend a week with me. My students loved it when Alex would accompany me; they adored him.

Then I was asked to teach a sophomore class in the illustration department. I did it! A step up and a little more walking-around money.

In the continuing-education class the average age of my students was around thirty. My new students were eighteen to nineteen. This proved more challenging. Half of my younger students seemed totally uninterested in either my teaching, their work ethic, or the class itself. Most of them seemed lost.

I may have had something to do with their lack of interest.

I was a decent public speaker, I was comfortable doing demos, and I worked hard to prepare a syllabus. I felt capable, yet not fully comfortable. I was thirty but emotionally twenty-five. I have a clear memory on the first day of class of telling my budding new artists that out of all the twenty-two students in that class, odds are only two of them would make it in the arts. I could've been wrong, but I don't think I was far off in that assessment. My thinking was that these young creatives would look around at one another and think, *I'm gonna be the one to make it!* Like *Top Gun*—a little competition to motivate their minds.

Well, I fucked up. A few students switched majors a week later. I guess I scared them straight. You may or may not know this, but less than half of the students who go to art school end up having successful careers in the arts. And if you're going to half-ass it in art school, your odds are worse.

On days when I was frustrated with my students—the days they wouldn't show up or came in late and then took thirty-five-minute cigarette breaks—I'd let them know they were simply wasting their parents' tuition money. When we had a live model posing in class and there was a model break (lasts five minutes), students would head outside to smoke, talk outside the building, or get a new piercing. In most cases, they took fifteen to twenty minutes—too long and disrespectful of me, the model, and the class. These "students" would return to find me at their easel finishing their drawings, which really pissed them off. But I couldn't help myself. *Fuck 'em*, I thought.

At the end of the year, the teacher evaluations came in, and they were not good (go figure). Most of the students found me too opinionated, were displeased with their grade (all of them wanted A's), and a lot of the students resented the fact that I would finish their drawings (while they were outside smoking).

One day the chair of the department asked me into her office to let me know that they wouldn't be asking me back to teach the following year. I understood, and I told her that I probably wasn't a good fit or a good teacher, no hard feelings. Still, for the kids who left art school because of me, I feel confident that I saved them thousands of dollars. But tuition pays the teachers' salaries, and my style of teaching was not good for business. A few of the students in my class left the illustration department and made the far easier quasi-lateral move to the painting department, which, in most schools back then, was horseshit. I suppose I am a bit opinionated.

I continued teaching at a different Philadelphia art school, Moore College of Art & Design and at Parsons School of Design in Manhattan, making the New Jersey Transit commute once a week. I had learned from some of my earlier missteps. I became a little less opinionated, more inspirational, a much better listener, and an empathetic educator . . . I think.

Despite the improved Mr. Bliss, teaching wasn't the career I ultimately wanted, and my freelance career was taking off. *The New Yorker* magazine was just around the corner.

Fifteen years later and seventeen *New Yorker* covers to my credit, I received an email from one of the students in that sophomore illustration class. She went on to make a career in the arts and was very successful. She went out of her way to find me and thank me for my instruction. She didn't think I was an arrogant asshole. I got through to her!

There were other students I connected with: Mel Kadel, a fantastic artist who lives in Los Angeles, and others from the Moore College of Art & Design and Parsons who went on to have careers in the arts.

These small successes are gratifying to me, and I still enjoy motivating young people to follow their artistic vision. The tricky part is making young people understand what part their failures play in the artistic long game. If you want to be successful in art, I feel you must embrace failure over and over and over again. Failing is an essential part of any success.

"UH. DAD, THIS IS 'WALKING-AROUND-MONEY' AND I NEED 'WALKING-AROUND-NEW-YORK-CITY MONEY.'"

2:10 pm

Post shower + in our brand new adjustable bed in Burlington, arrived an hour ago. Sofi is with Penny at the new Vet – Penny had tests done today. I officially have enough cartoon roughs to finish over the next 3 days – damn easy. 141 Keep going, try and get ahead so I can indulge in more watercolors!

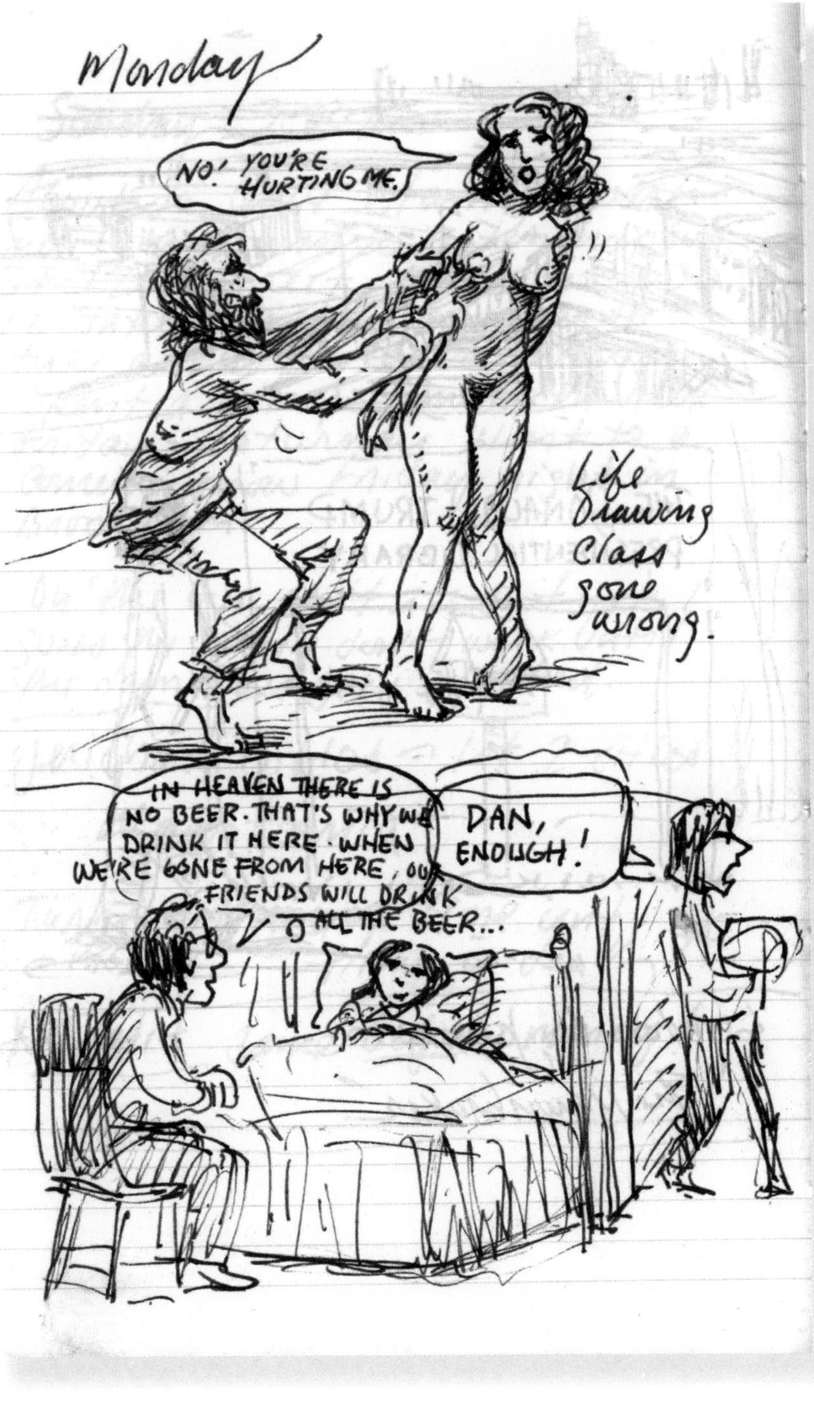
Monday
NO! YOU'RE HURTING ME.
Life Drawing Class gone wrong.
IN HEAVEN THERE IS NO BEER. THAT'S WHY WE DRINK IT HERE. WHEN WE'RE GONE FROM HERE, OU FRIENDS WILL DRINK ALL THE BEER...
DAN, ENOUGH!

MENDON THEN AND NOW

God how I loved fishing when I was younger. My siblings and I would go out on the ponds in Mendon Ponds Park, about fifteen minutes from our house. We'd take my dad's heavy-as-#@&! metal rowboat out. The thing had a small crack that my old man would periodically half-ass mend. But it still leaked, just enough to ruin anything you put in the boat, like a Kent cigarette

I pinched from the old man's studio or comic books or anything that you valued when you were thirteen years old.

I never caught much. I was there to swim, curse out loud, and smoke. My older brothers caught fish. Especially my older brother Charley—skinny bastard had a knack for dropping that lure in the perfect spot, between two lily pads, just off the bank in the sun.

Thirty-five years later I loaded that same shitty metal craft into the back of my dad's pickup truck and took my two-year-old, Alex, out on that pond. No fishing, just a pleasant row in the quiet sun. It was a beautiful summer day, and everything felt nearly right in the world.

I turned my head to grab a lovely yellow flower from a nearby lily pad, and the little guy toppled over into the murky water. One minute he was there, the next minute he was headfirst in pond shit. I jumped right in after him. He had a life jacket on, but that didn't keep him from being freaked-the-fuck out. When I pulled him up, he was covered in pond everything, looked like he'd dropped in from a Laurel and Hardy cartoon—total mess.

I laughed my ass off, and as scared as he was, my laughing made him laugh too, and we were both laughing together.

"GLEN, I'M NOT JUST YOUR EDITOR. I'M ALSO YOUR
BEST FRIEND, AND I'M TELLING YOU, LOSE THE CAT."

THE NEW YORKER

When I first began working for *The New Yorker*, I was heavily influenced by the work of Charles Addams, Peter Arno, and a few other cartoonists I admired. I loved Addams's lush ink and watercolor "drawings" and did my best to emulate his style. I was successful too (I could've been a forger).

Collectors saw my Addams-inspired work in the magazine, and I sold a number of originals. In fact, the week my first cover appeared, in late 1997, a collector bought it. I was getting paid twice. Once from the magazine, and again from a collector. That first cover made me eight thousand dollars in a week, and the royalties are still trickling in.

I was contracted after my second year at the magazine, guaranteeing me a small advanced stipend I worked against. In addition, I received residuals or royalty payments from the licensing of my cartoons through the Cartoon Bank, which was owned by *The New Yorker*. I still receive checks for cartoons published in the magazine from as early as 1999, and I hold the copyright on all my work.

My early originals for *The New Yorker* were quite big—fifteen by twenty-two inches. This was fine for the magazine, but I knew once I became syndicated in newspapers in 2005, this style wouldn't reproduce well. I had to rethink my art. I sized down, for speed. No more large works. A square-ruled six-inch box with lush ink and graphite would replace those big subtle watercolors. Some readers miss those larger cartoons of mine, but I never looked back.

I'd heard that Roz Chast took a lot of shit from some of the old boy cartoonists at the cartoon meetings. When Roz started, there were still a lot of tight-assed relics who frowned on her "crude" style. Charles Saxon couldn't stand Roz's cartoons. Told her as much to her face. I love Roz. I own two of her originals. Come to think of it, I own two Charles Saxon originals. Roz's were more expensive though.

I met Roz during one of my first cartoon meetings and happened to have a current issue of the magazine with one of her cartoons in it. The cartoon was of a tombstone, here it is:

I asked Roz if she would sign it for my mother, whose name is also Roz. I told her it was my mom's birthday, which was a lie. Roz looked at me and then looked down at her cartoon of a tombstone and then looked back up at me and asked, "This is for your mom's birthday?" I said yes, and then she signed the cartoon and thought I was insane.

I met all the cartoonists in those early days: Gahan Wilson (great guy, told me that the *South Park* creators ripped off his *National Lampoon* strip *Nuts*). Ed Koren (who became a lifelong friend). Danny Shanahan (great cartoonist, tragic end). George Booth (lit up any room). Victoria Roberts (draws and speaks beautifully). Lee Lorenz (always a jacket and tie). I really loved Jack Ziegler. He was a friend and remains my favorite cartoonist. I was devastated when he died. I miss him to this day.

There would be fifteen to twenty of us for the Tuesday cartoon meeting with Bob Mankoff, then the cartoon editor. I really like Bob as a cartoonist; I think he's terrific. But as much as Bob talked, and he talked a lot, I got very little substantive editing from the guy.

Once, when I was having trouble selling gags, I asked Bob what I was doing wrong. Bob told me my cartoon ideas were "too broad." I found this comment too broad. I asked if he could be more specific. He rushed off to play Ping-Pong (Bob is apparently one hell of a Ping-Pong player).

A lot of the cartoonists and other contributors at the magazine (including Michelle Urry at *Playboy*) thought the idea of a cartoonist being the cartoon editor was a conflict of interest. It certainly was, but for reasons unknown to me, Bob remained in place when Lee Lorenz left the gig. William Steig, who couldn't stand Bob, wrote to me once that he suspected Bob owned a piece of the magazine. Maybe. Bob was Machiavellian in his rise at *The New Yorker*.

Jan. 5, 1998
THE
NEW YORKER
Price $3.00
HAPPY
NEW YEAR
WELCOME
1998

60 Minutes did a segment on him. HBO made a de facto documentary film about him. A master at self-promotion, for sure. Can't fault a guy for that . . . right? I like Bob now that I don't work for him anymore, and he's a damn good cartoonist.

In those early years at *The New Yorker* I also worked for *Playboy*. *Playboy*'s cartoon editor, Michelle Urry, took me under her wing and showed my work to Hugh Hefner. I ended up selling quite a few cartoons to the magazine, though I got sick of Hef's feedback: "Tell him more like Arno." Michelle told me that Hef had a hard-on for the work of Peter Arno. I ignored him.

I was illustrating a children's book a year, cartooning for both *The New Yorker* and *Playboy* and a few other magazines. Throw in an occasional book cover gig and the selling of original art . . . I was out of debt! I had a balance in my bank account for the first time in my life. I will never forget sitting in my apartment on Second Avenue in Nyack, writing out my first premium check to Blue Cross Blue Shield. I had health insurance . . . I had made it. I was thirty-five years old.

for Instagram ↙

Tuesday 9:00 am Note to self:
Do not take LSD and look at
images/photographs of Mitch
McConnell's face—don't do it!

never know. Still, I've my eye on 2-
4 items that are solid investments
which I know I can sell once this
shit-storm is over. I may drop
150K... wait-n-see.

SEYMOUR HERSH

I first met Seymour Hersh at the offices of *The New Yorker* when the magazine moved from West Forty-Third Street to 4 Times Square. We met on the elevator.

Seymour asked me what I did for the magazine, and I told him I was a cartoonist and cover artist. He introduced himself as Sy, extending his hand. We chatted briefly, and I told him I was heading back home to Nyack. He asked me how I was able to come up with cover ideas if I didn't live in the city.

People are often curious how I'm able to capture the city, having never actually lived in Manhattan (my twelve years in Philadelphia doesn't count). I explained to Sy that I soak up the city on the days I visit. I walk everywhere, take photographs, and make sketches in my journal.

Sy was genuinely interested in this. He said his idea of a terrific *New Yorker* cover was like a "mindfuck." This made me laugh. Sy told me about a time in the eighties when he was living in the East Village with his family. One particular Sunday, Sy had to take his young son to an early tennis lesson and it happened to be the morning after the Village Halloween Parade. As Sy and his son exited their building, they discovered one leftover drunk parade participant stumbling and singing in the middle of the street dressed in full Nazi regalia, wearing assless leather chaps.

"That," Sy said to me "was a mindfuck—a New York City mindfuck."

We both laughed out loud. The elevator reached the lobby; we shook hands and parted ways. I'm still in touch with Sy. Every now and again when I receive one of his emails, I'm always amazed at how brilliant and hilarious he is.

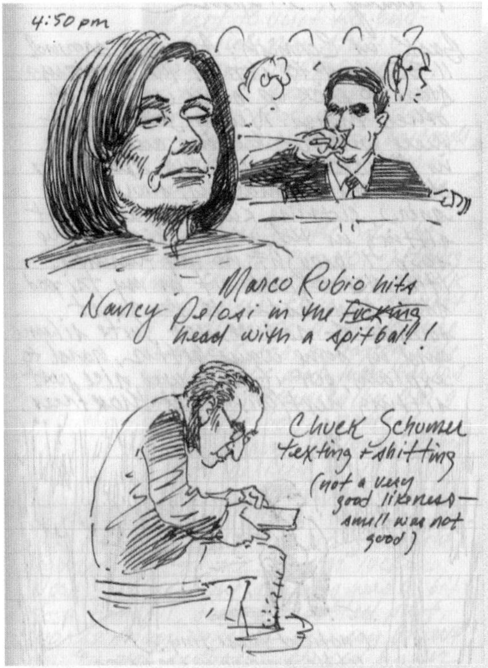
4:50 pm
Marco Rubio hits Nancy Pelosi in the Fucking head with a spitball!
Chuck Schumer texting + shitting
(not a very good likeness— small was not good)

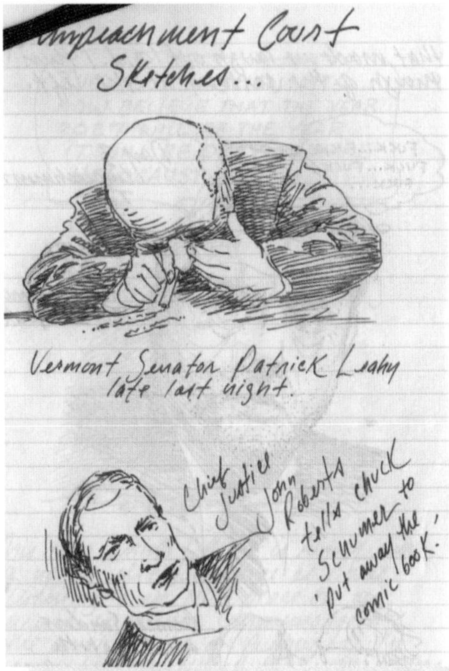
[redacted]mpeachment Court Sketches...
Vermont Senator Patrick Leahy late last night.
Chief Justice John Roberts tells Chuck Schumer to 'put away the comic book.'

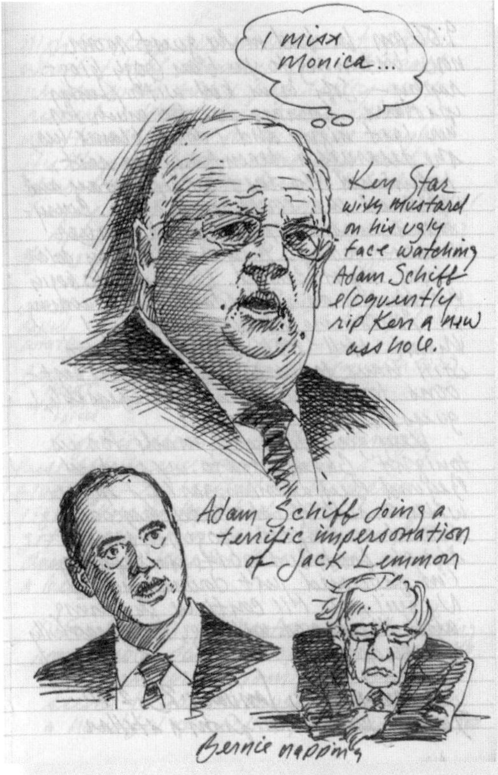
I miss Monica...
Ken Star with mustard on his ugly face watching Adam Schiff eloquently rip Ken a new asshole.
Adam Schiff doing a terrific impersonation of Jack Lemmon
Bernie napping

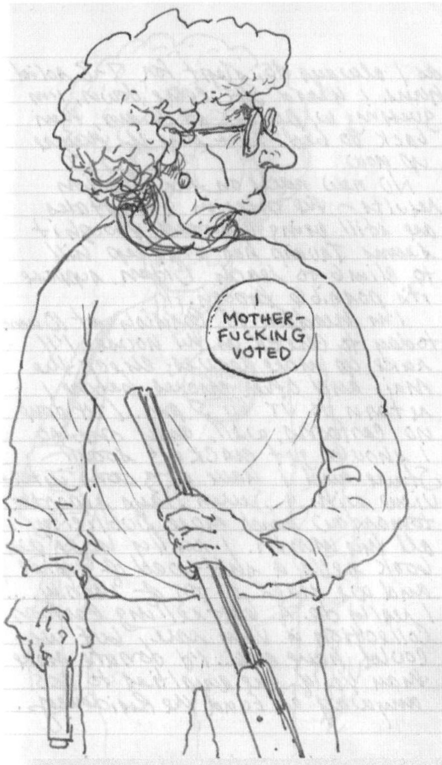
I MOTHER-FUCKING VOTED

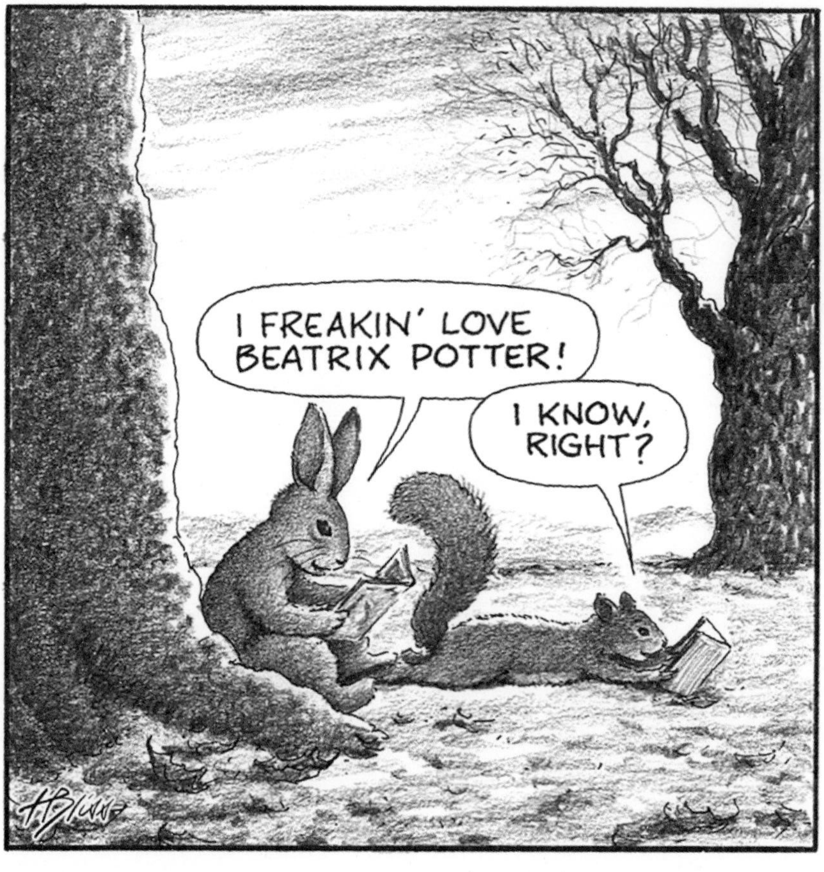
I FREAKIN' LOVE BEATRIX POTTER!
I KNOW, RIGHT?

CHILDREN'S BOOKS

Working for *The New Yorker* opened up the world of children's books for me. After my third cover appeared in 1999, I began a correspondence with William Steig. I initiated this with a fan letter, then we sent letters back and forth. In one letter he asked if I had considered writing or illustrating children's books. If so, did I need an agent?

I knew about the world of children's books. I wrote my MA thesis on Little Golden Books and followed a few of the more accomplished artists over the years. There is a long impressive history of *The New Yorker* contributors writing and illustrating children's books: E. B. White, William Steig, Ian Falconer, Syd Hoff, Leonard Weisgard, Roger Duvoisin, Marc Simont, Roz Chast, William Péne du Bois, and many more—but I hadn't considered a career in that area.

I was too busy working for *The New Yorker* and enjoying my single life in Nyack, New York. I was starting over, or trying to. My five-year-old son kept me busy. So did his mother. I had hired an attorney and was going back and forth to family court to secure my rights as a father—not easy.

I compartmentalized a lot at this point in my life, and I became very good at it. I kept my emotions in check and pushed forward with an earnest determination I've since lost. I was working myself out of debt and making steady progress paying off all those student loans. But when William Steig recommends something, one tends to check it out.

So I did. I met William Steig's agent, Holly McGhee, in Manhattan for lunch. We got along great, and to this day she is still my agent for children's books.

My first children's book, *A Fine, Fine School* by Sharon Creech, became a *New York Times* bestseller (still in print). Since then, I've illustrated twenty-six books for children, although I think after this book comes out, my career will be over and that's okay. I wouldn't be the first children's book author to have a few skeletons exposed. Tomi Ungerer comes to mind.

Why does my brain compel the rest of my body to draw this stuff? My god. I'm a 'celebrated' children's book artist (and author). What if some 7 year old sees this or worse, the kid's mother starts following me on Instagram?! All I can do is keep making my art and share it with others... I can't bring myself to censor my creativity — feels wrong. These are tough times for humorists and cartoonists. Oh. well. I think I'll jerk-off now.

ART

'psychic network of Solipcisms'

Looks like I'll be heading back to VT to lend Sobi a hand in dealing w/ Penny.

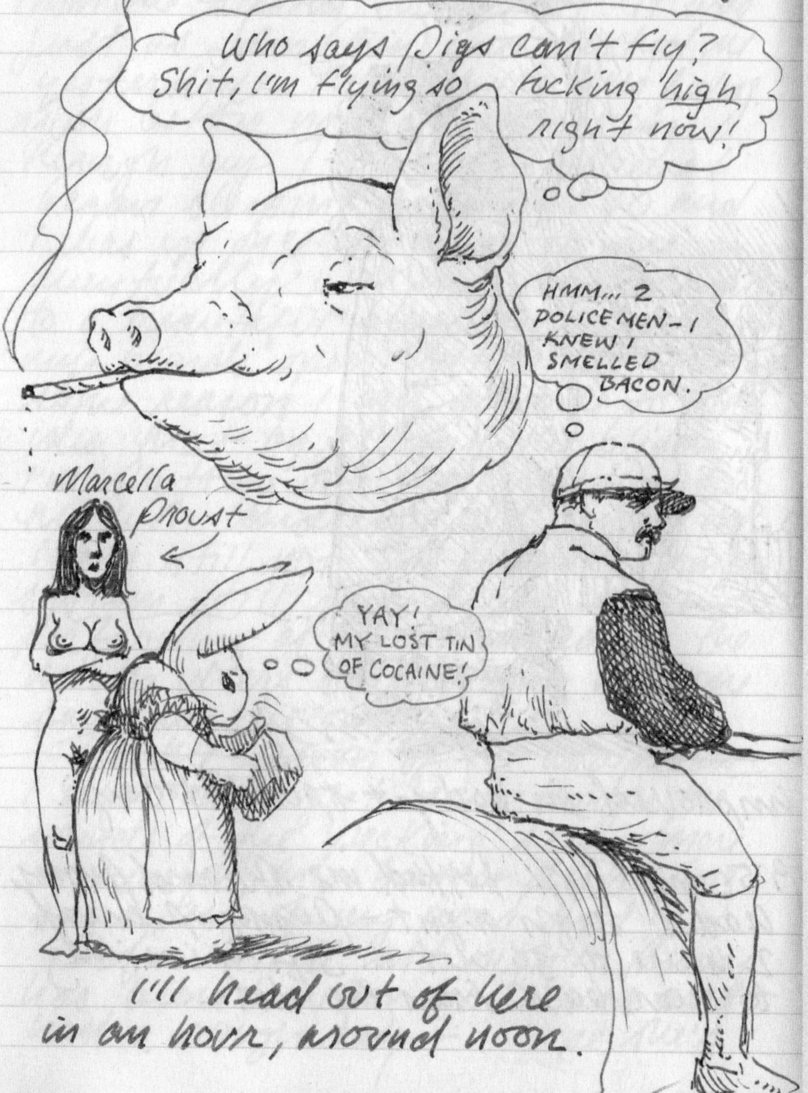
Who says pigs can't fly? Shit, I'm flying so fucking high right now!
HMM... 2 POLICEMEN - I KNEW I SMELLED BACON.
Marcella Proust
YAY! MY LOST TIN OF COCAINE!

I'll head out of here in an hour, around noon.

'The Huge Fucking Raven'

I am pleased that I have finally
reached a point in my artistic
development where I'm able to
conjure up some image and convey
it with some degree of accuracy.
In essence, if I can imagine
something, chances are good I'll
be able to draw it directly, in
the moment — a very satisfying
benchmark in any artist's journey.

"THIS GUY HAS THE BEST CATNIP IN NEW JERSEY—
DO NOT MESS THIS UP FOR ME."

COCAINE AND
CHILDREN'S BOOKS

I partook in harder drugs late in life. While most of my friends had tried a variety of substances early on in their teens and twenties, I was too frightened. I really didn't like to drink much, smoke too much pot (the combination of the two always made me throw up), or experiment with drugs that could kill me until I was well in my thirties. Where did I learn about cocaine? I learned it from you, Stephen King, I learned it from you! I had read Stephen King's terrific memoir *On Writing*, and in the book he talks about all the cocaine he snorted while writing some of his best books. Hmmm . . .

You're probably asking yourself, *How did Harry get the drugs? Who did he buy his cocaine from?* I'm not gonna answer that for obvious reasons. So just drop it.

There was a five-year span in which I was a cocaine enthusiast. Like Stephen King, I illustrated three of my best children's books while snorting the stuff. I never snorted cocaine for fun . . . well, not often. Rarely did I want to go out to a bar or socialize while using cocaine. I used the drug to get work completed, alone in my studio.

I would start snorting cocaine at ten o'clock at night and keep going till five in the morning, all the while working on a book deadline. I never did "fat bumps"—I paced myself. Maybe three to four small bumps an hour, usually accompanied with vodka on ice, throughout the night until sunrise. I smoked cigarettes too, but they were American Spirit "yellow pack," and they're way better for you than Marlboro or Camel Lights. I'm pretty sure that American Spirit cigarettes are actually good for you. The combination of a night of cigarettes, vodka, and cocaine was dreadful for my body, I knew this. . . . But, the work looked great (all the books are still in print), and I'm still alive.

You never want to do shitty cocaine. Sadly, most cocaine available to you will not be great. You never want to do any shitty drugs. If you're going to do cocaine, you want to get great cocaine—ideally, pharmaceutical cocaine, but you'll probably never get that unless you know Keith Richards. And even Keith Richards probably couldn't get it for you. Just know if you decide to put shit in your body, make sure it's really good shit.

I had two suppliers, one in New York and one in LA. New York was shit; LA was terrific. Usually overnighted by FedEx. Never answer the door when illegal drugs are delivered. Be sure to have your supplier select "no signature required" on the air bill. Just to be clear, what I was doing was completely stupid, and I could've been arrested, served time, or died! But the good Lord was looking out for me—thanks, big guy. I probably spent forty thousand dollars on cocaine over a five-year span—could have been worse, but a Prius for sure.

One morning, as I got into bed, my heart was racing and I didn't feel well (go figure). I had this thought that I was nearing some kind of expiration date, like a carton of milk that was going bad. I lay awake in bed frightened for at least an hour until I finally fell asleep at 8:00 a.m. That was the last time I snorted cocaine.

I woke up the next morning and told myself that I had too much going for me to risk on this fantastic drug. And I do mean fantastic. There are lots of things in this life that are fantastic and not good for you. I have no regrets regarding the drugs I've done. Well, one was regrettable—smoking heroin was regrettable. Made me awfully sick. Stay away from heroin. Overall though, I'm a fan of drugs.

I'm cognizant of the fact that this stance doesn't play well with children's book editors or librarians—though I've gotten high with at least one editor and three librarians—but it's how I feel.

Oh, I quit smoking too. These days I'm totally sober . . . except for booze.

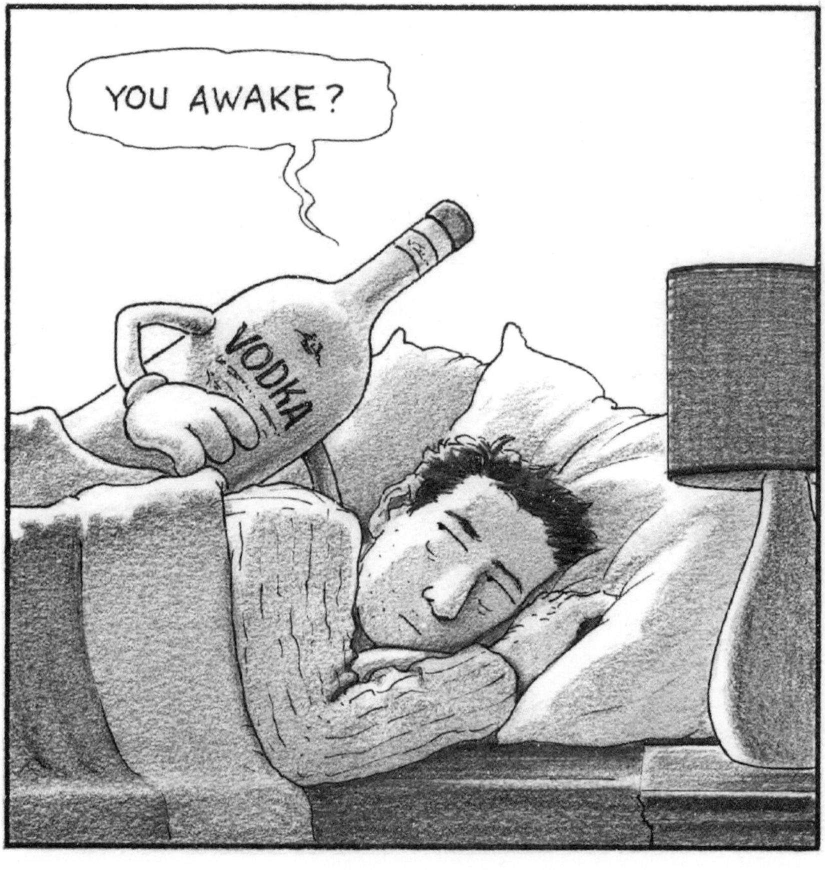
YOU AWAKE?
VODKA

THE FIRST STEP

I am an alcoholic. There, I admit it. Now leave me alone. My wife worries about my drinking, and sometimes I do too, but I don't know what to do. I've cut back. The truth is, drinking makes my life better. Don't we all want a good quality of life? Of course we do. Some find coffee improves the quality of their mornings, and others find that it's certain foods, working out, nature, meditation, money, drugs, or sex—so many choices! But for me, it's booze.

I didn't always like to drink. Up to the age of thirty, I didn't know how. I drank because it was what everyone else was doing—I drank to be social, to fit in, to be cool. I've come a long way from those early days, believe me. I'm a damn good drinker. I understand the chemistry involved, the alloying of my specific biology and that of the contents of the bottle. Also, I learned to control my drinking by watching others go out of control. I knew I never wanted to become an embarrassment to myself, my wife, kids, or, God forbid, Penny.

For years I practiced holding in-depth conversations under the influence of alcohol, worked hard to either bring a point home or have the "buzzsense" to capitulate. That's very important, to know when you're outsmarted or to simply acknowledge with a curious respect that you're not the sharpest wit in the room. How could you be? You're drinking.

HARRY BLISS: PLAGIARIST

I have been accused of plagiarism three times. Every time it made Page Six of the *New York Post*. Three days in a row, in fact.

In the spring of 2008 I had done a drawing for the back page of *The New Yorker*'s cartoon caption contest, in which I "borrowed" or "stole" or "lifted" Jack Kirby's work (a *Tales to Astonish* cover), though I tweaked it a bit, replacing Kirby's frightened man in the window with what Neil Gaiman called "a cheerful Harry Bliss man." But no question I "ripped off" Kirby's art in what I felt was an obvious homage to Kirby.

When the art ran in *The New Yorker*, all fanboy hell broke loose. Every Kirby geek in the United States weighed in on how a *New Yorker* cartoonist was taking credit for Jack Kirby's work. There's a long history of Jack Kirby never getting the credit he clearly deserved for creating so many Marvel characters. For many, my drawing was just another example of someone disrespecting Kirby's legacy.

Being on Page Six of the *Post* was a pretty big deal back then. The internet wasn't quite as ubiquitous as it is today—people still read this rag on the subway every morning. A lot of people. Page Six was great fodder for office watercooler conversations. Trump made many appearances.

I got an early-morning call from Bob Mankoff, my cartoon editor, and I explained to Bob that my rendition was a clear homage. I busted my ass try-

AFTER JACK KIRBY

"O.K. I'm at the window. To the right?
Your right or my right?"
Patrick House, Palo Alto, Calif.

ing to make it look like Kirby's cover. I assumed people would recognize the reference and know it was inspired by the Kirby art.

The magazine's PR person was busy that day. Bob said not to worry about it, and I didn't . . . too much. The truth is, I was upset. I'm a huge Jack Kirby fan, I always have been, and it's not uncommon for me to replicate artists' work that I have long admired in my own work as homage or out of respect. . . . But it's not always seen that way. I was worried and depressed all day.

The following day (5/23/2008 at 7:49 a.m.) I had made Page Six again.

The *Post* accused me again of plagiarism. The headline was "New Yorker Cartoonist a Real 'Copy' Machine." John Rau, an ad executive, wrote to the *Post* claiming *The New Yorker* was using one of his cartoon ideas from 2006. Rau's (crudely drawn) cartoon shows a man standing before a receptionist at "Hollywood rehab"—the receptionist asks him, "And the name of your referring publicist?" My (superiorly drawn) version depicts a woman going up to a desk, above a sign that reads "Hollywood Rehabilitation Clinic" and a male receptionist asks, "Were you referred to us by your doctor or your publicist?"

Same gag.

Now, this cartoon idea wasn't mine. When Bob was editor, every now and again, he would throw me a gag idea. I didn't sell often back then, once a month, and I didn't care because I was so busy with my children's book career. I was also syndicated, so *The New Yorker* was no longer a priority. But Bob knew that I drew beautifully, and he liked to see my work in the magazine. Bob called me weeks prior and gave me the gag over the phone, he told me it came to him from Bruce Eric Kaplan, a terrific cartoonist, who was also a writer for *Seinfeld* and the HBO series *Six Feet Under*. When the Page Six story ran on the second day, I got a phone message from David Remnick, the editor in chief of the magazine. . . . He was upset.

I was upset too, more pissed off though, and again I had to defend myself. In an email to David and Bob I explained that the cartoon idea wasn't mine, it had come directly from Bob, so I don't think I can be held accountable for this discrepancy. Did Bruce Eric Kaplan steal Rau's idea? Who knows? I doubt it. For anyone to think that they alone can have an idea and that this idea is exclusive to only their brain is naive at best. This kind of thing happened fairly often, back before everything was digitally archived and searchable on Google. Still, at *The New Yorker* it was rare. So on my second day on Page Six, I was once again depressed and angry.

Then, it happened again, sort of. The next day the *Post* ran "The Eagle Has Landed in Loony Toons Battle" as the Page Six headline . . . nice. But this time Rau was being accused of ripping off one of my cartoons. His website home page featured another crude 2006 drawing of an eagle feeding its young McDonald's french fries, and that looked a lot like my cartoon that featured an eagle feeding its young some McDonald's french fries . . . from a 2003 issue of *The New Yorker*. I got there first. It's not even a very strong idea.

From the *Post*:

Rau was especially red-faced because he had accused Bliss, a long time New Yorker and children's book artist, in yesterday's Post of ripping off one of his cartoons.

Rau went on to write "there were just too many similarities" regarding the Hollywood rehab cartoon, but he had a "change of heart after looking at the similarities between the eagle cartoons."

"That's incredible," he said. "Mr. Bliss would certainly be within his rights to say it's too much of a coincidence, but it is a total coincidence."

The article claimed Rau came up with the idea for the eagle drawing after going on a fishing trip on the Delaware River and watching an eagle return to its nest. As I said earlier, it's not a very good idea, and I'm sure hundreds of people have had it—they just don't know how to draw.

I was just glad the whole thing was over. Incidentally, Jack Kirby's biographer and former studio assistant, Mark Evanier, sent me a very kind email letting me know that if Jack were alive, he would've enjoyed my rendition and doubted seriously if Jack would have considered it plagiarism. On Evanier's blog he wrote that my drawing for the caption contest received many captions from Kirby fans, and many of them made reference to Kirby. *The New Yorker* should've known early on that something was up. Here's one of those submitted captions I still think is very funny and fits perfectly: *"What's that? You say you're a lawyer for the Jack Kirby estate?"*

Tales to Astonish artwork © MARVEL

And here are 3 ideas for cartoon that came from reading S.J. perlman — just a word or a phrase will open up my mind. Are they funny? I think so, but I can't be sure.

EXCTASY spelling !!

"HELLO EVERYONE. MY NAME
IS PHIL AND I'M ADDICTED TO
TELLING PEOPLE THEY'RE
ADDICTED TO THEIR DEVICES."

"LOOK AT ALL
THIS WONDERFUL
FALL COLOR!
ALMOST MAKES
ME FORGET
JUST HOW
#!@*-UP
THINGS ARE."

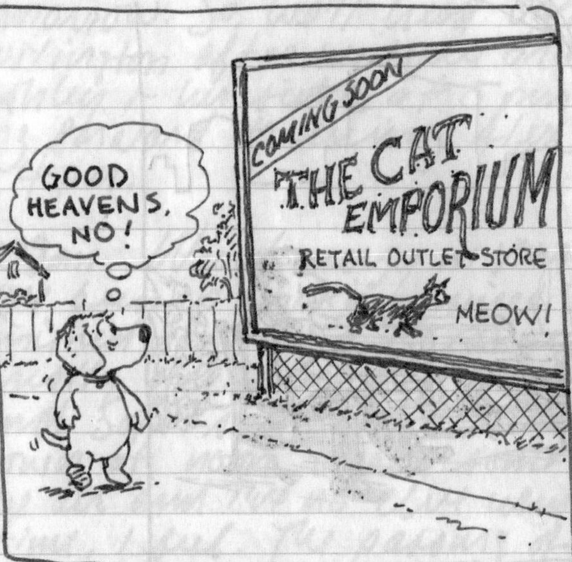
COMING SOON
THE CAT EMPORIUM
RETAIL OUTLET STORE
MEOW!
GOOD HEAVENS, NO!

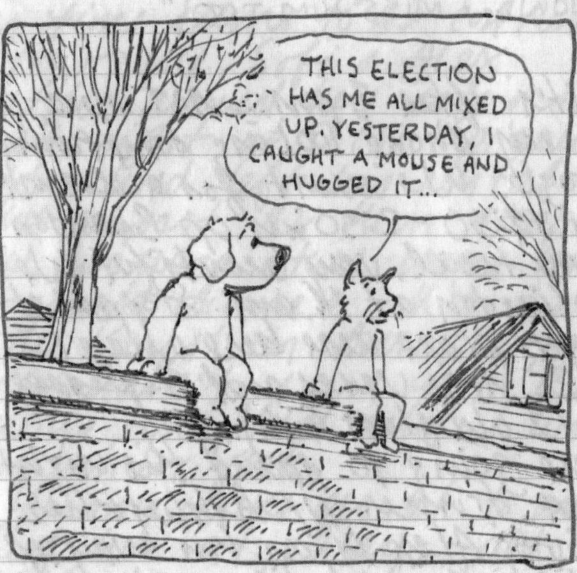
THIS ELECTION HAS ME ALL MIXED UP. YESTERDAY, I CAUGHT A MOUSE AND HUGGED IT...

"WHEN I GROW UP, I WANT TO IMPEACH A PRESIDENT."

FIRST LIBRARIAN

The year was 2006. The book was *Diary of a Spider*. It was the second in what I like to call the bug diaries trilogy: three *New York Times* bestselling children's books written by Doreen Cronin and illustrated by me. These books were and continue to be very successful—Amazon made an excellent animated television show based on the series in 2019.

In the mid-2000s the children's book business was booming. A fellow *New Yorker* cover artist friend of mine had written a fantastically successful debut children's book and was said to have been given a seven-figure advance for his second book. I would get sent out on book tours and stay at premier hotels, with town cars to and from airports, dinner at four-star restaurants, call girls (just kidding, I paid for these)—the full treatment.

It all seemed so strange to me—all the innocent children I'd meet and the money behind it—it felt uncomfortably incongruous. But I confess the eighty-thousand-dollar royalty check for *Diary of a Worm* felt good. Thanks, kids!!

I've never taken manuscripts just for the money. I have been offered big paychecks for a few children's books written by celebrities, and I've turned them down. At the height of my career, I took on a children's comic book for a very low advance because I was given full artistic freedom and the chance to work with Art Spiegelman and his wife, my cover editor at *The New Yorker*, Françoise Mouly. The book, *Luke on the Loose*, went on to become a bestseller

To Harry Bliss
With best wishes, *Laura Bush*

and is still in print. I hope it doesn't sound like I'm bragging here, because it wasn't so much about my integrity, it was just that I didn't want to do something I wasn't enjoying. I'd rather bartend or wait tables than sit miserably hunched over my desk for six months—no, thanks.

Back to 2006. I was invited to speak at the National Book Festival. I had done this event a few years earlier when the first book in the series, *Diary of a Worm*, came out. Doreen Cronin and I went to the White House and had dinner at the Library of Congress, where we sat a few feet from Condoleezza Rice and First Lady Laura Bush. Laura Bush had spoken in the White House pressroom earlier that day to a room filled with artists and authors from all over the country. I was impressed with her eloquence, intelligence, and genuine kindness (of course she has all of these qualities—she was a librarian).

After the dinner, when the desserts were served and people were mingling about the room, I got up from my table to introduce myself to Laura Bush. I carefully walked up to a Secret Service agent and asked if it was all right if I approached the First Lady.

The Secret Service guy didn't look at me; he stared out, scanning the room like the Terminator and said, "It's fine, sir."

I asked him once more because there was an echo in the Library of Congress, all that goddamn marble—I wanted to make sure I'd heard correctly. I repeated, "Is it okay to approach the First Lady's table?"

The Secret Service man kept his eyes on the room and said to me, "It's okay, sir, I'm not going to tackle you."

With that, I nervously walked to the table and met the First Lady. She was affable, warm, and seemed genuinely glad to meet me.

GOOFY'S WORLD

ANDREW WYETH

Years ago I sent a fan letter to Andrew Wyeth. He wrote back. The Wyeths, specifically N. C. Wyeth (Andy's father), were hugely influential for my family growing up. As a child, I marveled at the elder Wyeth's lavishly painted illustrations for *Treasure Island*, *Robinson Crusoe*, *Kidnapped*, and many other Scribner's editions. My uncle Harry, the de facto patriarch of the Bliss family of artists (ten working artists), spent most of his life trying to paint like Andrew Wyeth (with a fair amount of success, I might add).

To a fault, my uncle worshipped Wyeth. By the time my uncle's own visual voice emerged, it was too late. Emulating the artists you admire as part of your training is very common, but in time your own visual voice must

emerge—influences wash away, and then your unique vision is born. Some call this a "style," but I like visual voice.

If you look at early paintings by Duchamp or Gorky, you'll see that they too were influenced by painters they admired. Both Gorky and Duchamp were so good at mimicking other painters, I'd often wondered why they didn't get rich making forgeries. Check out Duchamp's *Portrait of the Artist's Father* in the Arensberg Collection at the Philadelphia Museum of Art. It could easily be mistaken for a fauvist Cézanne. Gorky literally had a Cézanne period. Look at his *Staten Island* and see for yourself. Andrew Wyeth's early watercolors were heavily influenced by Winslow Homer, but in time, like Duchamp and Gorky, he shed his influences and grew into his own. Personally, I'd all but forgotten the Wyeths in art school. Thomas Eakins, Brian Eno, girls, and marijuana replaced them.

Over a decade later, when I finally stopped waiting tables and started illustrating book covers, I became reacquainted with the Wyeths' work. Around this time I'd taken a trip to the Brandywine River Museum in 2002, and my appreciation for Andy's work took off. The museum holds most of the Wyeth family's most important works. Seeing his commanding brushwork floored me. It still does. There's a deep emotional presence in his process, and the underlying, abstract depth of design is profound. I know watercolor. It's been my primary medium for more than fifty years . . . Andrew Wyeth was a master.

In 2004, *Diary of a Spider* had become a bestseller, and in my correspondence with Andy I included a copy, which he liked. He invited me to get in touch with his assistant if I was ever in the area. My East Coast book tour was over and I was tired from all the travel, but I got in touch with Andy's assistant . . . and lied.

I told the assistant that I was still on a book tour and that I would be in the area. The assistant arranged the meeting date, and early one October morning I made the drive from Burlington, Vermont, to Chadds Ford, Pennsylvania.

I was met by the assistant at the end of a very long driveway and followed her up to the main house. Andrew and Betsy Wyeth greeted me in their home, where we all sat in front of a large stone fireplace. I wasn't as nervous as I thought I'd be. I was just glad to be out of the car and sitting down with two instantly affable human beings.

The conversation was kind and genuine, a sincere back-and-forth. We spoke for more than an hour, just the three of us, with a natural light falling across two of Andy's paintings on the wall. Betsy smoked, tossing her ashes into the open hearth. We enjoyed one another's company, nothing felt forced. At one point I asked if I could get a picture of me and Andy; Betsy took our picture. You can see in this photograph that Andy is not looking at the camera, and instead he's looking at me. I had this feeling that Andy liked my face . . . I dunno, but the guy made me feel special.

Then, Andy had this idea about staging a photograph. I had brought along a bunch of my cartoon roughs, which I had shown them earlier in our conversation. Both Andy and Betsy were taken with the roughs, and Andy especially enjoyed the crude quality of the ink line work. Perhaps the cartoons inspired them, because Andy suggested that he get on the ground and Betsy get up above him, straddling him as if she were going to kill him with her cane!

After that first hour, Betsy said she had to run errands—"I'll leave you two to continue to talk." Before she left, she gave me a pair of wrist warmers she'd knitted. She told me she knits often and makes these for her family to keep their wrists warm. I still have mine, and I wear them every now and again.

The next hour was just Andy and me sitting and talking about art. Though,

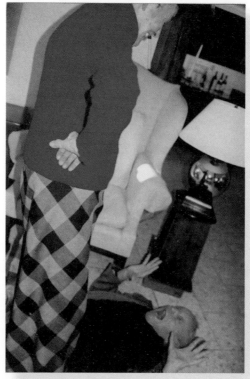

the first thing he mentioned after Betsy left was how grateful he was for her. He told me a story.

Early in his career, he had taken a portfolio of his work to *The Saturday Evening Post*, which was located in Philadelphia at the time. He showed his portfolio to the editor of the *Post*, who was taken with Andy's work and offered him twelve covers on the spot. This offer would have made Andy an instant success on par with Norman Rockwell. The money too was great. Andy went home to tell Betsy the news. At the time, Andy and Betsy were living in a cottage house down the road from his father's home in Chadds Ford . . . money was tight. Betsy said to Andy, "Andy, you don't want to be a famous illustrator with deadlines. You want to be a famous painter with the freedom to paint whatever you want." He declined the offer.

Andy told me how much he loved Edward Hopper, and said he was a very decent man. We discussed the chokehold photography has on the contemporary realist painters we know. He showed me an eighteenth-century marble bust he had in the adjacent room.

"Isn't that marvelous?" he said. Andy clearly loved this sculpture. It sat on a pedestal in front of a window looking out onto the Brandywine River.

After nearly two hours, he asked if I wanted to see a drawing he was planning for a watercolor: Betsy's hands knitting. He left and came back.

I held the drawing. "Wow, it's going to be beautiful, Andy," I said. Honestly, I didn't know what the fuck to say. I was just trying to stay in the moment, and I came up with the most sensible response . . . thankfully it wasn't gibberish.

Then, he mentioned working in his studio soon. I took this as a cue to leave, but Andy asked me something that, to this day, I cannot wrap my brain around. He said Helga was in his studio cleaning up for him. He asked me if I wanted to meet Helga. *The* Helga. The subject of his beloved series of paintings.

I hesitated, and in that hesitation I think Andy sensed some nervousness. He offered, "Maybe the next time, on first meeting, she can be a little rough." I took his cue. He walked me to the door. I thanked him for his kindness and hospitality and waved goodbye. This is how I remember last seeing Andy.

This is the last time I saw Andy—
standing in his Dutch doorway as
I drove away...

I never made it
back to meet Helga.

Andy passed on - 1/16/2009

KISSING ASS

When I returned home to visit my parents a month or two after spending the afternoon with Andrew Wyeth and his wife, Betsy, I found that my family, and in particular my uncle Ken, were quietly impressed. I clearly remember being asked about the visit by my uncle Ken, who had informed me that Andrew Wyeth once declined a visit from John F. Kennedy. I told my uncle Ken about my recollections from the visit. When I finished, Ken turned to my father with a look that said, "How on earth did your son pull it off?"

My father simply shrugged and said, "What the hell are you looking at me for? He's a really good ass-kisser."

I was put off by this, I felt a sting, but I was also entertained by it—it was funny. The old man has a good delivery, and I respect it. This was sixteen years ago, and since then I've learned to embrace my father's comment. I was once one hell of an ass-kisser. It's a skill, and it has opened many doors for me, the Wyeths' included, and those open doors led to wonderful opportunities. I did what I had to do to get where I wanted to go. I no longer kiss ass because I've got everything I need and want. Although, I do seem to recall a recent instance of me dusting off the old skill for my auto mechanic. Or was it the electrician . . . ?

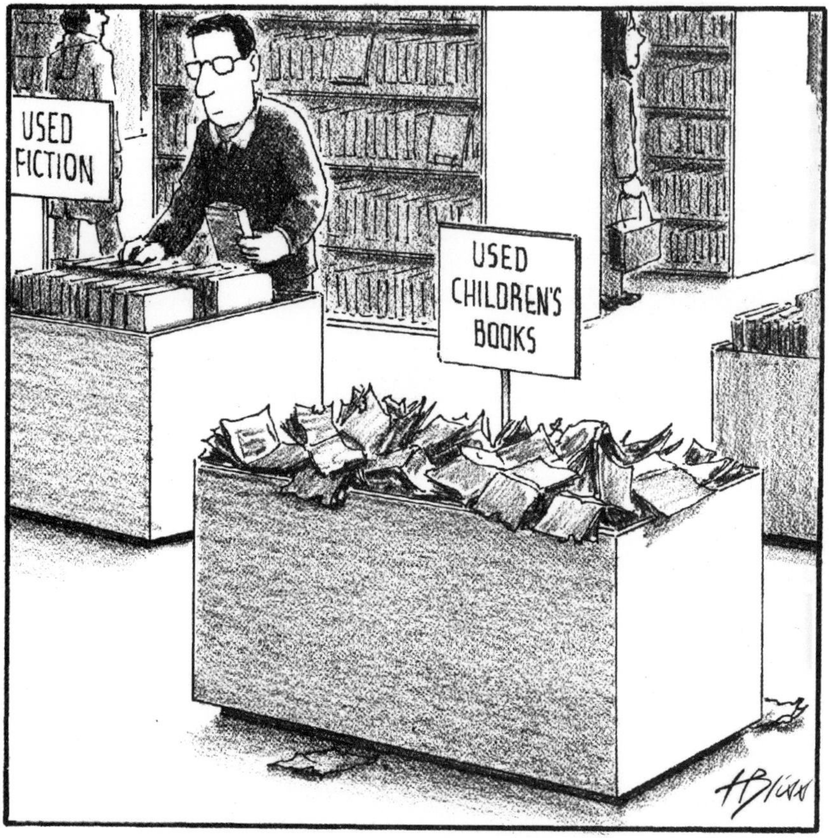
USED FICTION
USED CHILDREN'S BOOKS

THE SHOW MUST GO ON

I've traveled all over the world doing my dog and pony show in front of countless audiences, mainly consisting of elementary school children. I'd stand up on the stage and show images of my cartoons and children's books along with some biographical photographs. I talked about my career and what I love about drawing/reading. My intention was to inspire and entertain.

In the early days, after my first children's book was published, I was nervous and not especially good at public speaking. But, in time, I got better—a lot better. I learned that the really good cartoons, the ones that people really loved, would do the talking for me. Laughter is a terrific remedy for nervous energy. By 2010 I had curated what I'd felt was a crowd-pleasing show. Experiencing a gymnasium full of second and third graders cracking up became a wonderful new "high."

Once, early on, I drove two and a half hours from my home in Northern Vermont to a massive Barnes & Noble in Southern New Hampshire. My publisher had arranged an author event for my new picture book. I arrived at 6:45 p.m., allowing me fifteen minutes to set up and wait for the crowd to settle in. At seven o'clock I walked up to the podium, adjusted the microphone, and looked out at an audience of one little girl.

She sat alone holding my book, waiting for me to begin. I took a deep breath in, exhaled with a "the show must go on" determination, and started. And . . . I killed. That little girl was cracking up for the full forty minutes. I had her in the palm of my drawing hand: the silly voices for captions, my timing, just the right amount of irreverence—all of it came together for that kid. It was like a beautiful dance. After the show, I personalized her book—drew a little dog in it and met her parents (they'd been sitting in the back laughing too). I packed up my stuff and drove the two and a half hours north in the snow.

Corn
Chip Paws!

Penny Sleeps

Sofi once said she would give Penny an orgasm if she could, so Penny would know what it felt like.

out of the lake. Well, now I know —
loves to drink & get
drunk!... artists!

6:19pm Another break, this time
my relaxing on the sofa with Penny
is poised by a vodka & tonic &
some old bluegrass on the Spotify.

"Where the
fuck is
my dinner?"
— Penny

Seems, Joan
Didion
would like
the original
cartoon art I
made —

so, I will be
very happy to
send to
her. Griffin
gave me
her address
in NYC.

"CAN I HAVE HER NOW? HEY! <u>MY</u> TURN."

PENNY'S FALSE START

In the beginning, Penny was Sofi's dog. We had just started dating when Sofi, my now wife, adopted Penny. One day, when Penny was only six months old, Sofi called me—she was terribly upset and crying. She told me she had taken Penny to the vet after she became weak and lethargic overnight. Sofi was with her five-year-old daughter, Delia, at a nearby toy store when the vet called with an update. Penny had a rare autoimmune disorder. His exact words to Sofi were "You have a very sick puppy."

I drove over to meet Sofi and together we drove to the vet. As the hours passed, Penny was in decline. Sofi began staying with Penny at the vet all day long, from eight to four. She packed up her sleeping bag so she could sleep beside Penny on the floor, and then when the vet closed she would take her to an overnight place. In the morning Sofi would pick up Penny and head back to the vet. This went on for nearly a week. In the second week, they started giving Penny blood transfusions.

Unfortunately, Penny was allergic to the synthetic blood, so they had to find doggy blood donors. The transfusions would happen at the overnight clinic, and the vet would monitor Penny's condition.

It was exhausting for Sofi, but she held it all together. Powerful steroids were introduced, but after another week with no signs of improvement the vet asked us to consider putting Penny down. I thought it might be the right thing as well. I wasn't connected to Penny the way Sofi was back then, Penny was her baby. My primary concern was Sofi, and watching her pain was not easy. Sofi wanted to give the steroids more time to take effect; she wasn't letting go. The vet hoped the steroids would've helped, but there was no sign. Sofi, unwilling to give up hope, insisted on waiting another day.

The following morning Sofi had chicken with her. She held some in her hand for Penny, and remarkably, Penny was interested. She showed the first signs of strength by lifting herself up so she could eat the chicken out of Sofi's hands. Sofi believed that this was a sign Penny could recover. The vet was dubious.

The following day Penny started eating a little bit more. When Sofi was speaking to the vet, Penny stood up on all fours and began walking, following Sofi around the room for the first time. The vet looked at Sofi and said, "I think you were right."

Over the next ten hours Penny improved. That afternoon we'd never been so happy to see a dog take a piss on her own. Watching that disheveled miniature poodle return to life filled us with awe and joy. Penny was back.

Penny stayed on the steroids for a whole year, and although our miniature poodle turned into a tiny Hulk, it cured her of the autoimmune disorder. The steroids made Penny hilariously aggressive and demanding. She even caught a mouse and beat the hell out of it. She'd bark at us when it was mealtime and stand on all fours in front of the refrigerator with an attitude like a pissed-off drunk wanting another round. Sofi started buying her veggie hot dogs, and Penny went ballistic for these things!

Sofi saved Penny's life and gave me—and everyone who knew Penny—seventeen more beautiful years with her.

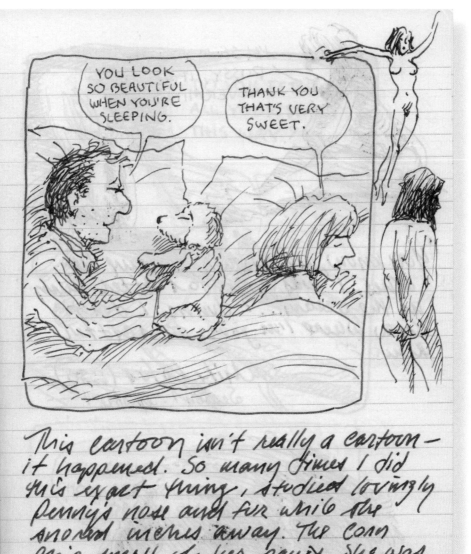

This cartoon isn't really a cartoon—
it happened. So many times I did
this exact thing, studied lovingly
Penny's nose and fur while she
snored inches away. The corn
chip smell of her paws. She was
beautiful.

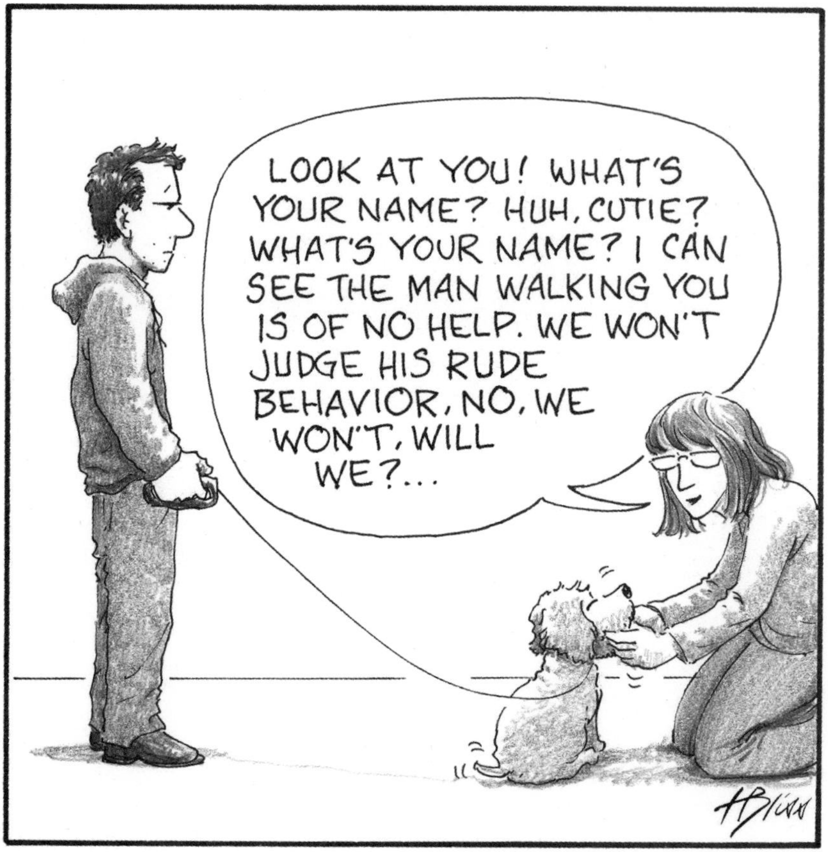
LOOK AT YOU! WHAT'S YOUR NAME? HUH, CUTIE? WHAT'S YOUR NAME? I CAN SEE THE MAN WALKING YOU IS OF NO HELP. WE WON'T JUDGE HIS RUDE BEHAVIOR, NO, WE WON'T, WILL WE?...
H Bliss

WHAT'S YOUR DOG'S NAME: BACKSTORY

Back when Sofi and I began dating, we both lived in Burlington near the University of Vermont. We would regularly take a short walk up to the campus, where Penny would run, sniff, and explore off leash.

Penny would get countless adoring looks from the students on their way somewhere. I'd spot these looks from a distance—melting expressions of awe. Sometimes, there was brief discourse, but mostly the undergraduates just wanted a quiet moment to love Penny. These interactions always made me feel good. I relished the whole dynamic—the way a small dog could bring a smartly dressed millennial with earbuds to their knees, helpless in the face of such powerful cuteness. I often wondered if these college "kids" had pets of their own back at home that they missed. . . .

This Penny adoration happened all over the city. Wherever we went, Penny drew unsolicited love from a countless variety of strangers. Once, after a walk by Lake Champlain, Sofi returned home to tell of a woman who asked if she could pet Penny, did so, and then proceeded to ask Penny—a dog—what her name was. Sofi told me she found this woman annoyingly ignorant to the fact that dogs can't talk. Sofi said she refused to indulge the woman with an answer if the woman insisted on posing the question to Penny. I pictured the whole scene and laughed. I thought this was fodder for a cartoon, and here it is.

MAURICE

I have been a fan of Maurice Sendak's work most of my life. *Chicken Soup with Rice* was an early favorite. This book is one of the first books that made me feel better. If I was sad, *Chicken Soup with Rice* made me not sad anymore.

We had a much-loved copy of *In the Night Kitchen* in our home too. I remember marveling at the surreal, dreamlike narrative of Mickey, the naked-boy protagonist, floating from his bed through the air and into a night kitchen, where oblivious Laurel and Hardy look-alike bakers attempted to bake the boy! The comic panel formatting, a clear homage to Winsor Mc-Cay's *Little Nemo in Slumberland*, was a joy to pore over. (I would later find out from a close friend of Maurice's that this book is a story about a little boy having a nocturnal emission. If you look at this book, it all makes sense.)

In 2003, *The New Yorker* published a cover of mine, "Lateral Pass." The cover featured football players in the huddle, hands on shoulders, save one player whose hand is on the ass of another player.

Sendak liked this cover so much he contacted me to purchase the original artwork. I had already sold the piece, but I had a fairly tight color sketch that I offered instead. He agreed. In the end we decided to trade artwork. Maurice knew that I was a hockey player through our prior phone conversations, and when I communicated to him that one of my favorite childhood books of his was *Chicken Soup with Rice* from the Nutshell Library, he re-created an illustration of the boy on skates sipping a bowl of soup, only Maurice gave the kid a hockey stick and hockey skates.

The piece hangs in my home across from a Garth Williams page from *Charlotte's Web*. Nearby is an original Arthur Rackham—good company.

I first met Maurice Sendak in 2007 on a drive from New York City back to my home in Burlington, Vermont. At the time of our meeting, I'd felt my children's book career was nearing its end. I had illustrated fifteen books and was feeling burned-out and tired of the coke-infused late nights slumped over my drawing board. I was mentally and physically in sorry shape.

I went to see him at his home in Ridgefield, Connecticut. I was naturally a little nervous coming up the driveway. Maurice's longtime caregiver, Lynn Caponera, met me at the door. I walked into the house and it all felt very familiar to me, not all that dissimilar from my own home in Cornish today. Eighteenth- and nineteenth-century oil paintings, drawings, and fine prints hung on the walls, along with copious books everywhere, vintage toys, and Maurice's latest works back from the printer, spread out on a large antique farm table.

Outside the windows were a remarkable old stone wall and impressive oak trees populated with countless scrambling squirrels, chipmunks, and chirping birds. Maurice said he enjoyed watching the squirrels from his studio window.

All the furnishings were antiques—old and wonderfully crafted. Two quiet old dogs, a German shepherd and a white Labrador, slept on a large well-worn area rug in the living room while we chatted. Maurice first talked about music, Chopin and Schubert, and a recent dream he relished. He was telling me that he had met Chopin in his dream. He went on about how pleasurable the experience of dreaming was for him. He was clearly excited and inspired.

I mostly just sat and listened, trying to digest everything. But somewhere in my brain I was thinking what a lazy fuck I was. Here's an eighty-five-year-old man twice my age, inspired and still producing beautiful work. And there I was, a crybaby quitter who relied on drugs to finish work.

Lynn served us cookies and tea while we conversed. We talked about dead artists we loved—Blake, Homer, Van Gogh, Stubbs—and some of the new artists making books for children. One in particular, had tried to suck up to Maurice, use him for his celebrity. He called people like this "star-fuckers." When Maurice said this, I replied that I hoped he didn't think I was there to fuck him, because I wasn't going to—no way. We laughed at the irreverence our conversation morphed into.

An hour passed and Maurice asked, "Would you like to go see what I'm working on?"

"Yes," I answered, "but I am not giving you a blow job." I didn't actually say that.

Maurice grabbed his cane, and I followed him past the kitchen, where there were innumerable vintage Mickey Mouse toys behind a glass cabinet— three dozen or more that Maurice had collected over the years. I've never met anyone who had so many variations of Mickey . . . a bit obsessive.

Off the kitchen, in a large living room, Maurice showed me intricate little toys he'd made with his brother, Jack, when they were kids in Brooklyn. Remarkable hand-painted mechanical whirligig improvisations, most still worked.

We walked through the kitchen, then a short hallway, and down seven or eight steps into Maurice's studio. He had a bed set up and a toilet so he could work without having to move around the house too much. The studio was below ground level, a cozy, large, sunken space with ten- to twelve-foot ceilings, well lit from the large windows' natural light.

We moved over to where his drawing table was, the heartbeat of the studio, where my eyes locked in on a remarkable little Blake-inspired watercolor. I can't remember what Maurice was saying when I discovered this artwork. This happens when I see art that I find miraculous. I tend to zone everything else out and let myself be consumed with the art. I'm not aware it's happening; it just occurs.

I leaned in closer, and I was blown away. I looked at the artwork and then looked back at Maurice.

He said, "What do you think?"

I told him it was incredible. There were additional watercolors on his desk, at least four or five, all illustrations for a poem his brother wrote. It would become Maurice's last book, *My Brother's Book* and is a tribute to Jack. I couldn't wrap my mind around how good these pieces were, delicate gems. If I was feeling shitty about myself earlier, I was now inspired. I thought, *If this old dude can produce this kind of work at his age, maybe I can too!*

Time passed too quickly. But before Maurice let me leave, he proudly showed me an erotic pop-up greeting card a friend had sent him of Mickey Mouse with a huge boner. Lynn was with us and we all cracked up. I had a four-hour drive ahead, and the sun would be diminishing soon, so we said goodbye and made a plan for another visit—there was so much artwork in that house, and Maurice loved to share it.

Returning home, I started fresh. I was going to power forward with Maurice as my beacon.

When I got the news that Maurice had died, I wept. I felt his presence leave this earth. I never made it back to see him, and I miss him still.

In 2014, two years after Maurice's death, I was awarded, along with Nora Krug, the Maurice Sendak Fellowship. The annual residency award was designed by Sendak for artist storytellers. (This award later inspired me to create my own fellowship residency program, the Cornish CCS Residency Fellowship for graphic novelists.)

Nora and I spent five weeks in near isolation on Sendak's 150-acre farm in Cambridge, New York. The experience was remarkable for me. Lynn (who now runs Sendak's estate), ran the program with Dona Ann McAdams. They were a tag team of warmth, hilarity, and over-the-top hospitality. There were movie nights in the barn—*Jaws* (my all-time favorite) with bats fluttering in front of the screen. Nora milked a goat. We ate the best organic food and laughed our asses off.

Nora and I were prolific too. She was midway through her debut graphic novel *Belonging: A German Reckons with History and Home*, and I broke out the watercolors.

I was surprised at my production. I painted landscapes, cows, pigs, and portraits, and read all I could in the same space Maurice lived and worked. I slept where he slept, surrounded by his book collection (all signed editions), his art, and his stuffed toys. On the bookshelf next to Maurice's bed were five or six Wild Things dolls watching over me. Each night, I dozed off next to a stuffed Max leaning against a lovingly worn out Mickey Mouse. No boner.

"WE WERE ALREADY IN THIS ROOM—I REMEMBER
THAT HIDEOUS RENOIR."

RENOIR

I have been to art museums all over the world—Moscow, Singapore, Dublin, Dubai, London, New York City, and many more. In all my travels over the years studying various masterpieces, along with an art education that began in utero (my parents met in art school), I've learned one thing that I believe to be irrefutable: Renoir was mediocre at best.

" HONEY, THE VIEW IS BEYOND WORDS,
<u>SO</u> PEACEFUL ON THIS ROCK FROM
WHICH I'M UNABLE TO MOVE UNTIL
I AM RESCUED..."

CORNISH

It's not a secret that I now live in the former home of J. D. Salinger. *The New Yorker* published a lovely piece about the residency program I started here in 2016. So, really, this is old news, but I'm reluctant to talk about it.

I didn't buy this house solely because it once belonged to Jerry. That would've been stupid. I wanted to get out of South Burlington, Vermont, and I was looking for a rural place to live. I have PTSD from all the yelling I experienced as a child, and I think that part of my brain resurfaced. I was beginning to find the noises of traffic, people, doorbells, planes, leaf blowers, all sorts of things you find in a rural suburban neighborhood increasingly difficult—I needed quiet.

I got a nudge from a fellow *New Yorker* contributor, Nancy Franklin, who posted on Facebook that she was surprised the Salinger house was still for sale after more than a year. I decided, mostly out of curiosity and because I wanted a break from cartooning for the day, to take the hour-and-a-half drive south on I-89 and check out the house. I got an appointment with a local Realtor, and we made a time to meet for a tour.

The minute I hit Plainfield, New Hampshire, and spotted Mount Ascutney off in the distance, something in me felt good. The name of the road I was driving on was Maxfield Parrish Highway. Maxfield Parrish lived in Cornish and painted the landscape throughout his lifetime.

I drove another mile and a half through winding dirt roads and up to the top of a small mountain in Cornish, and all the while as I drove deeper and deeper into the wooded landscape, that good feeling kept getting stronger. When I pulled into the driveway of the home, I was giddy. No noise, save the rustle of the leaves and a bird or two—quiet. Everything else after this was icing on the cake.

I bought the house, and I now live here most of the time. I adore this house and Cornish more than any place I've experienced in my life. I plan to die here.

Every summer, there's always a handful of people who drive slowly by the house and stick their hand out the window of their car to take pictures. A few bold people will stop, pull in my drive, and if I'm around they'll ask me about the place. (For the record, I don't like this. "Yes," I say, "this was the first home Salinger bought when he moved here. I now own it, and I have some yard work to do, but thanks for stopping by. . . .")

I'm a cartoonist. I'm not a rich man. I made my modest success by drawing pictures all alone in a room, a discipline I've been doing since I was six years old. I have some retirement money, and I plan to be working until I'm seventy or eighty, so I'm doing okay.

Yes, I bought a modest old home on twelve acres of land in God's country in New England, and that just so happened to have belonged to a really famous author. (And there's a tunnel in the house. I forgot to mention the tunnel. It's so freaking cool.)

Do I like the famous author's writing? Yes, very much so. *The Catcher in the Rye* is a perfect novel, one of my top ten of all time. "Nine Stories" is a short-story masterwork. "Seymour, an Introduction" lost me a little bit, but I return every now and again to try to decipher what it is he was getting at. "Raise High the Roof Beams, Carpenters" is also a favorite of mine. There are others. But I was never obsessive about the work, I just found the prose brilliant.

I suppose it's nice to live in a home where Jerry once lived, and every now and again I imagine his ghost is around me. . . . Yes, I think this. I hope his ghost approves of what I've done to the place, which is nothing. I am essentially a caretaker. All I do is preserve what was left here for me. That's what I do with all the art books in my home, preserve them and keep them in good shape. Why? Because I love them.

Sometimes, I read out loud, imagining that Jerry is listening. I imagine he enjoys Ring Lardner, P. G. Wodehouse, the occasional 1900s *Scribner's* article . . . I collect bound volumes of old *Scribner's Magazine*.

I don't think this is crazy but even if it is, there's no one around to tell me I'm nuts.

Famously, Jerry was reclusive and shied away from the public, we're all familiar with the reputation. Here's the odd thing about what has happened to me over the years since I've moved here: I am becoming a recluse. Only an hour ago, two men came to my door, the first visitors who weren't my wonderfully respectful neighbors in well over a year, and I immediately shooed them away. They were very nice gentlemen, dressed in suits, probably going to convert me into the Church of Jesus Christ, and that's fine, but as soon as I saw them pull into the driveway I became angry. As the two men were about to open the gate, I popped my head out and said, "No, thank you—not a good time," and then I shut the door.

I'm not proud of this behavior. And I'm not proud to be seriously considering getting a sign for my front porch that reads "No Solicitors." Years ago I would hate a person that had that sign on their porch, but now here I am.

It gets worse.

Even when my amazing neighbors (who want privacy as much as I do) wave to me from the street when I'm out back working—nice people, kind neighbors I rely on for things—even these people have become a distraction.

Essentially, people have become a bit of a nuisance. Sofi and I live half the time together at the home in Burlington, Vermont, and half the time apart—she stays at her lake house on Lake Dunmore, and I at my place in Cornish. She often says to me, "I worry about you." I wish she didn't worry about me. It makes sense that she worries about me. I think I am becoming eccentric, even strange, but I think I'm gonna be okay, and I really hope she stays with me, because I truly love her.

I guess what I'm discovering is that the need to be left alone is increasingly enveloping me. I don't fight it anymore. I just let it happen. I don't think I have a choice.

I'm viscerally happy alone here. I just want to stay here all by myself with my dog, draw pictures, read my books, drink my booze, and every now and again hang out with my wife and kids. That's all I wanna do for the rest of my life. Does this make me a misanthrope? No, I don't think so, because I'm on Instagram! I have followers, and we share things. I like people . . . who are far away.

And every now and again, say, once every two or three months, I will see a neighbor and I will smile and I will engage with them in a long conversation. We will chat about all sorts of things. I'll ask them about their life, discuss the Cornish Fair, tapping the maples, ticks, and when we part ways, I'll feel good.

Now that's not a misanthrope. That's somebody who likes to be alone most of the time, and every now and again enjoys the company of other people, just not very often, like maybe four times a year.

Is some part of me turning into Jerry? I'm not sure. Maybe.

It certainly wasn't planned. But I'm not going to fight it. My home and all the miraculous nature surrounding it is a constant meditation for me, and it's just what I need at this point in my life.

This week I managed to spend no less than 10 hours hiking in the woods, 2 hours each day.

Sometimes, when I'm out on one of treks through the Cornish countryside, I become fascinated. To be in a state of fascination is no small thing; it's wonder, awe and love, all piled on top of one-another. When I feel this, my inclination is to drop to my knees and thank whomever made it all possible. (Is it whoever or whomever?)

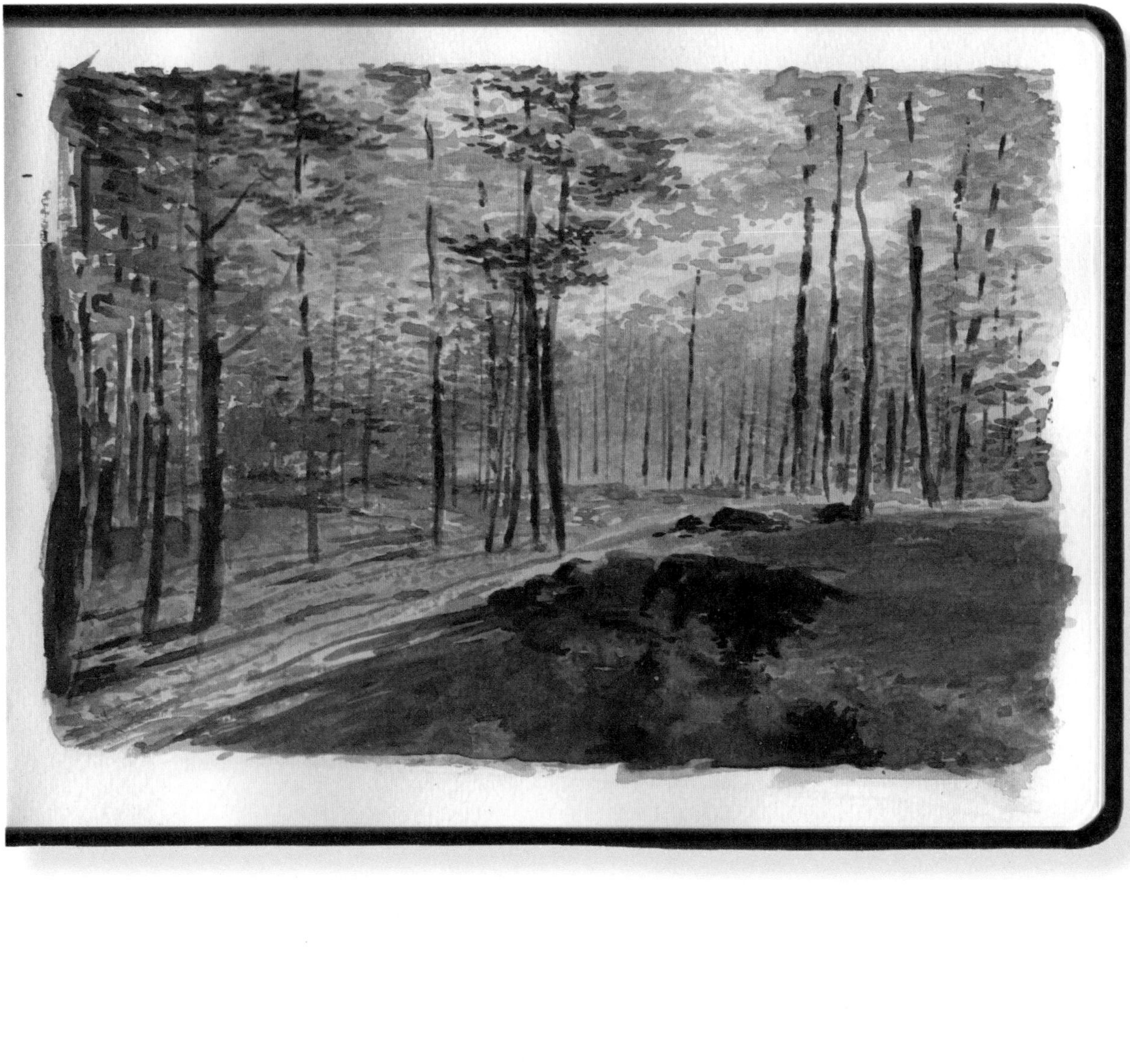

This isn't a bad memory drawing of
me in the woods last night at midnight — a transcendental walk
that I must repeat as often as I
can. Tonight, I go out, leaving Penny
here — too cold for her today.

Last night, the wind would move
over head, into the frozen, ice-coated
branches up high. Seconds after
these breezes, the sounds of ice
breaking off from these twigs wou-
fall onto the hard surface of the
snow, like crystals on a marble
floor — very cool sound indeed.

Here's a tree I pass at least once a week while I'm out in the woods... It has a goiter or burls and no one knows why these things appear.

nice shelter for a critter!

Some say it could be a bug infestation or some sort of stress caused by bacterial fungus or an infection. The goiter section of this tree was, at one time producing cells faster than the rest of the tree. The quick production of the cells creates an irregularity...burl!

Blow Me (Down) Bridge.

This is the Blow Me
Down Bridge
in Cornish — it's
a one lane
covered bridge
sketched.
As I was
drawing
the fucking
thing, a
guy

who owns the
land next to
it came out, moved my bike off his land
and made it clear he wasn't a fan of
tourists gawking on or near his land.
A woman was with him and I told him
I was sorry. He didn't respond. Then, I
told him I lived up the road. He left,
back into his house. I finished my sketch
and as I was leaving he came back out and
explained/apologized. We shook hands and
I was on my way. Kyle is his name - good old
boy.

'Ghost Tree'

Dingbton Hill nr Cornish

View of Dodge road heading to Lang-'setting' sun, the most lovely time of the day to meditate on the beauty Cornish has to offer—takes my breath away.

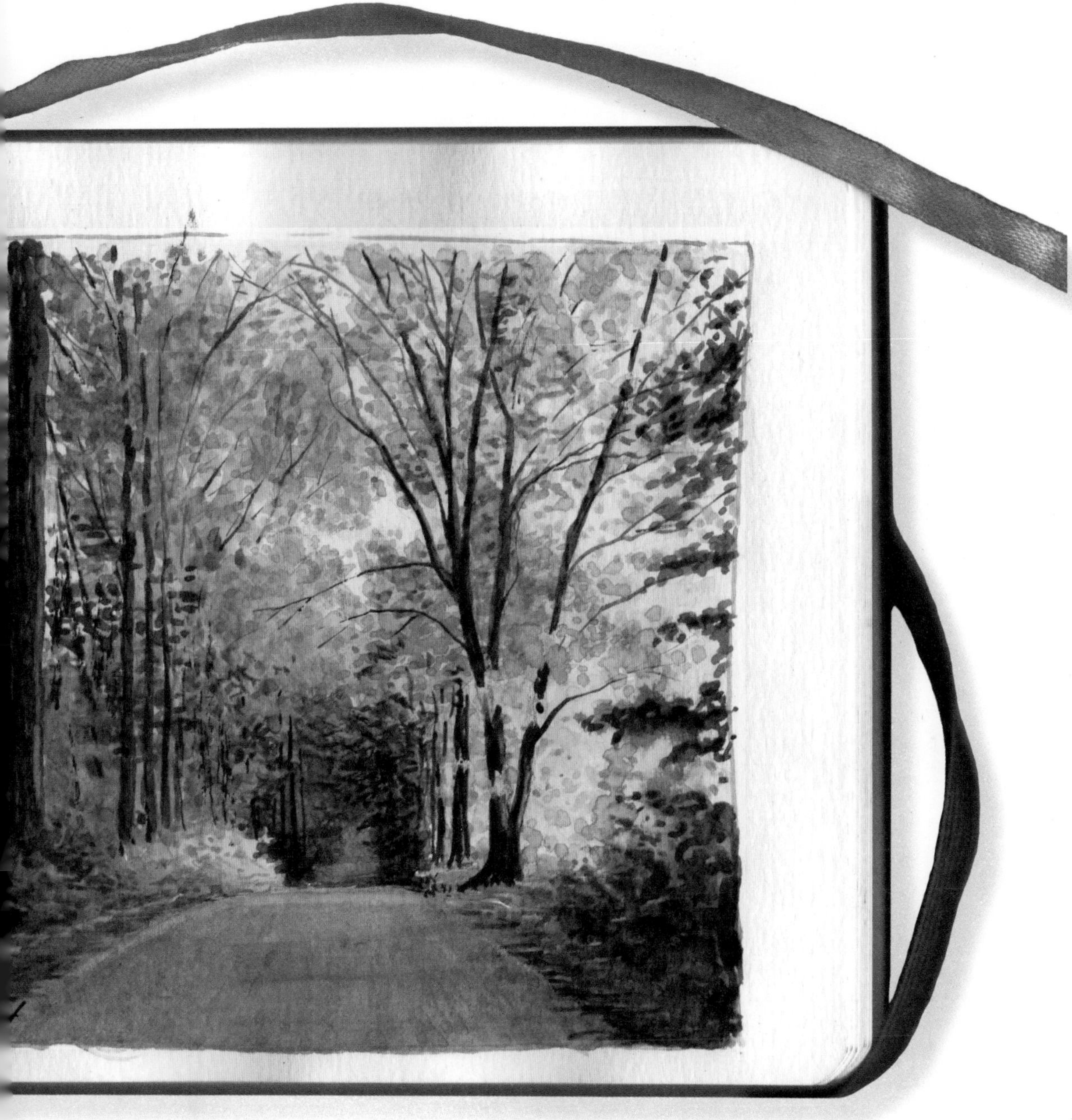

Tree on my land   Cornish *B*

my backyard +

"YOU GO IN, AND IF YOU DON'T COME OUT,
THEN I'LL KNOW I SHOULDN'T GO IN."

PREWAR TREE-HOLE APARTMENT

Every time I pass a tree with a hole in it I think to myself, *What a nice place for an animal to live.* Then I imagine the inside of the hole decorated with little fine-crafted animal furniture, a Franklin stove, and framed nineteenth-century English watercolors. A few tasteful oil paintings on the walls, a cherished landscape study by Constable. There's an exquisite Navajo rug, a tiny little tombstone blanket chest, wonderfully worn with a Roz Chast hooked rug on top. A cup of yesterday's chamomile tea sits beside a cozy armchair. In the chair sits some furry animal relaxing with a mid-century tumbler of bourbon, lost in a hardcover first edition of *Misery*.

It's all very Beatrix Potter (sans Annie Wilkes) I know, but I actually believe some version of this is going on. So much so that sometimes I'll look inside the hole and try to spy on the animal, which is a remarkably stupid thing to do. Some hostile rodent could rip my face off (and we're back to Stephen King).

Nonetheless, I take comfort in my notion that the smaller animals, like ourselves, enjoy their own creature comforts.

JOAN

Sometime last spring, the former owner of this house, Joan Littlefield, drove by and we chatted. On occasion, I will catch Joan's Prius driving by the house slowly. She looks closely to see if anything has changed or if I'm tending to her former landscaping. Neighbors say she stalks the house, but I know she misses this house and the property. Joan and her husband, Jim, a retired anesthesiologist who passed away eight or nine years ago, adored this place. Neighbors tell me Joan and Jim had at least three people working on the property at any given time during the year. Cornish, New Hampshire, is known for its gardens and has great pride in keeping up this gardening history.

On this afternoon, I asked Joan to pull in the driveway. I had questions. She got out of the car, and I asked her about the various plants that she and Jim had planted. She was happy to oblige me, visibly excited to escort me around her former home. We wandered around, and she explained the various flowers that she had planted.

We came to an area by the toolshed, off the garage apartment. Joan pushed aside some hosta plant leaves and pointed out a small stone where they had buried a pet. It was their little dog, Rex. The dog's name was crudely carved into the four-by-eight-inch surface of the stone. Joan began to cry. Penny was still alive then, but in poor health, so I felt close to Joan's loss. I stood next to Joan and considered a light hand on her back, but the moment passed.

We then carried on exploring the property until she got back in her car and drove away.

When I was alone, I walked back to the small tombstone and thought about her dog in the earth. I was glad the animal's remains were close to me. There was something comforting about it.

Walking back up to the house I was curious about Joan's sadness. Was Joan sad when she drove past her former home? Is this property, now my home, a reminder of her loss? If so, why keep revisiting the loss? Is it possible for her to move on? I don't think so. If after all these years a lost pet could still manage to bring such raw emotion to the surface, then letting go seems impossible.

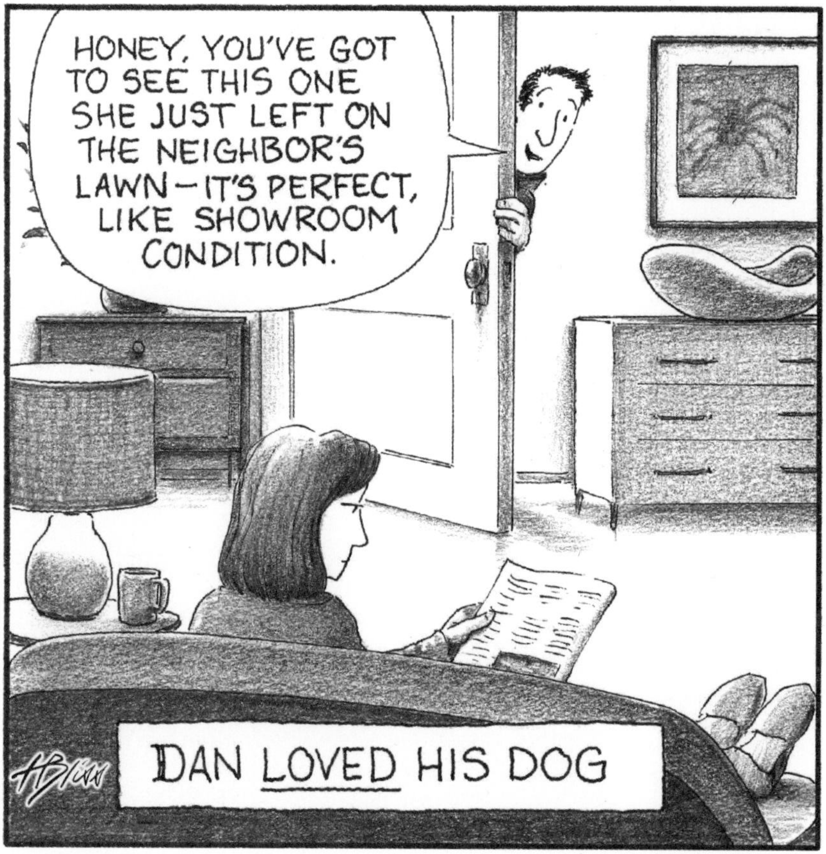
HONEY, YOU'VE GOT TO SEE THIS ONE SHE JUST LEFT ON THE NEIGHBOR'S LAWN—IT'S PERFECT, LIKE SHOWROOM CONDITION.
DAN LOVED HIS DOG

CONSTIPATED DOG REMEDY

One summer afternoon a few years back, when our sweet Penny was still clinging to this life with an impressive display of stubbornness, she was constipated for three days. This was a side effect of the medicine she was taking for Cushing's disease. So for three days my wife, Sofi, and I sat out in the front yard with her, waiting.

Penny had trouble assuming the position to shit. A prior fall had left one of her hind legs incapable of positioning. Oftentimes we had to assist her when she went, holding her tummy up to take the weight off the lame leg.

But on this late-summer afternoon, both Sofi and I knew something had to be done. We had read that three days of constipation for a dog could be dangerous. We'd expressed our concern to the vet, tried various foods, and were patient with our Penny, with no luck. So, we resorted to YouTube.

We found what we thought was a downright disturbing remedy that called for two matchsticks to be inserted . . . into Penny's anus. As Penny sat on the grass looking miserable, we read repeated renditions of this surefire "fix" on our phones. We decided to give it a try.

Following the directions, we pulled two matches from a typical matchbook. Next, we positioned Penny with her backside facing us and inserted the two matches—first in my mouth to wet them, then in her anus, sulfur side first. The instructions read "sulfur side goes in about halfway." We then slowly gave Penny some space (I'm certain she was as confounded by all this as we were) and waited.

In less than a minute she began doing her walking-'n'-pooping thing and out came three days of, well, shit. It took a few minutes, but when Penny had finished, Sofi and I went directly over to her and told her what a good girl she was. We were both (all) so relieved.

There on the grass, in full view of our neighbors, Sofi started laughing at the success of this ridiculous elixir and the whole situation. I laughed too until I noticed Sofi's laughing turn to crying. We picked up our Penny and went back into the house.

guy directly across from you on his phone; but the dog he was walking was stopped, looking at us with a look that said 'what the fuck did you just do to your dog's ass?!'.

Monday afternoon: Corinth.

Mother's Days continued...

9:35 pm In bed in Delia's Room w/
Penny. Just said good night to
Sofi. We went out for a nice dinner
in Winooski, the Waterworks. IT
was a long day - emotional for
Sofi, mostly because of Penny.

Penny hadn't pooped in 2 full
days and around 2 or 3 pm, we
were trying to get her to 'go'. no
luck. So, I went on line and
searched. I found one odd remedy
that involved 2 paper match
sticks, sulpher end into Penny's
ass...

matches in
rectum
you
have to lick
the sulpher end
to wet it first.

"the white"

Well, this
strange
remedy
worked like
a charm.
Penny
instantly
moved forward until
she shat out the 2 matches and
a medium-size stool.

— matches
— poop.

We were so
happy this worked.
Sofi started to cry right there.
I held her as she sobbed. From
across the street we saw a

YOU'RE LATE.

"'WORDLE' IN THREE TODAY."

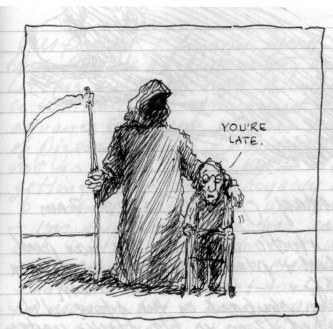

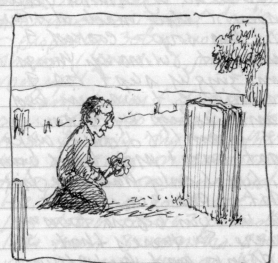

DEAD RECKONING

On a recent drive from Cornish to Burlington I was talking to my oldest brother, John, who, along with my sister-in-law Katie, is visiting our parents today. After my dad's previous failed attempt at suicide (when he laid in bed eating ice, willing it all to end), he is back to wanting to die. According to John, he is more determined than ever. I have my doubts.

Before I spoke to John, I spoke to my mother, who is the most self-absorbed person in the world. I was telling her about my mother-in-law, Elaine, and the recent stroke she suffered. I explained how difficult it had been for Sofi and her siblings. My mother said nothing—no response to this information, she simply rotated from what I said into a story of a twenty-five-year-old leg injury she sustained while at her fifty-year high school reunion in Los Angeles! This isn't an age thing—my mother has been this way for as far back as I can remember. It's more of a disorder, some kind of malfunction like someone who can't turn left or is colorblind . . . my mother can't ask questions. I can't ever recall my mother asking a question. I'm serious, nothing is coming to mind.

Here's an imagined excerpt of the platonic ideal conversation with my mother:

Harry: Hi, Mom, how are you and Dad doing? I haven't spoken to either of you in a while, although I wrote you a letter a few weeks back, did you receive that?

Mom: Of course we received your letter; we always love your letters and thank you so much for taking the time out to add those little cartoons—it makes us both laugh. Your father complains a lot, but I'm used to it by now. I suppose I do a fair amount of complaining too, but we still manage to love each other despite the occasional resentments. . . . We're hanging in there, Harry. Honestly, it's difficult for me . . . aging in these times . . . so much suffering, but we're grateful for every day we can see the sun and birds and hear about you kids! How are you doing? How is everything going with Sofi and Alex? How is your work going?

The highlight of the Cornish Fair

This kind of sincere back-and-forth dance of dialogue has never happened with my mother—never.

Since I left home, I have found romantic partners with the type of families I had always wanted. Loving, kind, and intellectually curious families who would look me in the eye, ask me questions and share intimacies. I learned from these families over the years. I grew because of them. In so many ways they saved me from the kind of sorrow that comes from living with family dysfunction marinated in narcissism.

I'm finding it interesting today, seeing the evolution of my existence through my parents. How we got started and where we are now and all of that stuff in between. Sure, it's depressing and often frustrating, but sometimes emotions can take a back seat to investigation.

Like when I tell my mom about her grandson and how well he's doing and she instantly changes the subject (to the mischievous squirrel she wants to drown for eating her zucchinis). I no longer get angry with her. I would be curious to know what's happening in her brain. Maybe I could convince Charley to attach an fMRI to her head while she sleeps.

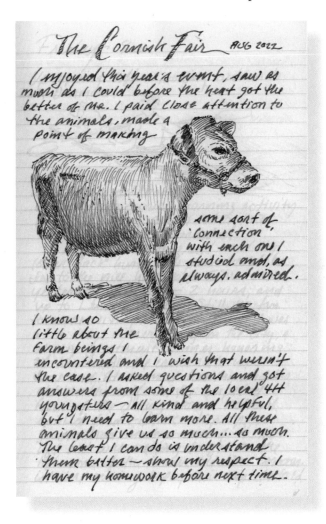

The Cornish Fair   AUG 2022

I enjoyed this year's event, saw as much as I could before the heat got the better of me. I paid close attention to the animals, made a point of making

some sort of 'connection' with each one I studied and, as always, admired.

I know so little about the farm beings I encountered and I wish that wasn't the case. I asked questions and got answers from some of the local 4H youngsters — all kind and helpful, but I need to learn more. All these animals give us so much... so much. The least I can do is understand them better — show my respect. I have my homework before next time.

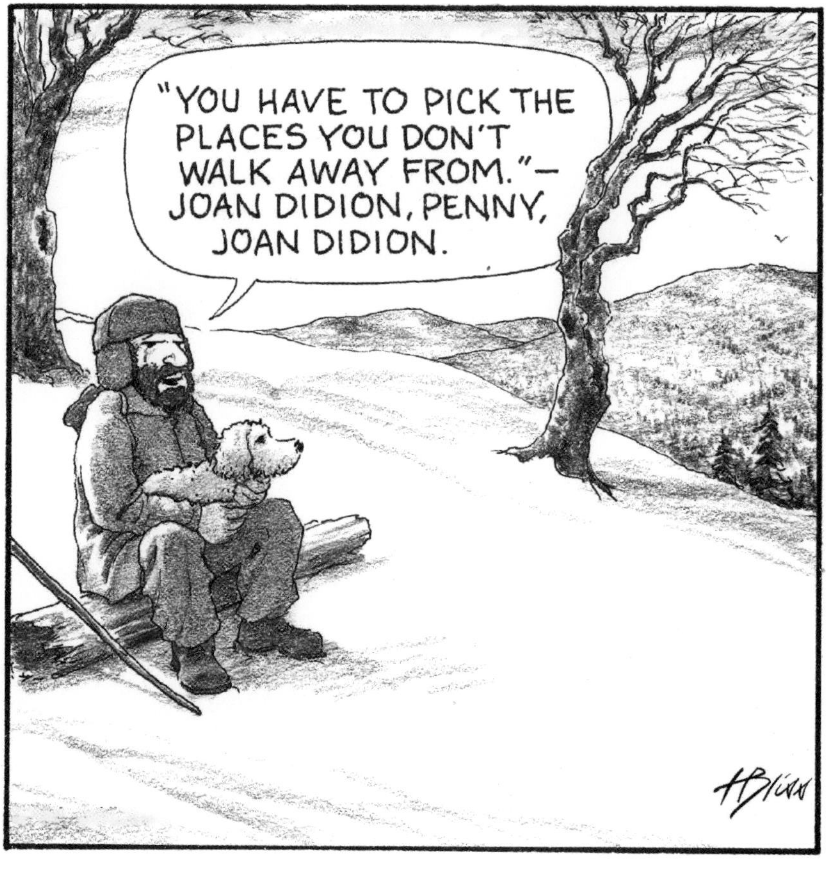
"YOU HAVE TO PICK THE PLACES YOU DON'T WALK AWAY FROM."— JOAN DIDION, PENNY, JOAN DIDION.

A COVETING

Lately I've been thinking about why I am compelled to make art. I've been making pictures my entire life, and it's only recently that I've started thinking about my motivations. I imagine my drive to achieve a certain level of success, keeping my head down over the drawing board all these years, has kept me from overthinking it.

I understand now that I am trying to hold on to a moment, covet the vision and keep it close so I'll never forget it. If I see a winter landscape and it pulls me in, so much so that I find myself freezing my ass off rendering the scene, it's because I never want to forget it.

I keep Moleskine journals for this very reason. At first, I simply wrote and drew things in these journals—cartoon ideas, dreams, psychedelic experiences. But after eight years and twenty-eight-plus journals I now realize that the underlying reason for putting it all down on paper is so I can recall my life. I make art in a desperate attempt to hold on to this life.

View of the Avon Gorge
There are fewer
things on this earth
that give me more
pleasure than watching
this pen in my hand
construct all these
marks to bring about
a view before my
eyes. Why am I
seemingly compelled
to keep at this task?
The only explanation I
have is that in doing
so, I am desperately...
foolishly attempting to hang on, covet this glorious life I know
will someday end. I record to hold close & relish before dark.

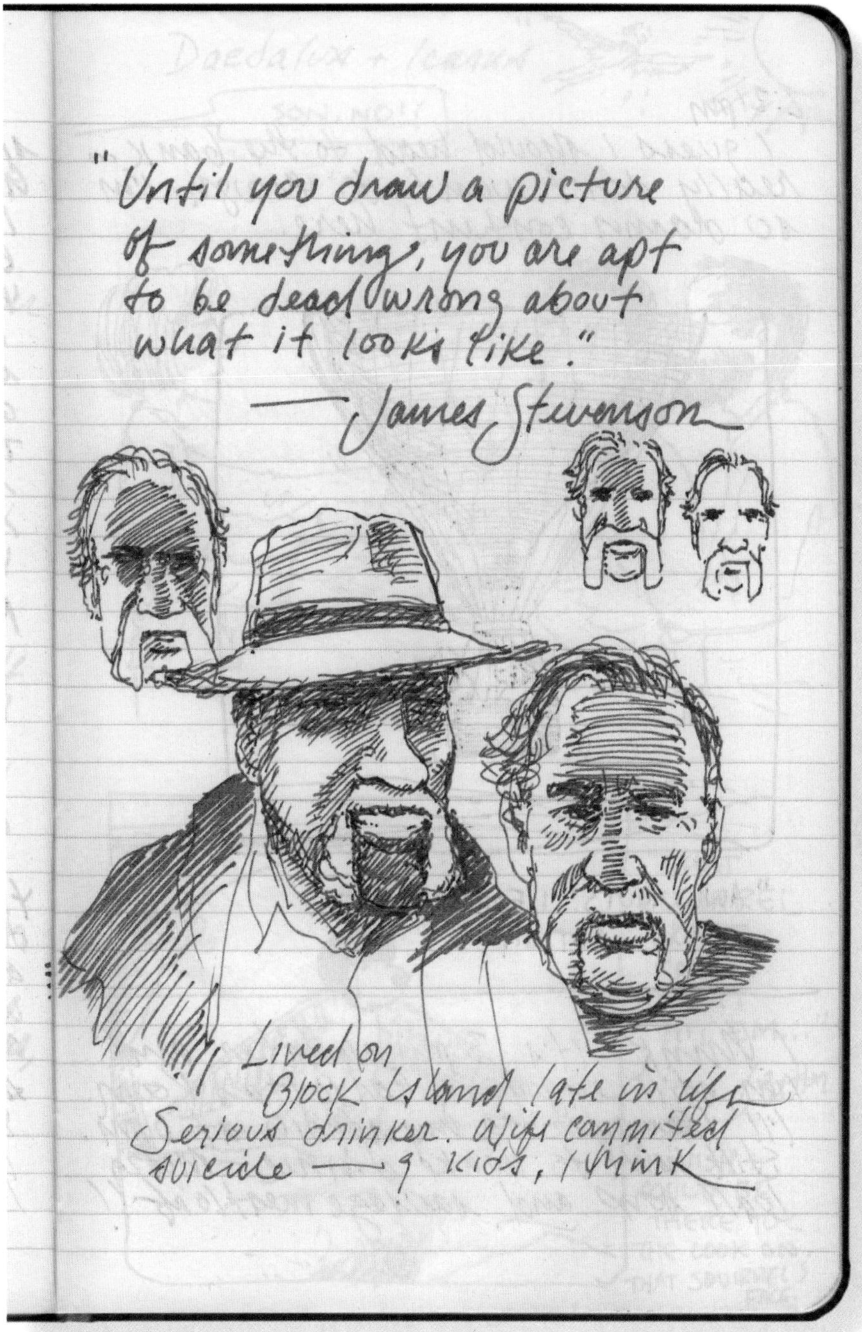

"Until you draw a picture
of something, you are apt
to be dead wrong about
what it looks like."
—— James Stevenson

Lived on
Block Island late in life
Serious drinker. Wife committed
suicide — 9 kids, I think

STEVE MARTIN

I miss Steve. I haven't talked to Steve in a while. He's busy working on season three of *Only Murders in the Building*, and it seems he doesn't have time for me. I don't take it personally; this happened the last two seasons of the show. Besides, after publishing two cartoon collections together, I needed a break from bookwork. Cartoons are easy, but the strips are more demanding. I still email him cartoons that I need captions for once or twice a week. He recently sent me back some captions for a drawing and added, "I've been so busy working. Working on a series is like being underwater."

There was only one time when I was struck by Steve's celebrity, and this was the very first time Sofi and I had lunch in the city with Steve and his wife, Anne. I have a clear memory of being nervous and perhaps a bit awkward, but it went okay. I made him smile. Sofi made him laugh, an actual laugh.

Seeing Steve Martin laugh five feet away is pretty cool. I've never told Steve how influential he was to me growing up—all the albums, films, *SNL* . . . massive impact on me. We've done interviews together where I've expressed this, so I'm sure he knows.

What he doesn't know is how much I want the Seurat drawing hanging in his hallway. And the Hopper. The Lucian Freud as well.

Early on in our collaboration I noticed Steve's deep knowledge of art. After the first book was put to bed, I bought an oil painting at auction by an American landscape painter named Henry Pember Smith. A "listed" artist

A color portrait of Steve, made when I was fifteen years old.

but self-taught and fairly obscure, I thought. When I sent Steve a photo of the painting, I was sure he'd had no idea who this artist was. He knew. Even used the word *shimmer* to describe the quality of light in Pember Smith's work—the perfect adjective.

I didn't know this at the time, but Steve started out collecting nineteenth-century American landscapes in the 1970s. Of course he knew who Henry Pember Smith was! Since then, I have sent Steve paintings at auction that I was going to pull the trigger on. He's given me feedback, told me to ask for the "condition report," suggested holding off and waiting for something more desirable. I trust his instincts. Anne's too. Together they have a remarkable art collection.

I never thought I would be checking in with Steve Martin about fine art purchases. Never.

When I'm with Steve and Anne, it's always comfortable and easy. Twenty years separate us. In my mind, I feel older than my age (it's not wisdom, more atrophy), and Steve's younger somehow, so we almost meet up. At least this is how I see our relationship.

When he's done working on the latest season of his show, we'll probably regroup and discuss the third book. Here's the thing: I don't give a shit. I don't care if Steve never wants to work with me again (huge mistake). I'll still miss him. I won't miss the famous Steve Martin. I'll miss the guy who calls me when I'm on psilocybin trekking through the Cornish woods to tell me a story about Harrison Ford, Eve Babitz, and blow jobs. I'll miss the guy who, after looking at one of our collaborative cartoons, sends me back an email response that reads "Makes Steve laugh." I'll miss the guy whose wife is a passionate birder who sends me ink she makes out of blackberries. His banjo playing. Watching him with his daughter and new puppy, Sunny. And that Seurat. Really will miss that Seurat.

I'll be glad when the interviews and TV stuff is over. I need to begin the finishes for the next book soon — by mid December, I hope to start on the first strip.

Mondays 8:00 am

Good Morning America zoom meeting about to happen — too early to be speaking to people other than my 1/2 sleeping wife and dog. I hope I don't ruin everything. Sofi and Penny are here in the room with me — both sleeping. Slept pretty well last night considering...

10:17 am Back relaxing in the guest room. GMA went well — glad it's over, too short, but I hope it sells books. At 4 pm we have a longer book event w/ Henry Winkler — virtual book signing and I'm looking forward to that... the Fonz!!

Denny
sleeping
Sunday Morn.

Denny
Again...
monday
10:30
am

one of Steve's—made me laugh...

Great Moments in Song Writing...

My Stuffed Shark!

4:20 am woke up, but I'll be going back to sleep. Just wanted to jot down a cartoon idea.

This morning's coffee has been sweetened with coffee-infused maple syrup. ♡

SHIT COFFEE COMPANY

Drawing Steve from Memory

Here's a sketch of the dumbest Raccoon in NH checking out the gun barrel of my neighbor, Clem's, .20-guage shotgun.

8:30 am The wife and dog are still sleeping. Curious if Kenny's had breakfast yet... getting late.

"YOU'RE RIGHT. THIS IS MUCH BETTER THAN PUTTING
THE OLD CALENDAR IN THE TRASH."

BURNING MAN

The other day I drove past my neighbor's land. They're in South Carolina for the winter, but I saw a man on their property standing in front of a large pile of tree limbs, sticks, and brush. Smoke was rising from the pile.

I wondered who the man was and why he was on the land, so I slowed to a stop and turned in. I pulled up just shy of his pickup truck and got out of my car. I approached with an affable demeanor, waved, and said hello.

He was a tall man—older, bearded with a kind smile. I told him I had just purchased the land that abutted my neighbors' property, the land he was now standing on. He was a longtime resident of the town, a former selectman who was doing some clearing for my neighbors.

Every now and again, when there was a quiet in our conversation, we'd both stare at the flame and smoke, which was just beginning to catch on. I'd never seen a pile of brush as large as this, that I imagined, once fully ignited, could get out of control. I mentioned this to the man, and he didn't seem to disagree. But we both understood this was unlikely in mid-February with a light layer of hardened snow all around.

As the man was talking about his mistrust in local politics, education, and the government, I kept admiring the fire. I became transfixed by it and found it difficult to look away. Even when the man turned to look at me with a query, I wouldn't take my eyes off the flames. I simply nodded in oblivious agreement. The heat from the fire felt good, and I moved a few steps closer.

The man too moved with me. We heard the fire, the crackling and fizzing of sap burning.

It occurred to me that at some point the man had stopped talking and, like me, was watching the small blaze catch on. We seemed to be hypnotized, unmoving like we'd suddenly been turned to stone. I thought about what we looked like from inside the fire, and I pictured us from this point of view. A strong wind came and turned the direction of the flames directly at us. We both jumped back, the man falling backward onto the ground.

"Jesus!" he said.

I helped him up, and he steadied himself. His eyebrows and beard were singed, and we both smelled burning hair. A cawing crow above us seemed to be laughing.

"Sonofabitch wind," the man said.

I nodded. "Well, I'd better hit the Price Chopper. Nice chatting with you."

He waved and returned his gaze to the burning pile.

Auction Day
LOOKS LIKE THAT BLISS FELLA JUST WON HIS-SELF A FINE SET OF BONE CHINA HE AINT NEVER GUNNA USE...
Man @ outdoor auction

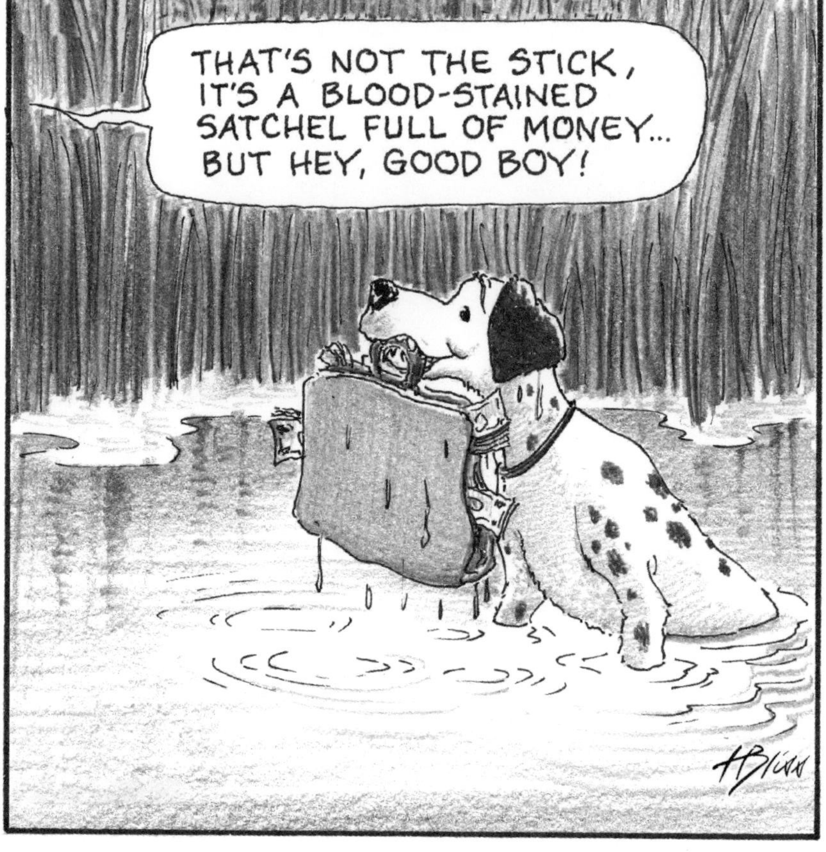
THAT'S NOT THE STICK, IT'S A BLOOD-STAINED SATCHEL FULL OF MONEY... BUT HEY, GOOD BOY!

PENNY ROLL

There was always a moment just before Penny rolled in some disgusting dead thing when my adoration for her transformed into horror. It all happened so fast. One minute she's happily off leash, carelessly sniffing the breeze while I drift along with not a care in the world, and the next minute (second) Penny makes the move.

If you have a dog, you're familiar with this move. Penny would lower her head, turn it to the side, and begin to rub the side of her noggin into whatever dead thing she'd discovered. Then, she would move forward with the intent of rubbing her neck, side, and eventually all of her back deep into the rotting carcass, squirming like an oversize furry maggot possessed, legs flailing up in the air . . . back and forth, back and forth.

All the cares in the world would return to me and it was directly home for a bath.

Another thing I never understood was the whole dog/stick thing.

I would guess that about half the time on our walks together, Penny would find a stick. What always interested me was the fact that once she'd found the choice stick, she always turned around and headed back home.

When she was younger, she would never let me find a stick for her. As she got older I was more successful in this odd apprenticeship. No small sticks. She'd grab sticks longer than she was, cumbersome and nearly firewood worthy. Always held on tightly with a strong, proud strut.

Once we approached my yard, she'd find a spot where the stick was to be laid down. This was never random, Penny put thought into this placement—not sure why. After this, we'd both head into the house.

Penny
profile

The sun is
out and thus
far, this
Friday looks
like a lousy
example of
all things beautiful
in New England
at this time of year.
Interestingly, I
have damn little work

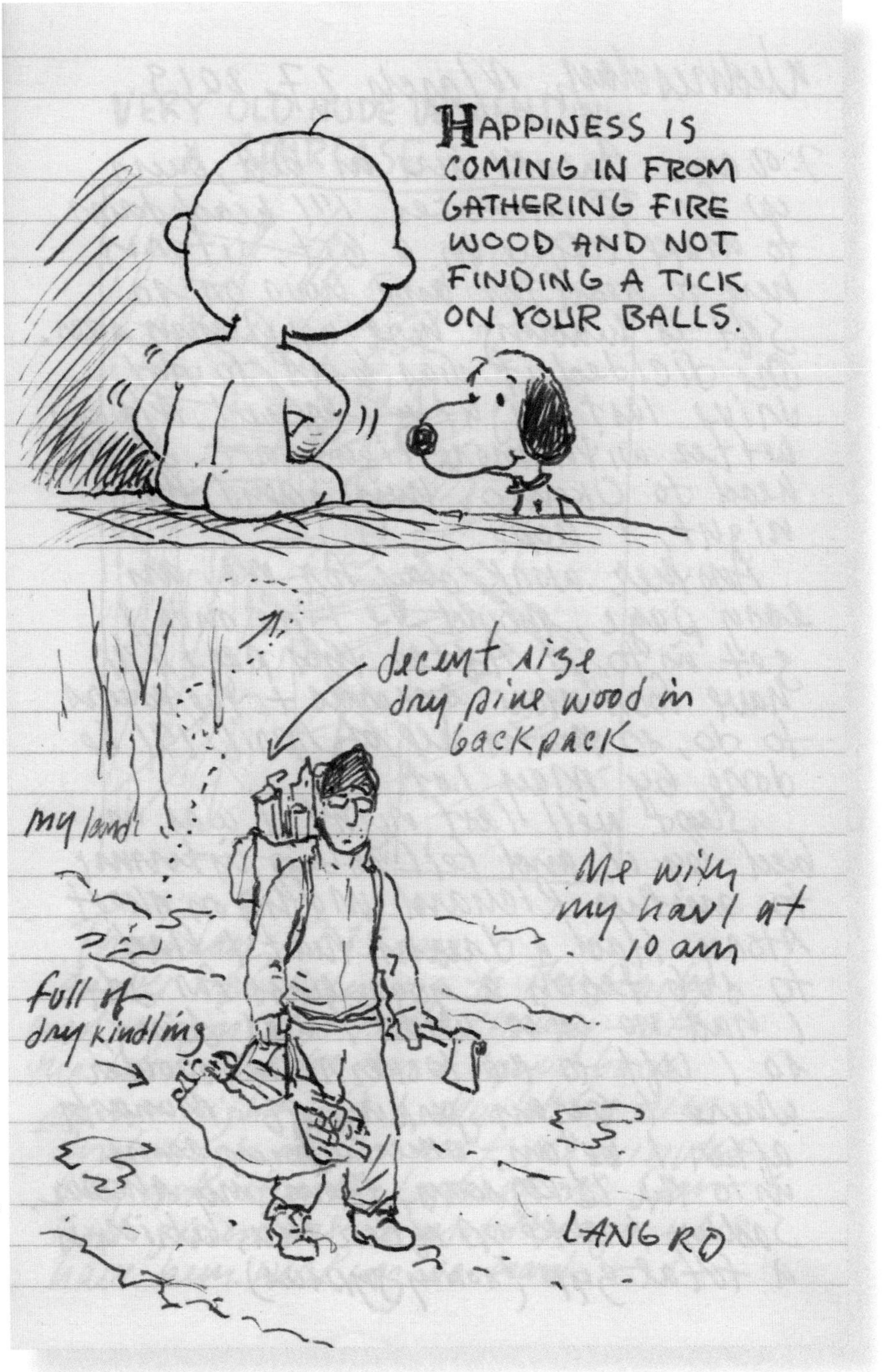
HAPPINESS IS COMING IN FROM GATHERING FIRE WOOD AND NOT FINDING A TICK ON YOUR BALLS.
decent size dry pine wood in backpack
my land!
Me with my haul at 10 am
full of dry kindling
LANGRO

"STILL THINKIN' ABOUT THAT SQUIRREL, HUH?"

KARL = WORRY

I've got myself into a pickle. I'm pretty sure I love a chipmunk. I find myself worrying about Karl, both when I'm away and when I'm here in Cornish. When I'm away, I worry that a bird of prey will swoop down and have Karl for lunch (or dinner at this point—been fattening him up with all the birdseed). This scenario is very unlikely—a hawk navigating at top speed through the trees, patio furniture, grill; plus with Karl's quickness it would not be easy. Now if this were an open field . . .

When I'm here, I'm worried he feels neglected. Sometimes, he looks downright lonely. He sits at the end of the stone wall looking off toward Mount Ascutney, all melancholy-like. Reminds me of Penny's sitting posture near the end. Generally, I feed Karl two or three times during the day. Today is no different. Earlier, just for fun, I served him the birdseed on my Wedgwood fine bone china (this china once belonged to columnist Liz Smith). When he finished, he jumped up on my leg and scared the shit out of me. Was he happy? Showing gratitude? Impressed with the china? I have no idea. Karl now lets me pet him on his soft back with the top of my index finger, which is very nice.

I know he knows who I am.

I was at the lake house for five days spending quality time with Sofi for our anniversary. Upon my return to Cornish earlier today, Karl rushed out from the back patio to greet me. I hadn't unlocked the door yet, and there he was, all perked up and excited to see me. I'm not kidding, he was actually

excited . . . and I was too. Something inside my brain tells me that having a chipmunk that makes me feel that good is strange.

After I got settled in, I unpacked some of the oak wood from Sofi's lake house. She had a sick oak tree cut down, and I periodically transfer some of this excellent firewood to my place in Cornish. Chopping up the wood wasn't easy in ninety-degree heat with a sore right shoulder. But I perked up halfway

This is the place where Karl sits at the end of the day — a stone from the retaining wall by the patio. Every time I see him looking off in the distance this way I become sad and I don't know why.

Mountai. of Vermo

Maybe in these moments of quiet chipmunk reflection I'm reminded of my mourning yet to come.

(Look of the bri side... very sa

Before the sun diminished, I was on the patio standing & looking to Vermont. I looked to my left and spotted Karl, essentially doing the same thing. There we both were together looking off into the atmosphere. I looked back, down at Karl and thought "I'd love to see his home." I wanted to shrink down and be with him in his place...

interestingly enough, I have a tunnel in my house too...

KARL, I LOVE IT! WHERE'S THE BAR?

Guest room.

Next

through the pile when Karl graced me with his presence. He'd made his way from our usual spot on the patio, around the back of the house, to where the woodshed is located.

This is the first time Karl has ventured away from the patio to spend time with me. I know I'm anthropomorphizing a goddamn chipmunk, but I can't help it. I just spent fifteen minutes on Google learning about the sleeping

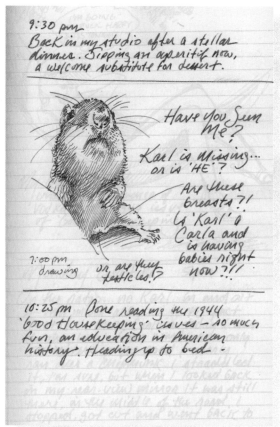

patterns of chipmunks. Their life span (two to three years). Diet. If they remember humans (yes). Other things you can look up yourself.

Last week, a friend of mine suggested that I get some peanuts for Karl. He said Karl will love the peanuts, and it'll be really funny because chipmunks like to stuff them in their cheeks and the visual would make me laugh. But I don't wanna do that because I worry Karl would choke.

I don't want to worry anymore. I was done with worrying. I've worried

7:13 PM Just back from a walk on my property & Lang rd, where I nearly ran over the injured chipmunk. I keep replaying the whole thing over — was it a red squirrel running off along the stone wall, leaving the chipmunk in the middle of Lang road?! I turned my 'flash-lyrt' on and searched the wet leaves by the side of the road. If I found a dead chipmunk, I'd have, at least, some closure. Jesus, my mourning for Karl is turning into a crime podcast!!

WHO THE FUCK KILLED
KARL?!

OSS POLICE LINE DO NOT CROSS POLICE LINE

Well, at least the bats are out. I love seeing my bats at dusk...

HI FELLAS!
KEEP AN 'EYE'
OUT FOR KARL!

The new chipmunk on the scene. Did this one murder Karl?

enough for two lifetimes. If Karl started choking on a peanut shell, what would I do? There's no giving a chipmunk the Heimlich maneuver. I'd have to sit there and eventually watch him (I honestly don't know if Karl is male or female) die and then every time I saw a peanut shell I'd think of Karl and get sad.

Oh, Karl, what have I done?!

". . . NINETEEN, TWENTY. READY OR NOT, HERE I COME!"

DEATH: B+

Captain James T. Kirk said, "Space: the final frontier. These are the voyages of the starship *Enterprise*. . . ."

I don't think so. The "final frontier" is death. Space is certainly a fascinating and ambitious frontier, but it's not final. Being dead trumps space.

We learn about space in school from an early age. Some of my earliest drawings are crudely rendered crayon depictions of rocket ships hurtling in space. I knew most of the planets' names before I knew my multiplication tables.

Why are we studying algebra or geometry when death is clearly a far more important topic? Is it too depressing a subject? I don't think so. Not at that age. Human mortality is without a doubt the most important topic in the history of the human race. It always has been and always will be. So why the fuck aren't we learning about it earlier in our lives?

Personally, I think high school kids would love it. Two semesters, the first covers the death of your parents, pets, relatives, and friends. The second semester would be your death. I can picture all the goth kids lining up to get into the class . . . there would be an overflow, a waiting list. The schools would have to hire more teachers to cover the topic, and they'd love it! It's fascinating stuff! Reincarnation. Afterlife. Cremation or burial? Ghosts. Wills. Decomposition! So many topics could be covered. The grim reaper as the school mascot? That might be cool!

And with the right teachers, young folks would move forward in their lives with a deeper understanding of what it's like to be alive. They would appreciate every moment, every breath, and they would live life to the fullest. Gratitude would fill the halls of the school, and pep rallies would be a celebration of life.

But we don't teach this topic in high school. We don't learn about death until, well, someone we love dies.

In my case it was Penny. But, soon both of my parents are going to be dead, very possibly before this book hits the bookshelves (Jesus, I hope so).

My older brothers, John (and his wife Katie) and Charley, are in their sixties now and dealing with the inconceivable difficulties of aging parents. With our mom and dad, this manifests in their unwillingness to be kind, listen, and let go of their irrational paranoia. They are just shy of impossible to deal with, so entrenched in loathing resentments.

Part of me is envious of our pals whose parents are already dead. What a relief. I'm sure it's tough too, when you miss your kind and loving parents—I'm sure that's not easy. But what if your parents are not nice, incapable of selfless love, manipulative, and narcissistic? What does one do then? I want answers!

Most of our teachers in high school were in their thirties, forties, and fifties, and some of them were probably dealing with aging parents, parents nearing death. They would've been right in the thick of it and could have communicated to us kids their firsthand knowledge, their sincere collection of elixirs or insights. But that didn't happen. We had shop and home ec.

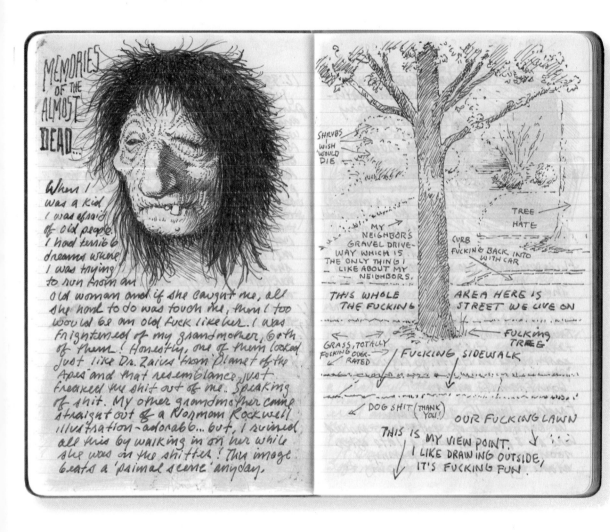

MEMORIES OF THE ALMOST DEAD...

When I was a kid I was afraid of old people. I had terrible dreams where I was trying to run from an old woman and if she caught me, all she had to do was touch me, then I too would be an old fuck like her. I was frightened of my grandmother, both of them! Honestly, one of them looked just like Dr. Zaius from 'Planet of the Apes' and that resemblance just freaked the shit out of me. Speaking of shit. My other grandmother came straight out of a Norman Rockwell illustration - adorable... but, I ruined all this by walking in on her while she was on the shitter! That image beats a 'primal scene' anyday.

SHRUBS WISH WOULD DIE

MY NEIGHBOR'S GRAVEL DRIVE-WAY WHICH IS THE ONLY THING I LIKE ABOUT MY NEIGHBORS.

TREE HATE

CURB FUCKING BACK INTO WITH CAR

THIS WHOLE THE FUCKING

AREA HERE IS STREET WE LIVE ON

GRASS, TOTALLY FUCKING OVER-RATED

FUCKING TREE

FUCKING SIDEWALK

DOG SHIT (THANK YOU!)

OUR FUCKING LAWN

THIS IS MY VIEW POINT. I LIKE DRAWING OUTSIDE, IT'S FUCKING FUN.

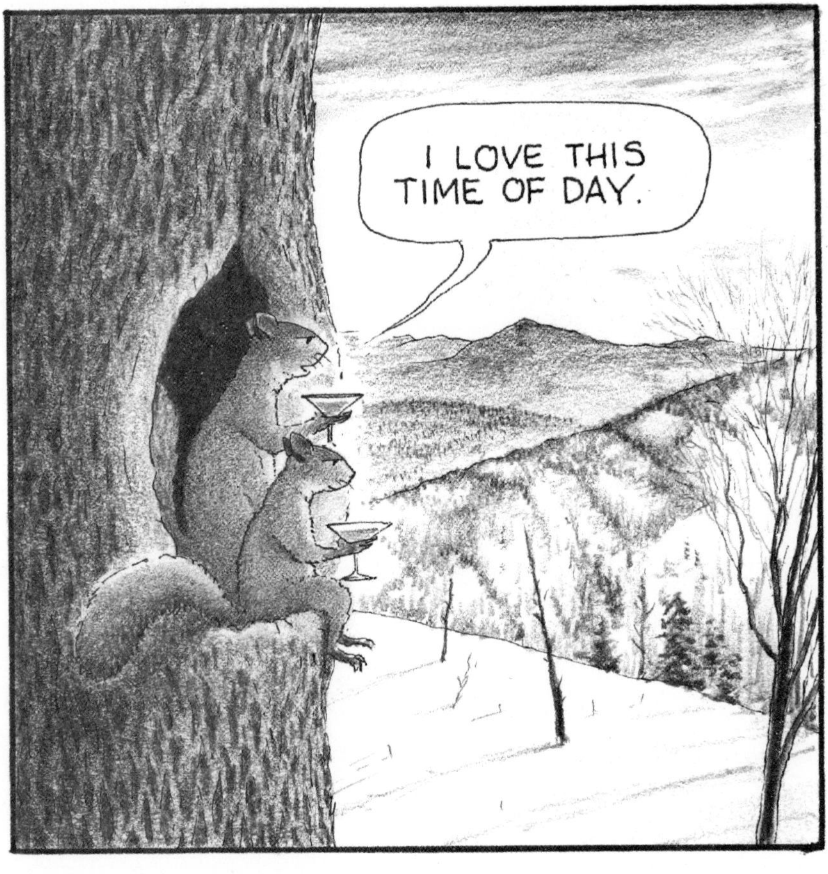
I LOVE THIS TIME OF DAY.

MORNING BRAIN
WITH SQUIRREL

I am fascinated by the brain. If I could do it all over again, I think I would've gone into neuroscience.

The other day, I was sitting with my wife in the kitchen. She was engaged in some magazine article while sipping coffee, I stared out the kitchen window at a squirrel clinging to the bark on the sugar maple in the backyard. The damn thing wasn't moving, it was just frozen there against the tree. Not even the fluffy tail was moving, and I thought the poor bastard froze to death overnight.

Then, I saw the tail move, and I got a little angry at the squirrel for fucking with me. I began wondering what that squirrel's life was like and how the squirrel was going to survive in the freezing cold. Where would it get its food?!

And then I started thinking about my parents, when they're going to die.

And then I started thinking about a couple of my friends, how they're struggling to make ends meet.

I was becoming miserable, and in no time I started thinking about the work I had to do, deadlines, and how I was procrastinating.

Finally, I looked away from the window and said to my wife, "I wish I could turn my brain off somehow!" She mentioned sleep (she wasn't totally present at this time) and I told her that didn't always work and that our brains still work while we're sleeping—we could have anxious dreams. She mentioned meditation (slightly more present with me) but that requires a lot of work. Then my wife, completely present and looking straight at me, deadpan, suggested death, and we both laughed.

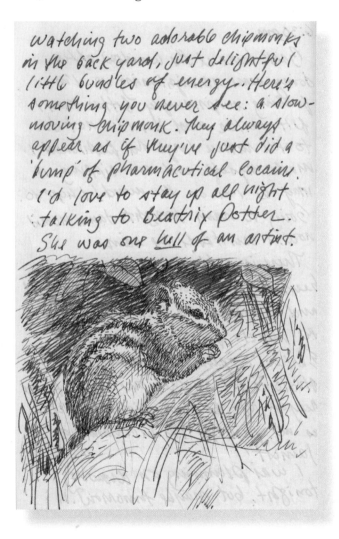

Sunday, February 9, 2020

I often wonder how certain animals survive in the cold. Adorable furry rabbits eat their own shit... not so cute. It seems their digestive systems aren't so effective, additional nutrients remain in their feces! gross!!

House cats, bobcats, hawks and other predators are out to kill!

These little bastards don't move much in winter. It's a way to conserve energy. Either this or they get lazy as fuck. Most hunters don't even notice the rabbit because they are very still, like a statue — a statue of a fucking rabbit freezing it's ass off.

KICK ME

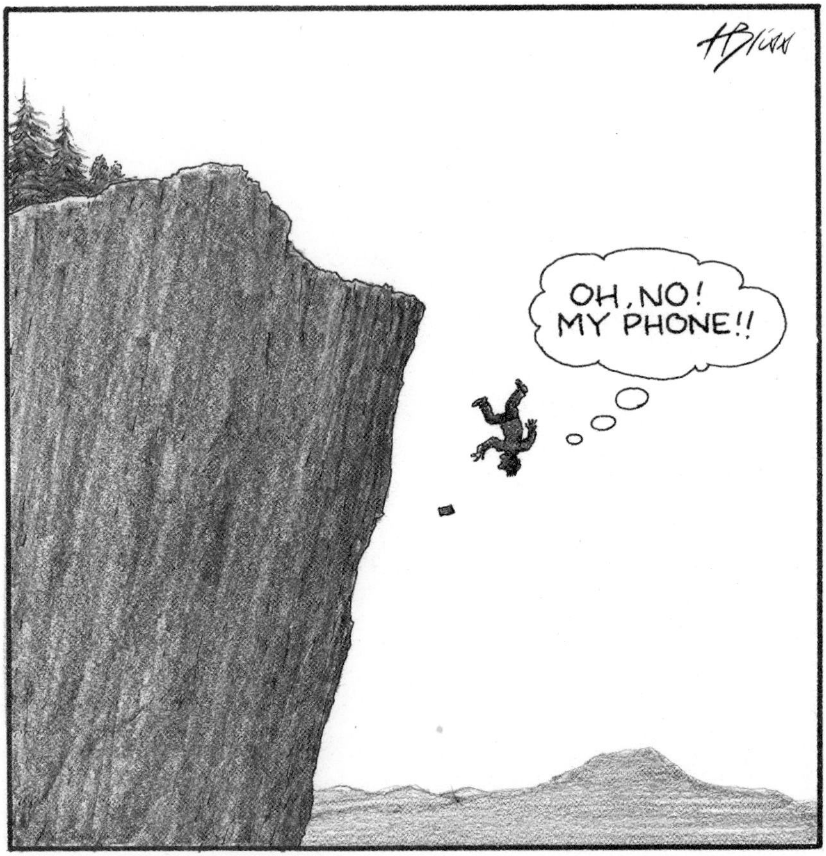
OH, NO!
MY PHONE!!

ROCKS FOR BRAINS

Yesterday afternoon I went for a two-and-a-half-hour hike in the woods. My home here in Cornish is rural, so I am surrounded by hundreds of acres of dense trees, rock, and snow. I have yet to come across another person on any of my walks. I like to think of my time walking as similar in some respects to a meditation. It's remarkably quiet. Aside from the wind and my own feet crunching in the snow, there is very little sound. An occasional something falling from a tree. Perhaps a squirrel.

I made my way along, mostly following a deer trail. I do a lot of talking to myself out there, I find it fun. Hell, I've even come up with cartoons while talking to myself in the woods.

After an hour or so, I came to the edge of a fifty-foot rock precipice overlooking a ravine below, beautiful. I always have a backpack with a thermos of my hot soup (I'm a Crock-Pot addict), my journal, a little tripod stool and other things I might need in case of an emergency, like a hunting knife in case I stumble across a hostile black bear. I set up my little stool and sat there quietly sipping my soup, hoping to spot a few deer down below. After the soup I decided to head down into the ravine below—why not?

I made it down the rock "wall" with surprising case, but not long after my descent I noticed the day's light diminishing. I didn't want to be out there in the dark—things get dicey. So I made the brave/stupid decision to scale back up the rock wall and head home. On the way up (with my crampons securely fixed to my boots) I came upon a noisy (pissed-off?) porcupine hiding in a rocky crevice—little guy was damn cute, scared, but cute. I continued on with unfounded confidence, neared the top . . . until I slipped and bounced back down that rock wall like a goddamn Slinky.

I landed on my ass in the snow and thank God for snow—it cushioned my fall. I spent four or five minutes just lying there thinking about what had happened and how bad it could have been. I took my time getting back up and carried on. For some reason, I felt self-conscious, and slightly embarrassed, but no one was around, except for the animals.

I'm sure there are a couple of squirrels, a little porcupine, and a few crows still laughing at what they witnessed—good times. My second attempt up the side of that wall of icy rock was a success, and I made it home bruised, but in one piece . . . just as the sun made room for the stars.

HAHAHA!

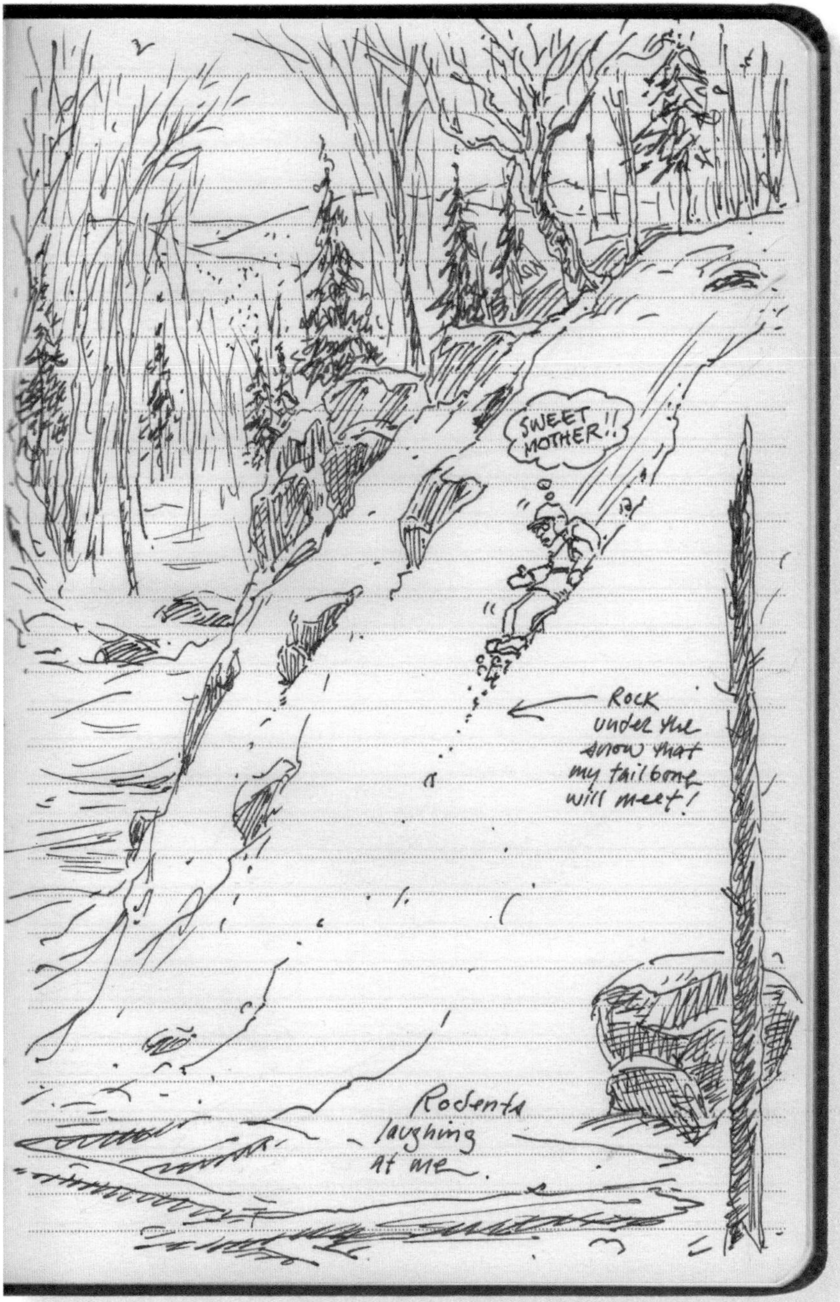
SWEET MOTHER!!
Rock under the snow that my tailbone will meet!
Rodents laughing at me

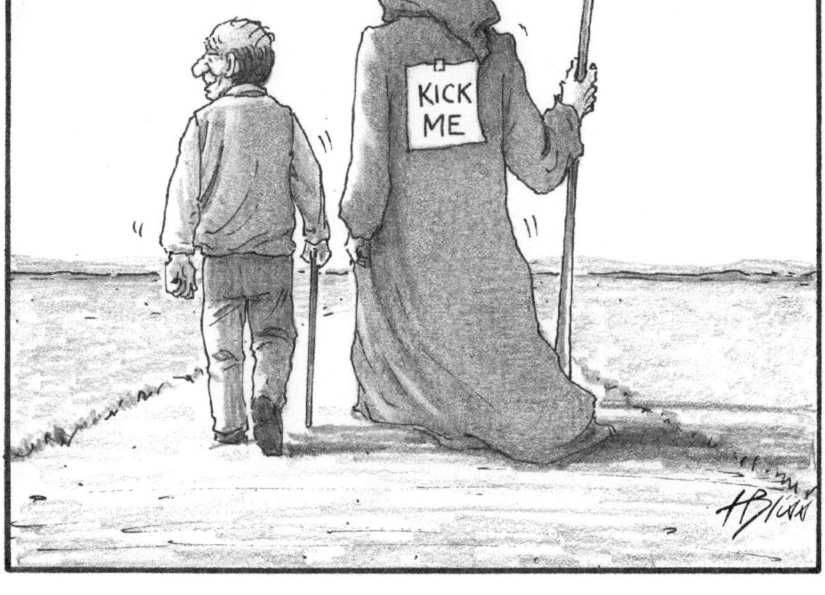
KICK
ME

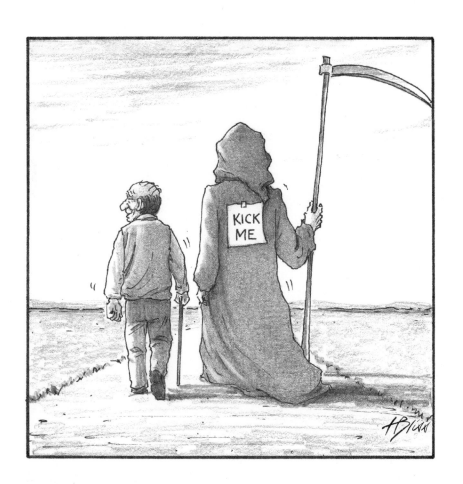

ED KOREN

Yesterday, I drove with James Sturm to visit Ed Koren. Ed has stage 4 lung cancer and has been in serious decline over the last two years.

I've been to his studio and home many times since I moved to Vermont in 1999. Ed was the only Vermont cartoonist I knew before meeting James, Alison Bechdel, Steve Bissette, and others. I knew this visit would be difficult.

A few months back, I sat with Ed in his studio. He already looked damn thin. He cried, telling me he was done—it's over. It was painful to see him in that state—a man who'd always been more active than most people half his age. In the past twenty years of friendship with Ed, he was always trying to get me to go biking with him or cross-country skiing. I always declined.

I declined because I knew I wouldn't be able to keep up with him. He'd bike for thirty miles or more three times a week. Ed, Vermont's first cartoonist laureate, adored being outside in the Green Mountain State. He was a volunteer firefighter for more than thirty years. He was friends with Senator Patrick Leahy, countless well-known writers, environmentalists, and anyone who showed an interest in preserving Vermont's historic landmarks. Ed Koren's contributions and legacy is etched into the history of the state.

Now, a wheelchair and walker have replaced the bike and skis.

"Another dropping of the hook into the old editorial sea" is one of countless notes we found while going through Ed's *New Yorker* roughs. This one from Ed to Lee Lorenz, his cartoon editor at *The New Yorker* for many years who recently passed away. Back in the day, before email, cartoonists sent in copies of their roughs with a handwritten note. Ed has hundreds and hundreds of these roughs with notes and correspondence all labeled in folders tucked away in his studio. The three of us looked through some larger images made in Paris. For years, Ed traveled annually as a guest artist to Paris to work on lithographs and etchings in a renowned printmaking studio.

One recent drawing struck me as poignant. It was like one of Ed's usual furry creatures, but different—a more existential expression, hints of Giacometti. The face seemed to be looking back at you, saying, *What's happening to me?*

Ed showed us one of his drawings, a cover for *The New Yorker*. He said this image will be carved into his tombstone.

Ed told us he had recently embraced stoicism, the acceptance of whatever comes your way. From his wheelchair, he motioned toward a large window at the back of the house, showing us where he'll be buried. The grave is next to his archive, a sturdy fireproof shed that holds most of Ed's art.

"A green burial," he said. "I'll be wrapped in a shroud and placed in a hole—that is already dug . . . covered with hay and soil." Ed told us that he had the "potion" upstairs that will end his life whenever he's ready.

When Ed spoke of his body in the earth, I thought of Penny, and how both Ed and Penny will break down. They will become other things, other life-forms. This thought lifted me up slightly. I suddenly imagined their lives not ending, but dispersing—spreading. Is Penny right now living as another organism(s)? Possibly. I believe the same thing happens to all once-living beings in the earth—they become other things.

As I communicated my thoughts to Ed and James, Ed said, "I will become other things. Do you know what I'll become?"

James and I looked at each other.

"A mushroom influencer."

This made James and me laugh. Ed went on . . .

"For sure," James added. "Maybe we'll get some good psychedelics out of that."

"Well," Ed steered, "we'll get some cartooning mushrooms. Whoever eats those mushrooms might turn into a great cartoonist."

When the time came to leave, we both gave Ed a hug. He made it clear that this could very well be the last time we would ever see him.

He said, "You know, I could last for a good long time . . . or not, so I was told by physicians and hospice people. I was throwing my life into cures, not cures, but stops for the cancer. That's somebody's life, but it's not mine." Ed then gestured to his drawing table and said, "My life is here."

He struggled to recall a line from Mary Oliver's poem "When Death Comes."

"'I was a bride married to amazement.'" Then he paraphrased an English poet: "I love my life. I love my life. I hate to say goodbye, But I don't want to say goodbye . . ."

He trailed off, then added, "You can do the best you can, and then you die . . . I'm looking at it—okay, I'm ready for you . . . but not really." These words hit me hard. James and I just listened quietly.

"The assassin!" he said, louder this time, as if he were pitching us. "In the form of a crab, holding a scythe, like a claw."

James said, "You're making cartoons!"

Ed said "I have to!"

HOLY SHIT! AL JAFFEE IS 99!
DO HUMORISTS HAVE A LONGER LIFE SPAN?

"I'M TELLING YOU! THEY DON'T KNOW ANYTHING!
NO ONE IS IN CHARGE!"

NOT KNOWING . . .

I like not knowing things. Not enough people, especially those with power or a platform, say "I don't know" or "I'm not sure." Over the years my opinions have taken a back seat to my queries. There are far too many nuances in this life for anyone to know anything. We agree or disagree and we have opinions. The rest is a crapshoot. Never trust anyone who can go a day without uttering a thoughtful and contemplative "I have no idea."

"THE ETCHINGS ARE IN THE LIBRARY."

MY HOME

It has only just recently dawned on me that over the years I have slowly turned my home in Cornish into a library and museum. My home is filled with art. On all of the walls and in flat files are the hundreds of works I've collected over the last forty years.

Each morning, I stand in front of the toilet admiring a beautiful nineteenth-century etching I picked up for ninety dollars on Pine Street (Philadelphia) in 1986. The drawing always impresses me.

Down the stairs on the way to my studio I pass my N. C. Wyeth oil, my most coveted work to date. I marvel at the palette, the subtle articulation of the forms, all masterfully painted.

Opposite the Wyeth is a Robert Crumb drawing I stop to look at—the ink is so thick on that vellum, it's nearly sculptural!

Above the stairs is a Sunday *Bringing Up Father* strip that floors me every time I pass by it.

There's an Arthur Rackham, Maurice Sendak, Garth Williams (from *Charlotte's Web*)—all hanging at the bottom of the stairs. There's a room I call Carlota's Room, because it was originally Augustus Saint-Gaudens's granddaughter's summer cottage. This is where all the nineteenth-century landscapes hang, along with two Thomas Rowlandson drawings.

Oh, I almost forgot, a lush impressionist oil by Frederick Mulhaupt. There's more too . . .

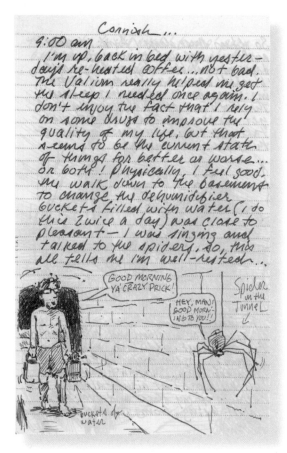

In addition to the art, there are all the books. Some books I've had since I was seven years old. I continue to buy books. I bought a nice oversize book on George Bellows earlier today. The only places I've ever felt at peace in my life were museums and libraries, and it seems I have turned my home into one of these places.

Some days I wander around the house, poking my head in and out of the rooms, just perusing the bookcases. I'll stop every now and again to look at an oil painting, study a passage I've not yet fully indulged in or a comic strip hanging on the wall—that *Bringing Up Father*, a *Pogo* strip, *Peanuts*, or *Krazy Kat*. Oh, there's a book on Georgia O'Keeffe's watercolors that I haven't picked up in years, I think I'll look at that. I can spend most of the day doing this and it's pretty wonderful.

I think I'm retired!

LITTLE WEREWOLF

I would often sneak up close to Penny while she slept to study her. I was always fascinated by the way the hair flowed from her nose. I thought she looked like a miniature apricot werewolf.

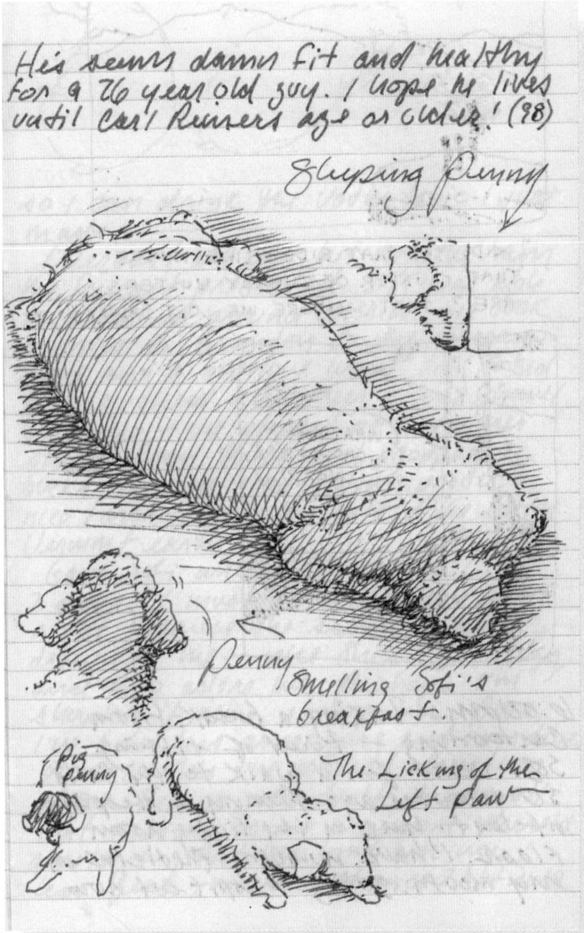
He's seems damn fit and healthy
for a 76 year old guy. I hope he lives
until Carl Reiner's age or older! (98)
Sleeping Penny
Penny
Smelling Sofi's
breakfast.
Pig
penny
The Licking of the
Left Paw

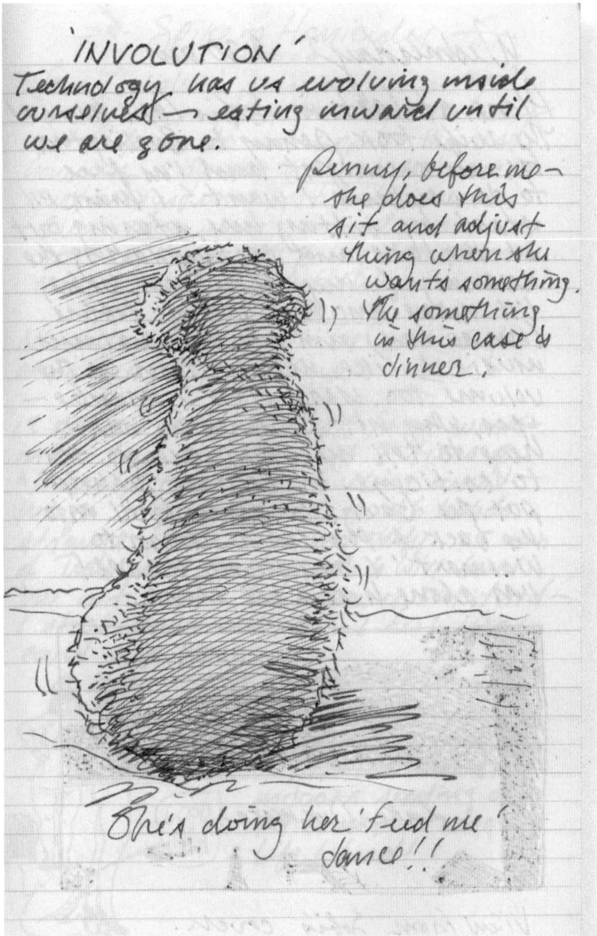
'INVOLUTION'
Technology has us evolving inside
ourselves — eating inward until
we are gone.
Penny, before me—
she does this
sit and adjust
thing when she
wants something.
The something
in this case is
dinner.
She's doing her 'feed me'
dance!!

ERIKA

I was recently visiting my son, Alex, in Brooklyn, where he lives and works as a filmmaker, editor, and performance-venue coordinator. We were walking on a warm, sunny April afternoon and I was telling him about this book I'm writing, the one you're reading now, and I asked him about his cat, Erika.

Erika lived with Alex for six or so years until she was diagnosed with cancer—she died two years ago. Erika stayed with me for a weekend when Alex had film work to finish and needed a cat-sitter. I'm allergic to cats, but I agreed. Erika mostly kept to herself, but she was affable—even funny. She would pounce on something in the other room when I was in my studio, and when I got up to see what she was doing, she was magically on the third floor looking calmly down at me with an expression of *What?*

Anyway, I asked Alex about putting Erika down when her time came—she was very sick, and the quality of her life was miserable. My son doesn't wear his emotions on his sleeve; he's reserved. I admire this quality, and I wish at times I was more like him in this way. I asked Alex what it was like in that moment when the life left Erika.

Alex told me it was horrible—the hardest he'd cried in his life. He said he was devastated. Like me with Penny, Alex held Erika in his arms when they put her down. I pictured Alex holding Erika as we walked that day along

Prospect Park. It was such a beautiful spring day, everything beginning all over again. Despite this, my heart grew heavy with that familiar longing, right there in the middle of all that beauty.

"REMEMBER THAT TIME WHEN MAMA SAID,
'IT'S EITHER ME OR THAT DOG'?"

THE LAST YEAR
AND A HALF

For the last year and a half of Penny's seventeen years of life she had both diabetes and Cushing's disease. The combination of these two conditions and her age would ultimately bring us to make the difficult decision to end her life in October 2021.

Sofi and I, but mostly Sofi, had to deal with a day-to-day routine of repeated insulin needles into Penny's frail fifteen-year-old body. The countless ear pricks to draw a drop of blood to read her blood sugar level were made more complicated by the Cushing's. The tiny punctures in Penny's ears were stressful, sometimes emotional. I was spending much of my time in Cornish, and as Sofi lived primarily in Burlington with Penny, she did most of this work. Penny received two shots of insulin each day, in the morning and at dinner. I would give Penny her insulin when Sofi was out of town or if she was with me in Cornish, but overall I couldn't handle it.

I was unable to draw blood from our dog's ears, I didn't have the stomach for it. When Sofi couldn't get enough blood to come out of Penny's ear to test for, she had to prick it again . . . and again. I stood by and watched, praying to myself that she'd get enough blood to test the first time.

At the time, we saw the quality of Penny's life was not terrible—her tail wagged on occasion, she'd bark for dinner or if we played with Penny. But these necessary daily tasks took a hell of a toll.

Some relief came when our vet suggested FreeStyle Libre, a glucose monitoring device that we inserted into Penny's skin once every fourteen days. The device provided a real-time reading of Penny's glucose levels. This less painful monitoring was much easier, but it wasn't cheap, and it was strange to see Penny with what looked like a mechanical plug in her.

The last few months of our dog's life were painful. We struggled to accept the fact that the situation was no longer sustainable. Sofi's life revolved around caring for Penny. I grew concerned for Sofi's quality of life.

We agreed it was time to let Penny go.

For the last two days of her life, Penny ate steaks I lovingly prepared for her. She still had an impressive appetite. I loved watching her eat those steaks. No more bloody ears, plugs, or needles.

It's strange, I still have a box of unused syringes in a cabinet in Cornish. I can't seem to bring myself to throw the damn things away.

10/24/20

Quinny is still hanging in there, though she's never acted this old before — she'll be 17 before long. Friday morning, I picked her up off the bed to take her down for breakfast & to go out. I made a quick stop to pee and, as I was sitting on the toilet (yes, I sit to pee in the mornings), she did the same! She pissed right there on the bathroom mat/rug in front of the sink.

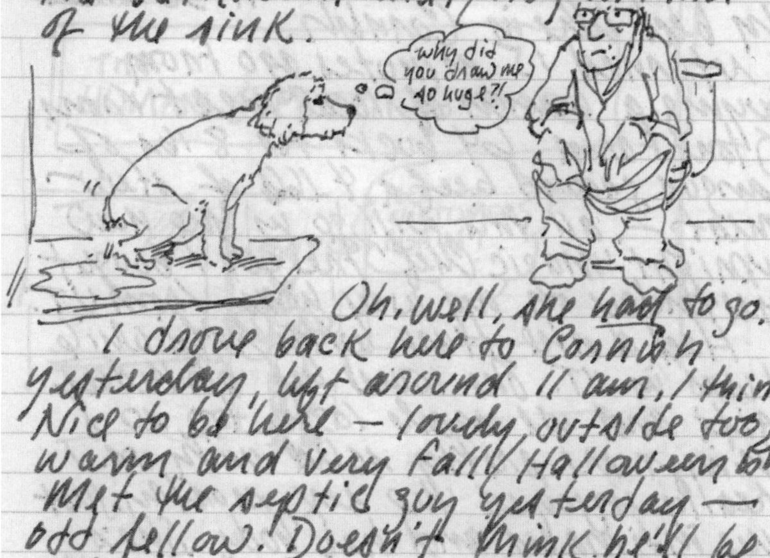
why did you draw me so huge?!

Oh, well, she had to go.

I drove back here to Cornish yesterday, left around 11 am, I think. Nice to be here — lovely outside too, warm and very Fall/Halloween-ish. Met the septic guy yesterday — odd fellow. Doesn't think he'll be able to replace my current septic tank — a logistical problem. SO, he feels repairing the current tank may be the best route — returns here Monday morning to do the work.

AN IMPORTANT DREAM?

August 21, 2022, 8:34 a.m.

Today I fell back asleep for just over an hour and had a dream I was visiting a friend of Sofi's, a gregarious older woman in her sixties. The woman was on a couch with Sofi and Sofi's daughter, Delia, and they were looking at something—maybe a photo album. I was opposite them in the living room, slightly distracted by the woman's dog.

She had a cute dog, about the same size as Penny, only her dog was purple and made of a very soft fabric. The fact that the dog was purple and made of cloth wasn't strange in the dream, it just was. While the woman was talking with Sofi and Delia, I was admiring the dog. In time, I began thinking of Penny and began to cry.

When I woke from the dream moments ago it occurred to me that since Penny has passed, my dream crying has been complete crying. In the past, when I cried in my dreams, I never fully cried. I was always holding back tears, fighting the emotion. For reasons unknown to me, I couldn't bring myself to emote in that unconscious state. I'd wake with a heavy chest that was physically devastating.

In the dream I had a full-blown cry. It had a beginning and an end. And when I woke, the feeling was of a satisfying catharsis, a cleansing of sorts. I'm just realizing this now, but it feels significant to me. I can now recall another recent dream where I cried intensely and again, upon waking, felt an emotional catharsis.

This all started after Penny passed. Perhaps there's some connection to that moment and my dream crying. The day we put Penny down I was hovering over her body, and I cried like I have never cried in my life. I wailed.

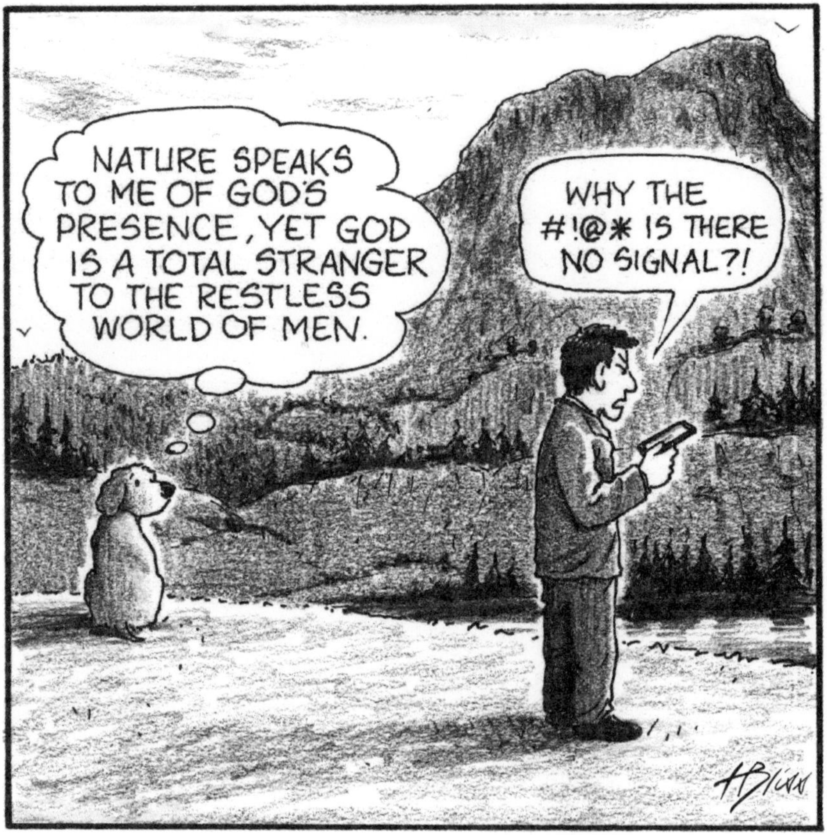
NATURE SPEAKS TO ME OF GOD'S PRESENCE, YET GOD IS A TOTAL STRANGER TO THE RESTLESS WORLD OF MEN.
WHY THE #!@* IS THERE NO SIGNAL?!

THE TREE CLUB

Last night at midnight I went for a walk in the woods. Earlier in the evening, when the snow finally stopped and the sun left the sky, I noticed that it was going to be a clear night—the North Star was crystal clear and moonlight was already casting shadows on the packed snow. I finished some cartoon work, made dinner, and watched the rest of *L.A. Confidential,* which I had started two nights ago (it takes me multiple nights to watch films; I'm old).

Around eleven thirty, I layered up and walked across the road from my house, up into the woods. It was damn cold, but the moon had lit everything up and the entire landscape was like a Parrish painting, just miraculous. I crunched through the snow, looking up to witness the icy limbs of the treetops, all glistening from the moonlight. It was as if they were illuminated from within.

And no, I wasn't tripping. At a certain point, making my way deeper into the woods, I grew tired. I knelt down in the snow. As I was resting there on my knees, breathing relaxed, I felt as if I was suddenly compelled to be submissive to some quiet force all around me.

I looked around, and the trees seemed to be reaching up toward the night sky. Were they showing reverence? Gratitude? Had I just crashed some kind of silent tree/moon ritual thing? I had no idea, but I wanted in. Again, not tripping.

Kneeling in the snow, I shot my arms up toward the moon, like tree limbs.

Truthfully, I felt amazing. I don't know what was happening, but there was some energy, some correspondence, which took place between me and those trees. Was this some sort of initiation? Had the trees let *me* be a member of their exclusive club?

I took a few deep breaths and lingered there a bit longer. I didn't want to leave. If my face wasn't so damn cold, I'd have taken a nap right there in that snow. But, I got up, gave a nearby white pine the kind of hug I reserve for my wife, and headed back home.

"BEHOLD, PENNY. THE 'WI-FI DEAD ZONE.' "

Wednesday, February 16, 2022

7:15 am

Up in bed, been up for 20 min
utes following 6½ hours of deep
sleep, not as many hours as I'd
like, but I feel well rested. I
was in bed and asleep around
12:30 am following a terrific
11:30 - 12:15 walk in the moon-
lit woods across the street. I
was in awe of the moonlight...

I was on my back on
the snow looking up at a full
moon. I'd gathered a few pieces
of wood to burn on my trek
as I always do. I'd of stayed
here longer, but the hard snow
beneath my legs and ass began
to soak through, so I headed
back to the house. So very quiet —
silent. only light wind.

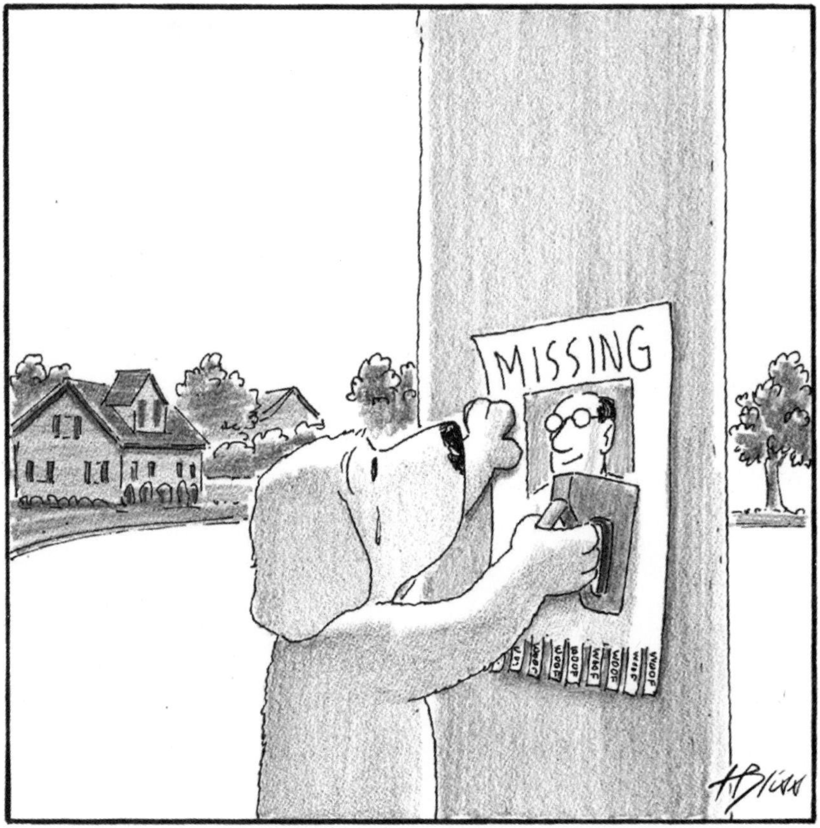
MISSING
WOOF
WOOF
WOOF

ED

My dear friend Ed Koren died the other day. I was alone in Burlington when I got the news. I was expecting it, but I wept anyway.

A local friend and reporter reached out to me for a comment for Ed's obituary. I didn't have the emotional energy to respond at first, then I recalled the first time I met Ed. It was 1998, a week or two after my first cover ran. I was at my debut *New Yorker* holiday party, which took place at Balthazar in Manhattan. Tina Brown was the editor in chief then, and she was notorious for exceeding the magazine's budget on these swanky soirees.

The place was packed with writers and celebrities, and I was very nervous. Kathy Osborn, another cover artist whose work I've always admired, pulled me out onto the dance floor, but I was/am a terrible dancer and I was perspiring. . . . It was not good. Afterward I tried to quell my anxieties with vodka, but I only became nervously intoxicated, and anxious.

My new cover editor, Françoise Mouly, knew I was nervous, so she kindly took me by the sweaty hand and introduced me to all *The New Yorker* cartoonists, writers, friends. . . . I can still smell the Shalimar she was wearing that night. I chatted with Peter de Sève, Carter Goodrich, Ian Falconer, Roz Chast, Bob Mankoff, Sam Gross, Gahan Wilson, Susan Orlean, and Victoria Roberts. I was dizzy from all the interactions.

Somewhere out on the dance floor, Salman Rushdie danced with at least two supermodels (this happened at every subsequent *New Yorker* holiday

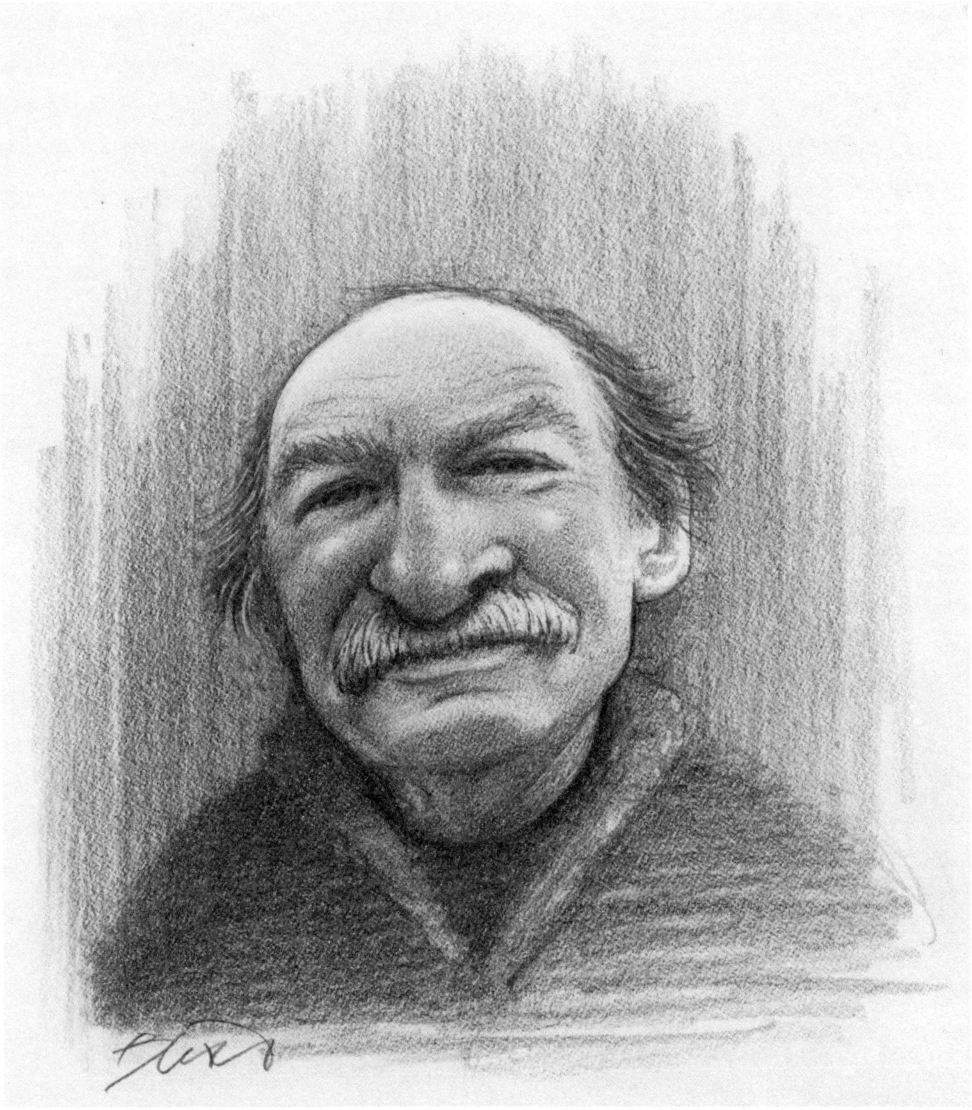

party). Then Françoise walked me over to meet Ed Koren. Among all the who's who New Yorkers looking fabulously intimidating, here was a volunteer firefighter from Vermont in a tweed jacket, blue jeans, and a rosy-cheeked smile. This legendary *New Yorker* cartoonist whose furry characters I grew up loving, shook my hand and my nervousness began to ease away.

Ed was warm, kind, and affably brilliant. I told him I was planning to move to Vermont to be closer to my son. At the time I was living in Nyack, New York, just north of Manhattan. Ed insisted I visit him when I relocated. The following year, I did just that, and for the next twenty-three years, we were friends.

I will miss Ed Koren for the rest of my life.

JUNIOR: AN INTRODUCTION

I suppose it's time for me to write about my new puppy, Junior. I'm watching him right now in the backyard, tethered to his leash, which is wrapped around the porch post. Sometimes, I let him roam around off leash in the backyard, but I have to keep an eye on him because on occasion, he wanders out onto the street and the cars come by—I worry. When we go for hikes he's off leash. He can come and go—sniff, dig, explore all he wants. Although, it's hard to keep him from eating deer shit. I can't blame the little guy. Deer droppings look delicious, like little chocolates. I can't think of another animal that has more edible-looking shit.

Overall, he tends to stay close to me and listens. Junior is a standard Aussie shepherd, and this breed is loyal and damn smart. He's a beautiful mix of mocha-brown and white, with stunning ochre eyes—the Timothée Chalamet of dogs. Sharp baby teeth. I have the scars to prove it.

He is a handful though, I didn't know this when I got him. Sofi was the one who really dealt with Penny when she was a puppy; I came along after most of the heavy lifting was done. Now, it's my turn and I'm finding it very challenging. Those of you who have raised a puppy know how difficult it can be. This is especially true if you are pushing sixty and are used to having a lot of time on your hands to do whatever the fuck you want, which has been my

life for the past fifteen years. Sure, I have to draw cartoons . . . but I'd hardly call it stressful.

This son of a bitch has me up at 5:00 a.m. He wants my attention all the time. It's only been six weeks, and I've given names to all of his goddamn toys. One is a stinky rag that I call Purple Guy. There's Nitty—a knitted hat he enjoys destroying. A rope with a knot I call Chief Brody, and a few others. He started humping a gray towel that hangs outside my studio. Every time I catch them in action, I stop and say, "Get a room, you two." Me? I haven't pleasured myself in ages. I'm in bed at eight. Up at five. I'm out back in five-degree weather waiting for him to do his business, looking up at the stars in the clear sky above and asking myself, "What have I done?"

I love Junior. I'm pretty sure he loves me. But puppies will piss you off.

Today we were headed over to my friends' house for lunch, about a mile walk.

I couldn't get Junior on the leash when it was time to start out. He thought it was a game and he kept running away from me. This went on for fifteen minutes until I became so frustrated and angry that I completely lost my temper.

When I was finally able to lay hands on the speedy fucker, I grabbed him by his neck and pressed his head against the porch and let him know I wasn't in a game mood. I don't like when I get angry like this, I don't like that I fall into this behavior—reminds me of my father. Still, a part of me feels like he needs to know who's in charge. I hate it, but I think it's necessary.

When I finally got the leash on him, he was afraid of me, which felt terrible.

He kind of walked to the side, a little farther away than usual. After a few minutes, I gently pulled him close on the leash, held his head in my hands and told him in a calm voice I was sorry. I kissed his head and stroked the side of his face, and made sure that he was staring in my eyes. I don't know if he understood me, probably not, but I had to try to show him I loved him. He wasn't afraid of me after this. We continued on our walk.

Each night, when the cartoons are drawn, bones sufficiently gnawed, the vodka put away, Junior heads to his crate—a damn cozy nest littered with a blanket, a soft old pillow, a pair of my underwear and a gnarly old Elmo he found God knows where. If I weren't allergic to him (manageable), I'd let him sleep in the bedroom. But he's really taken to sleeping downstairs . . . or maybe he just wants to be alone with his gray-towel girlfriend. Whatever, I think it's good to have a little space. I cover the crate with two of my older coats. He looks adorable lying down in there, his little head on his huge paws.

I love that I get to witness something like this before I head upstairs to my bed. I always tell him I love him and wish him sweet dreams. I put on "sleep" Spotify for him—plays all night.

I'm doing my best.

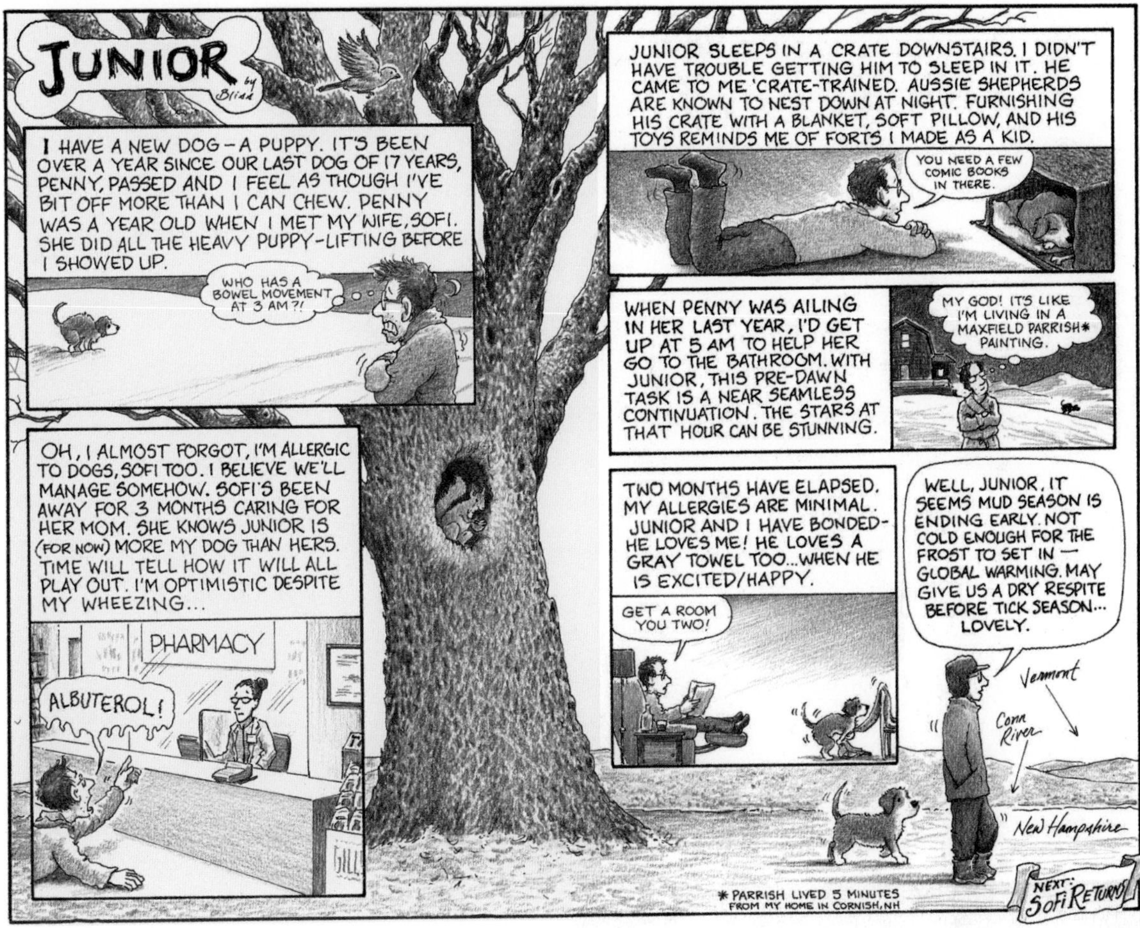
JUNIOR
by Bliss
I HAVE A NEW DOG—A PUPPY. IT'S BEEN OVER A YEAR SINCE OUR LAST DOG OF 17 YEARS, PENNY, PASSED AND I FEEL AS THOUGH I'VE BIT OFF MORE THAN I CAN CHEW. PENNY WAS A YEAR OLD WHEN I MET MY WIFE, SOFI. SHE DID ALL THE HEAVY PUPPY-LIFTING BEFORE I SHOWED UP.
WHO HAS A BOWEL MOVEMENT AT 3 AM?!
OH, I ALMOST FORGOT, I'M ALLERGIC TO DOGS, SOFI TOO. I BELIEVE WE'LL MANAGE SOMEHOW. SOFI'S BEEN AWAY FOR 3 MONTHS CARING FOR HER MOM. SHE KNOWS JUNIOR IS (FOR NOW) MORE MY DOG THAN HERS. TIME WILL TELL HOW IT WILL ALL PLAY OUT. I'M OPTIMISTIC DESPITE MY WHEEZING...
PHARMACY
ALBUTEROL!
JUNIOR SLEEPS IN A CRATE DOWNSTAIRS. I DIDN'T HAVE TROUBLE GETTING HIM TO SLEEP IN IT. HE CAME TO ME 'CRATE-TRAINED. AUSSIE SHEPHERDS ARE KNOWN TO NEST DOWN AT NIGHT. FURNISHING HIS CRATE WITH A BLANKET, SOFT PILLOW, AND HIS TOYS REMINDS ME OF FORTS I MADE AS A KID.
YOU NEED A FEW COMIC BOOKS IN THERE.
WHEN PENNY WAS AILING IN HER LAST YEAR, I'D GET UP AT 5 AM TO HELP HER GO TO THE BATHROOM. WITH JUNIOR, THIS PRE-DAWN TASK IS A NEAR SEAMLESS CONTINUATION. THE STARS AT THAT HOUR CAN BE STUNNING.
MY GOD! IT'S LIKE I'M LIVING IN A MAXFIELD PARRISH* PAINTING.
TWO MONTHS HAVE ELAPSED. MY ALLERGIES ARE MINIMAL. JUNIOR AND I HAVE BONDED-HE LOVES ME! HE LOVES A GRAY TOWEL TOO...WHEN HE IS EXCITED/HAPPY.
GET A ROOM YOU TWO!
WELL, JUNIOR, IT SEEMS MUD SEASON IS ENDING EARLY. NOT COLD ENOUGH FOR THE FROST TO SET IN — GLOBAL WARMING. MAY GIVE US A DRY RESPITE BEFORE TICK SEASON... LOVELY.
Vermont
Conn River
New Hampshire
* PARRISH LIVED 5 MINUTES FROM MY HOME IN CORNISH, NH
NEXT: SOFI RETURNS

PUPPY UNIVERSITY

I signed Junior up for puppy training. Each Saturday I drive the twenty-five minutes to Lebanon, where the training facility is located. There are six other dogs in the puppy training class, all adorable. There is one instructor, Sarah, and she has an assistant, Courtney, both very nice and very good at working with the dogs and their owners.

These training sessions are probably more difficult for me than they are for Junior because when Sarah instructs us what to do with our dogs, my attention deficit disorder kicks in just like it used to when I was in elementary school and I forget what Sarah said. I feel like an idiot because I have to go up to Sarah or Courtney afterward and ask them to repeat the instruction . . . for me! I never thought I would be nervous for myself at puppy training, but that's where I'm at.

At the end of the training session, for the last ten minutes the dogs get to play.

"Okay, let them off leash for playtime," Sarah instructs.

There is one dog, slightly larger than Junior, a fluffy rust-colored female named Rue who Junior loves to chase back and forth. The owners are grateful for the playtime because they know that it tires their puppies out. And it's true what they say, a happy puppy is a tired puppy.

Another puppy in the mix is a lovely chow chow named Stevie, who is completely blind. Stevie has to stay behind a sectioned-off area with his owner, so no playtime. I feel sad for them. I see all the other dogs playing, and there's this one beautiful blind dog all alone. At one point, Junior went over and sniffed Stevie through the partition—they sniffed each other's noses—tails up, wagging. I went over too and spoke to Stevie's owner. She (I never recall dog owners' names, never) told me Stevie came to her blind; he's a rescue who had three prior homes.

As the woman was telling me about her dog, she became emotional. She apologized for "getting weepy." I didn't mind. I told her it makes perfect sense to feel so strongly about her dog. I knelt down and let Stevie sniff my hand through the partition, then Junior came over, joined in. We stayed there until Sarah ended playtime. On the drive home to Cornish, Junior's eyes closed and he slept. Watching him sleep made me wonder if Stevie was able to dream.

DAD GOES AWAY

"It's all going down right now. They're taking him away. Mom is stopping cars in the street and telling people I came to steal the house." This was the text my brother John sent me on Sunday.

Two days ago, our father was taken away in an ambulance after rolling off his mattress and spending the night on the floor of his bedroom (Rachel's old bedroom, where she spent most of her childhood listening to our parents fight). He had fallen at least three other times in the past month. Now he is unable to walk. We would later learn he had suffered a leg fracture.

When my brothers found him on Sunday he was still on the floor of his bedroom in pain and dehydrated. According to Charley, our mother's only job Saturday night was to supply her husband water, and she failed to do this. She brought him the water in a thermos, but he was unable to remove the top. In some ways this is a blessing in disguise because he's safer in a hospital at ninety-three than he is at home with his wife, an eighty-seven-year-old woman without compassion.

I spoke with the doctor Monday following a blood transfusion and was told that Dad would need to have screws put into his leg to keep it stable. As the day progressed, Dad seemed to be in relatively decent spirits. He had an appetite, joked with the hospital staff, and was watching *Gunsmoke* with John when I called.

When John and Charley first found Jack lying helpless in his own urine, our mother was convinced they were coming to steal her house. She grabbed her walker, marched out of the house, and headed up Colony Lane to Mr. Buck's house, a widowed neighbor we've known for fifty years. While she was talking to him for over an hour, Mr. Buck texted John that he felt like "she might stop talking soon" and he'd be able to walk her back down to her house.

A couple of days later, I tried to call our mother half a dozen times. No answer. Yet my mother keeps calling Katie, John's wife. Katie is without a doubt the nicest human being I've ever met. But Katie will not talk to Mom because she mistreated her—the one person in her orbit who had compassion and patience for even the craziest of old women.

I feel she's intentionally not answering my calls. She knows I won't tolerate her manipulations. There came a point in our relationship when applied knowledge kicked in, and I suddenly found myself winning arguments. I was like Gerry Cooney boxing Muhammad Ali for years, and suddenly, one afternoon in my mid-forties I knew how she moved, what her strategy was, and I was able to work Mom into the ropes, corner her and leave her with nowhere to go. I think she knew that in this case, I wouldn't let her manipulate the situation. I would force her to be honest and truthful. And in the end, she never could be. And that's when she would hang up on me.

My genuine fear is that Mom will burn the house down or she will methodically destroy all of my father's art, including his beautiful gouache illustrations depicting his rural childhood in the 1940s. I too have artwork in that house that I worry about. Not that my mother would destroy it, but a fire certainly would. If and when the time comes for our father to be released from the hospital, he will be discharged either to my older brother Charley's house or to a retirement home.

My mother's future remains uncertain.

Dad June 6th 2023
Charley's Living room
(passed on June 8th)

Mom
June 7th 2023
Living room
Henrietta NY

Cannot capture the lost sadness
                    here - Maureen
                    has such
                    a unique
                    sad
                    beauty.

Maureen is up!   Maureen
I guess she's tried
to leave before. She cried a few times,
which is so tough to witness. Hard for
me not to console her. I was attentive
to both roomies. Mom paid 1'd of
made a 'good doctor'... ha!
    Junior is being so good on this trip
— I owe him so much & he knows it.

RUNNERS

I just returned from Highland Hospital in Rochester, New York. I was visiting my father (fourth floor) and my mother (seventh floor) with my sister-in-law, Katie.

Next week my dad is being relocated from the hospital to my brother Charley's home, where he will be in hospice for his remaining days. How many days? We're not sure. He turned ninety-three in March. But all the logistics are set and he seems to be in good spirits—looking forward to smoking his pipe on Charley's porch, watching the birds.

My mother is a completely different story. These two respective stories, of my mother and father, should never have met, but they did, and I am here because of it.

I was not prepared to witness my mother in the state she was in today. When I visited her at the hospital she seemed uncharacteristically sedated, but she was still her insistent, manipulative, controlling, uncooperative self. Hours ago, Katie and I witnessed a dramatic shift. A clear altering of her personality.

When we first walked into the room, my mother was finishing up her lunch. There was an attending hospital aide standing watch. My mother is down to eighty-two pounds, so they need to make sure she eats. When she looked up and saw Katie and me, she put down her plastic fork, carefully pushed her food tray away, and said, "Let's go." My mother thought we were there to take her home.

We were not there to take her home.

Katie and I awkwardly told her that the hospital won't let her go yet. After a psychiatric evaluation last week it was determined my mother lacked what the hospital called "capacity." This means she can't be trusted to care for herself. Any decisions go to the next of kin, and that would be my father. There are some questions about his capacity to accept that role. Failing Jack (great name for a band) the role is assigned to my oldest brother, John.

For someone who has spent most of her life in control, this current state of existence is her hell. She cannot come home unless she has twenty-four-hour care. We're working on it, but it could take weeks. If you're old enough to have a parent that is going through this or has gone through this, you know it is an extremely difficult time.

After hearing the news that she wasn't leaving, my mother sat back into her chair, started eating a piece of lemon meringue pie, and asked us not to talk. As soon as she finished, the nurses came in, removed her tray, and informed us she was being moved to another room.

I realized this could very well be the last time I would see her. She had a terrible congestive cough and appeared to be diminishing before my eyes. Was she faking it? Possibly. It wouldn't be out of the ordinary for this behavior to be called up from her arsenal. But maybe not. Maybe she wasn't faking this time.

Before today, I hadn't thought this way. She seemed resilient, stubborn, slow, but strong-willed. The drugs my mother is taking to "help" her with her dementia is making her both better and worse at the same time. She seems to be less combative, but more sedated and out of it. As a son who had to put up with years and years of manipulative, controlling unsolicited mother advice, I'd wished for a more sedated mom. But not like this.

Once situated in her new room she told the nurse she had to use the bathroom. The nurse, a very kind young woman, assisted her. During the twenty difficult minutes this took, I met my mother's roommate, Maureen.

During mom's slow trek to the bathroom, Maureen noticed me, winked, and called me over to her bed. She quietly told me I was attractive and asked if I would help her sit up. I did. Better. Then she asked me to move the blankets off her, which I did. I was surprised to find her exposed legs not unattractive. She pointed with her finger, at her feet—asked me to take her socks off. I did. I noticed her sparkly French pedicure. In no time, Maureen was asking me to adjust her legs so they could swing closer to the side of the bed.

As this was happening I realized: Maureen was what the nurses call "a runner." That's why they had moved my mom into this room—she was a runner too. They're both intent on getting the fuck out of there.

I liked Maureen very much, and I whispered in her ear that I would be back tomorrow to draw her portrait. I don't know how much of this she was able to understand. She came in and out. At times she became adorably frustrated, like a sad child. We spoke very closely, as if I'd known her in some past life. She had a short shoulder-length black wig on, and it looked nice. She had a charming vanity about her. I could tell by looking at her that she was once very beautiful.

After my mother was all set in the bathroom and made the journey back to bed, I turned my attention back to her. I sat close to her and we chatted for a short while. Katie and I adjusted her pillows and she laid back. I caressed her head and whispered to her while she found a light sleep. I looked over at Maureen; she was crying. These two women, "runners," are profoundly unhappy. I cannot imagine what suffering they're facing.

On the way out I went back to Maureen and put my hand on her ankle. She wasn't crying anymore. I told her "I'm looking forward to seeing you tomorrow."

SATURDAY, JUNE 3, 2023

As of yesterday evening, my mother is back home, released from the hospital after eight days. She is again surrounded by countless things that have grounded her for the past fifty years. I'm hoping after some time there her mind will ease and the dementia-induced paranoia she experienced at the hospital will lift.

Our newly hired caregivers, Olga and Oksana, were there when Katie and Mom arrived at the house around 5:00 p.m. It seemed as though everything was going smoothly yesterday afternoon, texts sounded good, even a photograph of Mom out on the front porch—she was talking and looking like her old self. But at nine o'clock, after I returned home from a presentation I gave at a local library, things were far from smooth.

My mother wanted the caregiver to leave the house. Oksana tried to explain to Mom that she had to spend the night in the house with my mother. Mom picked up the phone, threatening to call the police. She didn't call the police—instead she went out the front door of the house and across the street in the dark to a neighbor's house, where the neighbor called the police. Frantic texts followed between Olga, Oksana, myself, and Katie, trying to figure out how best to proceed.

At about nine thirty I was on the phone with my mom, speakerphone. Mom had fallen outside the neighbor's house, an EMT at the scene let my mom talk to me. I calmly instructed her to go back home with the caregiver and get some rest. Mom said she understood everything I was saying. Then, after a few minutes she turned to the EMT and told him that I had instructed my mom to go back to the house and that the caregiver was supposed to leave. The EMT responded clearly and kindly to my mom. He explained that she needed to go back home with the caregiver or she would be returned to the hospital.

Oksana reassured me a bit later that everything would be okay, that my mother has dementia and was returning home after a hospital visit—her behavior wasn't out of the ordinary.

The next morning Oksana texted me that my mother had not slept. She was up all night.

To think of her not sleeping is disturbing, but I find comfort in knowing that at least my mother is in her home. She is losing her memory, and her "self" is deconstructing within her, and we are witness to it. All I want at this point is to alleviate her suffering.

I need to go to Henrietta to see my mom.

SUNDAY, JUNE 4, 2023

As of last night, Oksana and the other two caregivers are gone from my mother's home. My mother would not allow them to spend the night; she became angry, broke three windows, and they were unable to control her.

Shortly after nine o'clock I called and woke John and Katie—they drove to Mom's house. Mr. Buck, the neighbor up the street who Mom trusts, showed up at the house after John and Katie. Mom's sister-in-law Greta had called and calmed her down. Miraculously, the police didn't make an appearance. Around 10:00 p.m. I spoke with Mr. Buck on the phone and we both agreed to leave Mom alone in the house. There didn't seem to be any other option besides calling an ambulance and having Mom removed from her home and returned to the hospital.

Junior and I head to Henrietta tomorrow.

Thursday May who cares?

When I walked into my mother's hospital room and saw her sleeping — I thought she looked dead. This look didn't change much after she was up. She cried at least 2 times. She wants out of that hospital. I don't care if it's all an act, which I doubt it is, I need to get her back here in her house asap. I feel off, all out of whack — in some surreal space where I am surrounded by death. My mom's skin looks as if it will fall off her at any moment, like her bones are covered by aging + rotting pumpkin skin. Only, it's not a pumpkin rotting, it's my mom. This was at 10 am. I had to leave with junior at 11:15 to drive to Charley's house in Leroy to meet the guy who dropped off dad's hospice bed, wheelchair + hoist. Both parents. The same time

I asked Dean if his daughter-in-law, Olga — John's wife, could find someone to live here with mom for a month. I offered 20K...cash. I hope someone will help I need help.

Wednesday 6/7/23 11:55 pm
I drew this of mom at 3:00pm while she
slept in her wheelchair. We returned from
the art museum at 1:30 and she was sleeping for most of our outing. At 7:30 pm she
                                    was in an
                                    ambulance
                                    headed to
                                    Strong Memorial
                                    hospital. She
                                    won't return
                                    home again. I
                                    tried to keep
                                    her in her
                                    home... I did.
                                    But it
                                    wasn't
                                    meant to
                                    be. She
                                    needs more
                                    help than we
                                    can offer.

WEDNESDAY, JUNE 7, 2023

So much to put down here—the past few days have been incredibly difficult.

I arrived in Rochester on Monday and drove directly to my mother's house.

I found her on the garage floor, scooting on her hands and rear end, trying to find her way through the kitchen door. It sounds terrible, but it's actually not. My mother is very methodical. She understands the physical limitations impeding her former independence and has devised ways around it. The chores that were once fairly effortless now require her to invent a quasi–Rube Goldberg system. She will place chairs or stools in various places from the bedroom to the kitchen so that she can hold on to them, perhaps sit and take a break along the way. It may take her twenty-five or thirty minutes, maybe longer to get from one room to the other.

Once in the kitchen, she will sit on a small wooden stool. She will move or scooch the stool along the kitchen floor to get various items. I witnessed Mom in action earlier today making some strange sort of stew. A can of beef vegetable Campbell's soup, frozen tilapia, sweet potatoes, and other food things she scavenged from the refrigerator. She asked for my help only when her twenty-five-year-old microwave refused to cooperate.

My intention was to be patient with her, respect her, and provide assistance. I didn't want to criticize her. I wanted to help her. I think I did a pretty good job because she capitulated to most of my suggestions. I left her with this weird fucking dish cooking on the range, which, remarkably, probably didn't taste too bad. Mom is a decent cook.

Tuesday morning I went directly to my mom's house and spent most of the day with her. I went to see my father at Charley's house at 4:00 p.m. My father was sleeping when I arrived. He must be very close to the end, because he looked like a dead man.

Before I left, I stroked his head and kissed him, told him I loved him. He didn't respond.

I left and returned back to Henrietta to stay with my mother until Kristin, a caregiver who had looked after my father at Highland Hospital, came over to meet Mom.

Earlier today when I mentioned Kristin would be coming back to stay with her, Mom said that she liked her very much. This makes me happy. Mom remembered! I want them to get along. My mother needs someone she can trust other than me, Katie, and (on and off) John and Charley.

Now I am back at my Airbnb in downtown Rochester, nursing a vodka. Junior is sleeping next to me. Some part of me feels as though he understands what I'm going through; he seems to be as exhausted as I am. Surprisingly, Mom has been rather sweet with Junior. She doesn't like it when he comes too close, but I can tell she likes him, she smiled at him a few times.

I am getting texts right now from Kristin. It seems my mother has insisted on going downstairs to my father's old studio. I specifically told my mother she's not allowed to go down the stairs, but she's doing it anyway. She told Kristin to get out of her way, and Kristin is texting me that she's worried my mother is going to fall. I have to get in my car and drive the fuck over there and manage the situation.

When I arrived at the house at 7:17 p.m., Mom was downstairs on the floor of my father's studio. Kristin and I eventually got her back upstairs, but she wanted to leave the house, to go out into the street. We did everything we could to dissuade her from this, but she insisted and began calling both of us names and yelling "HELP!" This was a complete Jekyll and Hyde situation from what I experienced earlier in the day. This was a very hostile, frightening woman. She was filled with bitterness, resentment, even hatred. I realize it's all part of her dementia, but it's still difficult.

She sat down in her wheelchair and began pushing herself down the driveway. I got in front of the wheelchair, stopped her, looked her in the eyes and said, "Mom, please stop. If you don't stop doing this, I'm going to have to call the ambulance and they'll take you back to the hospital. Please stop doing this."

She told me to drop dead and get out of the way.

"Mom, you have two choices: get back in the house and listen to us, or you can keep trying to run away and go back to the hospital. Which do you want?"

She defiantly answered, "the hospital." Maybe she thought I was bluffing. I wasn't.

"Okay, Mom, I'm calling the ambulance to take you back to the hospital."

I did, and now she's gone.

Sofi had told me what she has been going through with her mother for all these many months, the exhausting work of caretaking she and her sister Nina continue to endure. I now understand their experience. It is beyond my comprehension how ill prepared we were for any of this. Caring for your parents in the last years of their lives is so difficult, it consumes all the energy we can muster. And we do it knowing eventually we will all be our parents. Will I have dementia? It's genetic. . . . Will Alex have to go through what I'm going through?

My mother will die soon, and my father will most certainly die sooner. We all die. I understand and accept this. But how we prepare for this reality, how we set in motion the transition of our gradual departure from this life is profound, and we need to get all our fucking ducks in a row sooner rather than later. Later is dreadful.

THURSDAY, JUNE 8, 2023

As I was packing up the car this morning to head back to New Hampshire, Charley left a voicemail telling me our father passed away.

OBITUARY FOR JACK L. BLISS

OBITUARY NUMBER ONE, WRITTEN BY MY DAD

Thank God, I'm dead! This goddamn world is shit. I've had a good life, god-damnit, and I have no regrets. I had a wonderful mother and good brothers, talented kids, and I served my country . . . dammit, I had a good life, don't kid yourself. God bless America!

OBITUARY NUMBER TWO, WRITTEN BY JACK'S WIFE, ROSLYN BLISS

Oh, please, I can smell that repulsive pipe of his. He's poisoning me still, you know that? Here, look at my forearm, there's a bruise from when he grabbed me three months ago. It's still there, here, look. He was good-looking though, very good-looking. He had an affair with a woman who cuts his hair, I know this. He said he goes to Tinker Park for his walks, but he's lying, he had a girlfriend.

OBITUARY NUMBER THREE, WRITTEN BY OUR FAMILY DOG, IGOR

Woof, woof, woof, woof, woof, woof, woof, woof howl!

FRIDAY, JUNE 9, 2023

Back in Cornish as of yesterday, early evening. Sitting in the recliner in my studio now after feeding Junior. Both of us relieved to be back home. I cried yesterday on and off. The emotional reality of the role I played in sending my mother back into a hospital hit me hard. It reminded me of the role I played in ending Penny's life.

I still don't like myself for what I did to my mother. If she dies in that hospital, my heart will be forever bruised. I will never get the image of her on that ambulance gurney out of my mind. She looked right at me. She looked sweet and innocent. I am devastated by the fact that my mother is in that hospital. Some part of me will never recover from this. I am crying all over again.

I've been feeling pretty odd the last 48 hours. Odd as in 'what's the point of doing anything anymore? I feel like I've already lived a life and now, I'm just making an effort to stay in the game, even though the sport bores the hell out of me. I'm becoming a recluse. Jesus, just like Salinger. Christ, I never planned this, but it's happening and I'm not sure there's much I can do to alter the course I'm on. I just need to stay married — it's important for me not to lose Sofi.

My girl, Penny.

FUTILITY

Lately, I've been thinking about why my father stopped painting or why any artist stops creating. At some point my father stopped drawing, and that's something I can't fathom. Drawing for me is like breathing. I'd like to be drawing when I take my last breath.

Tonight, I looked out the window at the landscape here in New Hampshire. The last rays of a remarkable orange sunlight fell across the valley, landing on three white birch trees in such a way that is beyond my abilities to capture. This happens each day at least once. I can see what I'm looking at in oil paint, imagine it rendered in a brushy, impressionistic realism—Willard Metcalf comes to mind. I can envision this, and it seems enough. It has to be; I'm not a painter.

There must come a point in every artist's life when they understand they can no longer capture what they see. Any attempt to try is a willful dive into futility. The mature artist won't fight this reality. Acceptance will open time. Time better spent in observance—the taking in. (I'm suddenly thinking of John Lennon's "watching the wheels go round.")

While watching the sunlight diminish I thought to myself, *This is bittersweet*. Because once an artist understands that what they're seeing is beyond their abilities, simply seeing becomes all they now need to do. It's like death. The artist capitulates to the realization that their skill, talent, ability—that thing they've spent their whole life perfecting is behind them, out of reach, somewhere in the past. I guess that's why the old man stopped.

"HANDS DOWN, THE BEST TREE
IN NEW HAMPSHIRE TO PEE ON."

CAPTURING NATURE: WHY?

I was out yesterday for a walk with Junior, the same walk along the creek we usually take. It's a fantastic little trek.

He loves to bounce around in the shallow water, and I enjoy exploring different stones just beneath the surface. When the sunlight hits the water in places, the stones are illuminated and pretty fascinating to study. I've been collecting stones from my various hikes for the past five years. I'm also attracted to stones clinging to the roots of felled trees. If a large pine has fallen (most felled trees are pines) in the woods, its roots are exposed and attached to those roots are countless rocks. Most of them are very old—50 to 150 years. When I check out the various stones from the roots, I feel a bit like an archaeologist. I'm convinced one day I'll find a Clovis point or two.

At first, I'd bring home four or five stones, including some large ones if I happened to have my backpack. There have been hikes where I've had fifteen pounds of stones in that backpack. I figured it was good exercise, but I also felt like an idiot. Half the time I'd return home exhausted only to find the stones inexplicably less interesting. Idiot. These days I am far more selective. Stones have to be particularly interesting to me, have some unique shape or color.

Yesterday, after about forty minutes, I stopped, turned around, and looked at the stream—the way the light was hitting the blue of the trees cast shadows onto the snow. I stared at this for at least five minutes, leaning on my walking stick while Junior played.

6/25/23

Here is Junior watching
the wilder life beyond the screen while
I do my best to capture his beauty...
I try and I fail. How can I capture
it? I am, after all, a mortal.

I thought to myself, *This would make such a fantastic painting*. I imagined a painter, maybe the great Cornish Colony impressionist Willard Metcalf, in 1880 sitting in the spot where I was standing, painting the scene plein air. I thought, *What a fucking pain in the ass it must've been to drag all his shit up here, set up in twenty-five-degree weather, just to paint a creek*. What motivated Metcalf? When he returned home with the painting, exhausted, numb from the cold, his efforts falling short of his inspiration, did he think to himself, *Idiot*?

This whole thing of capturing nature through painting or hoarding stones seems like a fool's errand. Why are we compelled to take some piece of nature with us? In the midst of my thoughts, Junior came bouncing back to me, soaking wet and muddy. Before I had time to move, he pounced with his huge front paws on my belly, knocked me backward on my ass and into the creek.

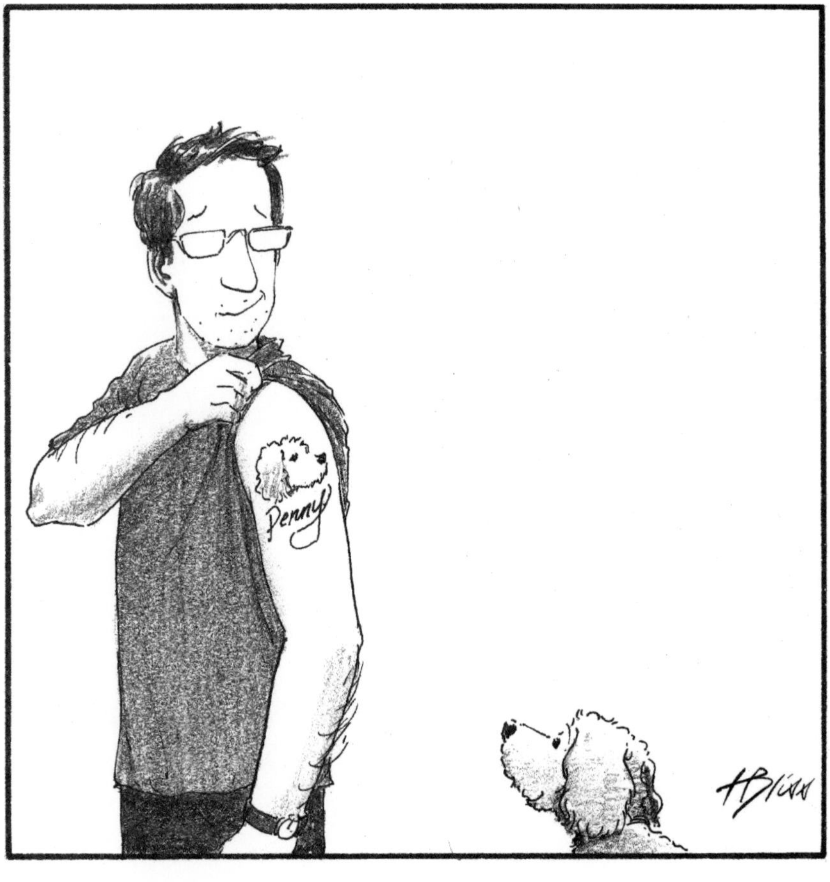
Penny

DOGS

So much has been written about dogs—our deep connection to our beloved pets. It's profound, and profound things need to be written about.

My love for Penny was profoundly tender. When Penny passed, the tenderness remained. I held it somewhere in my heart for more than a year. And then I found Junior, and my heart released, in bits and pieces, that tenderness I held for Penny. I think Penny would've liked Junior. She always got along with "boys." His puppy energy wouldn't be tolerated, and she'd shut him down quickly, but in time she'd have come around . . . I think.

I recently asked my friend Dan about his commitment to his thirteen-year-old terrier, Theo. I was curious what the long-term effects are.

Dan said, "Dog ownership is a heart-opening exercise, and the habit of kindness and the years and years of beneficial walks and caresses have made me a better person. I love the person that has been so good to him. Theo has taught me 'self-care.'"

I asked Steve (Martin) about his dog, Roger. He wrote: "We love our pets, our uncomplicated companions, the ones who allow us to talk to ourselves without sounding crazy, the ones we can fully love without hesitation, the ones who are our counter glow. I do not think of the last eleven years of my life as defined by the movies I made, or successes or failures of any kind. During that time, I lost both my parents, renewed family relationships, loved

* Boat landing at the Cornish side of
the Connecticut River...
    Watched this man lovingly dip
a very old dog into the Connecticut
River, clearly his dog... made me
sad. I considered talking with him,
let him know I felt his pain. I
didn't. I left the man & his dog alone.

and lost and loved and won, lived my entire fifties, and emerged as a fuller and more available person. But that eleven years, as my emotions rose and fell, had a vital constant, and I will always think of it as the era of Roger."

My vital, constant era of Penny lasted for seventeen years. She taught me so much. So much. I'm still discovering what I learned from loving her.

Back then, there was sincere joy, for the unknown, in far away places I knew I'd discover if I could only escape, and I knew I would, one day.

This is Charlie's dog sleeping outside of Charlie's Boathouse off North avenue here in Burlington. The way this dog was just resting it's tired old bones made me think it knew it wasn't long for this life. Sometimes, a dog will have this look of wisdom in it's eyes and it's very sad. I didn't want to leave this animal, I just wanted to stay with her until the end.

And yet another work with a man and
his dog in nature. I've lost track of how
many images I have created over the
years — hundreds. Why? I no longer
fret over the reasons why or if
readers grow tired of this Bliss
trope — it's in my DNA by now.
Still, I am curious. Is this all
because of Penny? I'm inclined
to believe this and now that she's
gone off somewhere, the need to
render her grows more potent...
good old Penny!

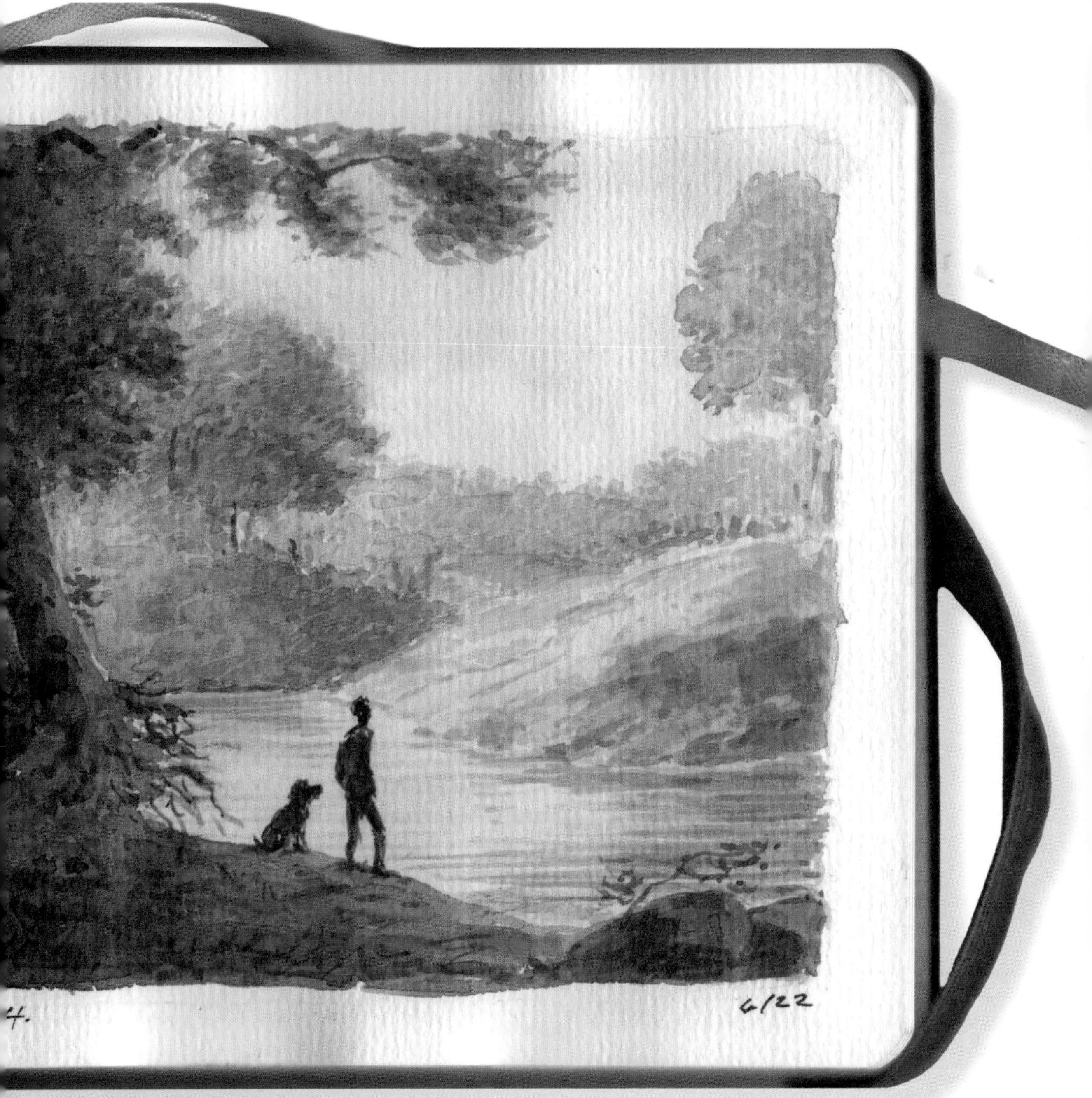
4.
6/22

DYNAMITE SH

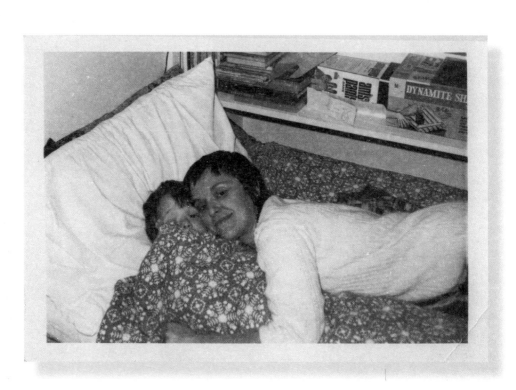

VOICES

Last week Sofi and I were together in Burlington trying to reconnect after being apart for a week. I had Junior with me, his third trip to Burlington.

Sofi has come around with Junior. I see her resist the urge to love him because of her allergies—understandable, we are both allergic to most dogs, and Penny had been an exception. Despite this, sometimes she gives in, petting him lovingly.

It's not only because of the allergies. When I was first considering getting Junior, Sofi didn't think the timing was right. Because her mother's stroke happened so soon after losing Penny, we never had a chance to simply be alone for an extended period of time, to travel together. Take ecstasy! To reconnect.

I didn't listen. I wasn't seeing very much of Sofi; she was gone for weeks on end caring for her mother, and I was alone in Cornish. I couldn't be upset with her. But I thought having Junior would fill a void, which it did . . . overfilled it, in fact. I wasn't prepared. Sofi warned me, but it's too late now—I love him. Sofi does too. Naturally, each time she gives Junior affection, letting him kiss her as she rubs his soft coat, she has to wash her face and hands. He's a beautiful dog, tough to resist.

Today we took Junior for a midday walk. We usually go to the Burlington golf course with his ball launcher—it's a great workout. We bring treats to train him to return the ball each time, though Sofi has a better success rate than me, and I know she relishes this fact. She can be competitive.

But today we decided to go to the east woods, the place where we used to take Penny. We have fond memories of her on these trails—she loved this walk. The trails are wonderful, maintained by the University of Vermont. We were the only ones there that day, and after a few minutes of walking, I could see that Sofi was enjoying watching Junior. We talked about our memories of Penny. Her playful energy, rear-end summer soaks in the cool stream along the trail, her happy bark.

As we walked, she watched Junior, then gave him a voice, Penny's voice.

Suddenly she stopped. She told me she'd promised herself she would never use Penny's voice or any voice for another dog after she died. I understood Sofi's reluctance. I felt similarly. Our voice for Penny was sacred, I guess.

We walked along for another four or five minutes, and I thought to myself, *I think we should do a voice for Junior. I think Penny would've liked that. This way, we can keep Penny with us—she'll always be with us, whenever we want.* I liked this idea of our bringing forth an omnipresent Penny. I communicated my thoughts to Sofi and she listened and didn't outright reject them, which was promising. I'm hopeful. She had the perfect voice for Penny, it always made me laugh—always.

We continued walking along with Junior, tossing sticks to fetch.

EAR WHISPERS

Earlier this week I drove up to see my mother for what I thought would be the last time. I drove with Junior from Cornish to Burlington to pick up Sofi, and from there we all headed west through the Adirondacks to Rochester.

That first night we went to see my mother at Strong Memorial Hospital. Mom was sedated and unresponsive, as has been her condition for the past couple of weeks. Morphine was introduced a few days ago. I sat with her and said some things into her ear. She looked frail and close to her end. I stroked her head and kissed her forehead before I left. I could've sworn I smelled Shalimar, her lifelong fragrance, near the back of her neck.

I promised my mom's brother Mark to FaceTime with him so he could see his big sister once more. I made this happen, but it was very difficult for me. I had the phone up to Mom's face, speaker on, and Mark spoke to Mom as I quietly cried. I tried to say goodbye to Mark, but even that was difficult for me. I consider myself fairly strong, but I cry, and lately I've been crying more and more.

That night, after John's shift with Mom, I spent six hours with her. John and I sat together for about an hour and talked. He held Mom's hand under the covers as we watched *First Blood* with subtitles.

After John left around 8:30 p.m., I made myself comfortable in the reclining chair next to Mom. I turned off the TV and read to her, then went through some assorted family photographs John and Katie had left in a ziplock bag. I

went through each one and talked about them as Mom slept. Her breathing was heavy at one point, and I got up and asked the attending nurse to come in. The nurse said it was normal and that my mother was comfortable.

I went to the outer room to get some ice from the ice machine. I returned, sat back in the recliner, took out the flask from my backpack, and poured vodka over the ice. After the first sip or two, I felt better. I sat with Mom, stroked her head, and spoke softly in her ear. I told her how much I loved her and how sorry I was for not understanding how brilliant she'd been all along. I knew—we all knew, but I didn't tell her enough, didn't reward her with the simple gratitudes that never made it past her son's stubborn judgments. At around midnight, I fell asleep. I tried to spend the night with Mom, but I left at about 1:45 a.m.

The next morning I went with Sofi to see Mom one more time before we made the drive back to Cornish. When the time came to leave, Sofi stepped out so I could be alone with Mom. I spent the remaining moments whispering into her ear for the last time. I sang a song for her, a song she used to sing to me when I was a little boy. I then kissed her forehead and left.

The drive home from Rochester to Cornish was brutal. We encountered all sorts of rain and thunder. It took us two and a half extra hours to get home. Nearly eight hours in a tiny car. When we pulled up to the house, we were exhausted.

We let an understandably hyped-up Junior out of the car, walked out back, and as if Murphy's Law was hovering above us like the sword of Damocles, Junior located a porcupine and went right after it. I screamed at the top of my lungs for Junior to stop, and ran after him up the side of the sloping hill, slipping and falling on the wet thicket. I was covered with all sorts of shit, but Junior, fortunately, didn't get to the porcupine.

Today is Saturday, July 22, 2023, and I'm here with Junior. Sofi is in Burlington with her daughter, Delia. Today, at 5:40 p.m., my mother passed away. My brother and my sister-in-law were with my mother when she passed. We were expecting it. On Thursday, Mom's doctors had said they didn't anticipate more than a few days—a week at best. Earlier today, John said the doctor came in and saw signs. These signs meant that death was near—hours.

As I waited to hear from John, Junior went after another porcupine. If your dog gets porcupine quills stuck in its snout, it can cost up to $1,000 at the vet, and every time they pull out a quill, it draws blood from the dogs nose—it's extremely painful. When you have an eight-month-old puppy, there is no way to deal with a porcupine other than to kill it. This is what I had to do with my .22. Then, after hearing of my mother's passing, another porcupine showed up. Junior noticed it and was about to go after it, until I yelled and diverted him. Once I dragged Junior into the house, I put that one down as well. I cried on my knees, by the stone retaining wall, watching the last twitches of the porcupine's life. I said aloud I was sorry just like I said to Penny when she died.

This has been one of the top ten shittiest days of my life. There has been so much death around me in the past year, and I'm not sure what to make of any of it. I don't have a therapist, no one with the tools to handle what I'm going through. I can talk to Sofi, and she's very helpful. . . . I may need more. I think for now I will let everything that has happened in these past five days sit within me, feel it all when it surfaces, and reflect with as much intelligent sincerity as I can muster. I know the loss of my mother, Roslyn Cohen, will haunt and inspire me for as long as I live. A few years back, I did a comic strip for the *New York Times* "Modern Love" section. In the strip I made fun of my parents' marriage. I was proud of the writing and the art.

My mother liked it. She taped a copy of the full-page strip to the kitchen door; it's been there for the past few years. In the strip, I mock my parents for writing critical notes to each other. They did a lot of this in the last decade of their lives together. Communication fell away and was replaced by angry notes and instructions.

In the past few months I've come to realize that my mother wrote copious notes. These notes weren't so much for my father; they were for her. I believe her dementia had been going on for years. It's possible she has been dealing with it for a decade. Her notes, meticulous gardening, and quasi hoarding were keeping her grounded.

She had not left Colony Lane in at least two years. All the while my siblings and I have been calling her crazy, nuts, or manipulative. But the truth

is, she was sick. She didn't know what she had, how could she? Dementia is a condition in which you slowly lose the self you once knew. We all jokingly call our mothers "crazy" or "nuts," and perhaps my mother had behavioral issues that were odd or controlling—no doubt, but she was also suffering. My mother was frightened of what was happening to her until she lost the ability to be rationally frightened. Fear, paranoia, memory loss, delusions, and God knows what else became part of her world.

It is this reality that haunts me. This is something I will never forgive myself for. How could I know? This will stay with me always.

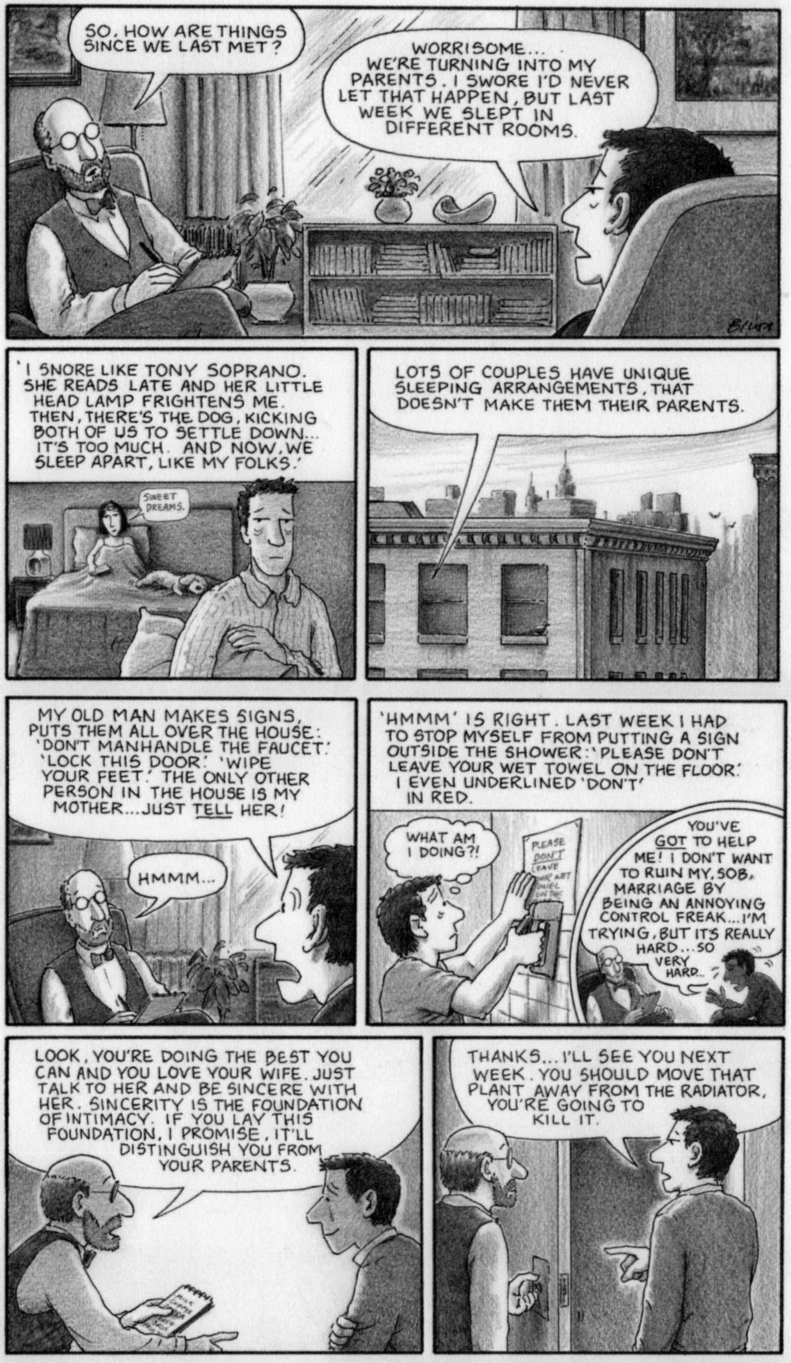

SO, HOW ARE THINGS SINCE WE LAST MET?
WORRISOME... WE'RE TURNING INTO MY PARENTS. I SWORE I'D NEVER LET THAT HAPPEN, BUT LAST WEEK WE SLEPT IN DIFFERENT ROOMS.
'I SNORE LIKE TONY SOPRANO. SHE READS LATE AND HER LITTLE HEAD LAMP FRIGHTENS ME. THEN, THERE'S THE DOG, KICKING BOTH OF US TO SETTLE DOWN... IT'S TOO MUCH. AND NOW, WE SLEEP APART, LIKE MY FOLKS.'
SWEET DREAMS.
LOTS OF COUPLES HAVE UNIQUE SLEEPING ARRANGEMENTS, THAT DOESN'T MAKE THEM THEIR PARENTS.
MY OLD MAN MAKES SIGNS, PUTS THEM ALL OVER THE HOUSE: 'DON'T MANHANDLE THE FAUCET.' 'LOCK THIS DOOR.' 'WIPE YOUR FEET.' THE ONLY OTHER PERSON IN THE HOUSE IS MY MOTHER... JUST TELL HER!
HMMM...
'HMMM' IS RIGHT. LAST WEEK I HAD TO STOP MYSELF FROM PUTTING A SIGN OUTSIDE THE SHOWER: 'PLEASE DON'T LEAVE YOUR WET TOWEL ON THE FLOOR.' I EVEN UNDERLINED 'DON'T' IN RED.
WHAT AM I DOING?!
PLEASE DON'T LEAVE
YOU'VE GOT TO HELP ME! I DON'T WANT TO RUIN MY, SOB, MARRIAGE BY BEING AN ANNOYING CONTROL FREAK... I'M TRYING, BUT IT'S REALLY HARD... SO VERY HARD...
LOOK, YOU'RE DOING THE BEST YOU CAN AND YOU LOVE YOUR WIFE. JUST TALK TO HER AND BE SINCERE WITH HER. SINCERITY IS THE FOUNDATION OF INTIMACY. IF YOU LAY THIS FOUNDATION, I PROMISE, IT'LL DISTINGUISH YOU FROM YOUR PARENTS.
THANKS... I'LL SEE YOU NEXT WEEK. YOU SHOULD MOVE THAT PLANT AWAY FROM THE RADIATOR, YOU'RE GOING TO KILL IT.

EPILOGUE

Alex and his girlfriend, Sarah, are here in Cornish to help me put this book you're reading together. I always knew this book would be a sort of curated journey that included writings, drawings, and cartoons—all threaded together with the hope of connecting me to you. Alex had told me that while he felt good about the book, he thought the last few essays were a bit of a downer, and perhaps I could end this book on more of an upbeat. I wasn't sure how I felt about his advice, but I've been mulling it over. I don't like manipulating readers. I wanted the journey of this book to be as sincere as possible, a frank reveal of events that made me who I am at this moment in time.

Yesterday I attended a memorial service for a local Cornish woman, Claudia Hohenberg Yatsevitch, who had died last year. She was ninety-four. I relate this because I feel there is something "upbeat" buried within the experience I had at the service. The Yatsevitch family have deep roots in Cornish. They have much of their land in conservation easement, and I often ride my bike up to their family cemetery. I've done watercolors on their land, near their farm where Claudia lived for many years. The memorial service was at my friend Colleen's barn up the street, and I walked there around 2:00 p.m., leaving Junior alone in the house, audibly sad at my departure.

It seems there have been more than a few deaths over the past two years. Too many. Maybe I'm at that age. The age when death becomes peripherally more profound. Paul Reubens (Pee-wee Herman) died a week ago, and he's

393

still being memorialized on social media. Maybe there haven't been more deaths and it's just the ubiquitous media landscape that makes it feel that way. I don't know, and I don't really care so much anymore. I only know I've lost things I loved. Penny started it all. Then Mom and Dad, Ed Koren, and some Cornish folks—some I knew, and some I didn't get a chance to know.

When I arrived at the barn, I saw most of my neighbors were there. There were also many people I had never seen before, people who knew Claudia and were there to celebrate her life. I went into the barn and looked at all the photographs of her through the years. She had grown up in Vienna, but came to the United States in 1938 at the urging of an uncle, who insisted her family leave before the Nazi occupation. She lived in Cornish for more than sixty years. She had married twice and had five children. Looking at all the photographs reminded me of my mother. Emotion welled up in me, like a heavy wave cresting in my chest.

One of Claudia's daughters came up to me and asked who I was. I told her, and we talked for a bit. She was very kind to me and explained that Claudia had suffered from dementia. When the dementia became too much for Claudia, she told her children that she no longer wanted to live. She stopped eating and, soon after, passed. I wanted to have a longer conversation with Claudia's daughter, about losing her mother to dementia, but it wasn't the time.

Moments later, we were all asked to have a seat in the barn, where fifty or so chairs were set up and a microphone.

Prayers were lovingly recited. Songs were sung. Memories shared of Claudia's odd-looking dog, Smiley, who chewed off a number of car license plates. Someone recalled that you could always identify a Yatsevitch car driving in Cornish because of the teeth marks on the license plate. Some spoke of Claudia's unconditional love of all animals (she fed wild turkeys), her calm energy, and the visceral reverence she had for Cornish. Like me and my mother before me, Claudia wasted nothing. She recycled and reused everything—though I doubt Claudia was the hoarder Mom turned into. Claudia had to haul bags of coal to the basement furnace. Before this task, she'd empty the ashes from the furnace, carry them out into the winter air, and reuse them—carefully distributing them to make a path in the snow. Clever reuse idea for traction, but the kids would inevitably track the coal back into the house.

After about an hour, we were all still sitting quietly, a soft breeze through the open barn doors kept everyone comfortably peaceful. No more volunteers to get up and share Claudia stories or recollections, just a quiet resignation that seemed to replace any awkward pressure to get up and speak. In the quiet I thought again of my mother and tears almost fell, but didn't . . . I held off until I returned home, where Junior was there to console me.

I think my mother would've liked Claudia.

"THANKS FOR COMING.."

ACKNOWLEDGMENTS

This book wouldn't be possible without the support and expertise of Deb Futter at Celadon and her terrific staff. Gratitude to my agent, Esther Newberg, who believed in me. Heartfelt thanks to my sublime friends/family: Sarah Wilson, Alexander Bliss, John Butler, Delia McConnell, Sofia Dillof, and my best friend, Junior.

ABOUT THE AUTHOR

Harry Bliss is the creator of the internationally syndicated *Bliss* and a cartoonist and cover artist for *The New Yorker*. He is coauthor of two *New York Times* bestselling books with Steve Martin and has written and illustrated more than twenty-five books for children. He is the founder of the Cornish CCS Residency Fellowship for graphic novelists in Cornish, New Hampshire.

CELADON
BOOKS

Founded in 2017, Celadon Books, a division of
Macmillan Publishers, publishes a highly curated list
of twenty to twenty-five new titles a year. The list of
both fiction and nonfiction is eclectic and focuses
on publishing commercial and literary books and
discovering and nurturing talent.

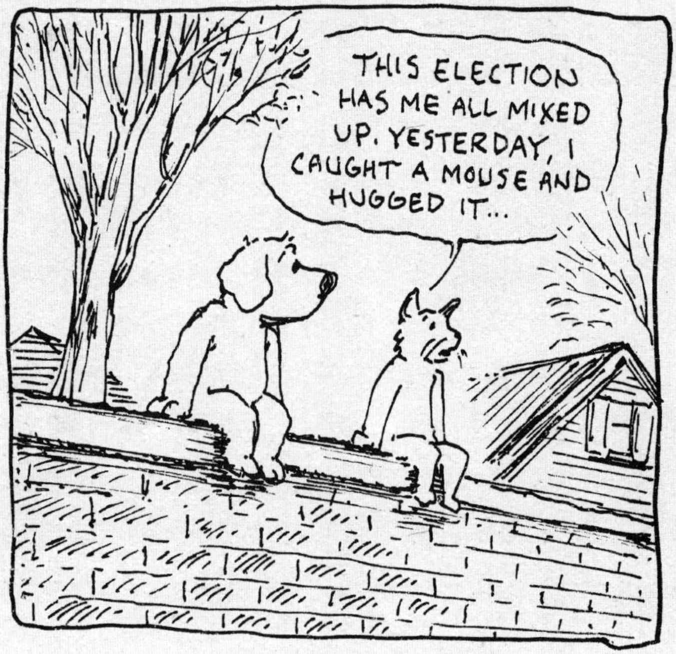
THIS ELECTION HAS ME ALL MIXED UP. YESTERDAY, I CAUGHT A MOUSE AND HUGGED IT...

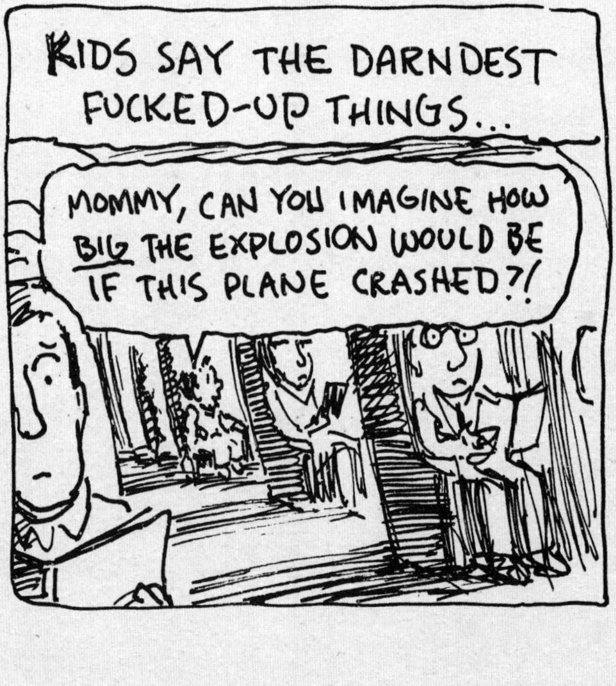
KIDS SAY THE DARNDEST FUCKED-UP THINGS...
MOMMY, CAN YOU IMAGINE HOW BIG THE EXPLOSION WOULD BE IF THIS PLANE CRASHED?!